STRAIGHT TEXAS

Straight Texas

Edited by

J. Frank Dobie
Mody C. Boatright, Associate Editor

Publications of the Texas Folklore Society Number XIII

University of North Texas Press
Denton, Texas

Copyright © 2000 by The Texas Folklore Society

All rights Reserved

Copyright © 1937 by The Texas Folklore Society
Facsimile Edition 1966
Southern Methodist University Press
Second printing 1977
Third printing 1984

Printed in the United States of America

Permissions:
University of North Texas Press
P. O. Box 311336
Denton, Texas 76203
(940) 565-2142 FAX (940) 565-4590

Library of Congress Cataloging in Publication Data

Dobie, James Frank, 1888–1964, ed.
Straight Texas.

Reprint of the 1966 ed. Published by Folklore Associates, Hatboro, Pa., which was a reprint of the ed. Published by the Texas Folklore Society, Austin, and issued as no. 13 of its Publications.
 1. Folk-lore—Texas—Addresses, essays, lectures. 2. Names, Geographical—Texas—Addresses, essays, lectures. I. Boatright, Mody Coggin, 1896–1970, joint ed. II. Title. III. Series: Texas Folklore Society. Publication no. 13.

GR110.T5D62 1977   390'.09764   77-8134
          ISBN 0-87074-164-0 (cloth)
          ISBN 1-57441-097-0 (paper)

PREFACE TO THE REPRINT EDITION

STRAIGHT TEXAS is a varied and rich collection. It was published in 1937 and has been out of print too long.

In his article on Texas place names J. Frank Dobie presents a wealth of stories about his people and his land. This form of presentation is unusual for him, but the material is transmitted with his characteristic liveliness and gusto. Texans were looking back over their past in 1936, their hundredth year of independence from Mexico. Dobie observed the occasion with his sixth book, *The Flavor of Texas,* now a very rare item. In this book and in the article on place names, his love for Texas is evident, but this love needed no centennial for its quickening. In 1920 he had resolved to collect the tales of his land and people, as Lomax had collected the songs.

Other articles and contributors might be mentioned also. A. W. Eddins had contributed tales since Stith Thompson edited the first volume for the Society in 1916. Charles L. Sonnichsen, who went on to become one of the leading interpreters of the Southwest, made his first appearance as a contributor to the Society's publications. Tressa Turner's collection of folk superstitions is a valuable early work, which has recently been followed up by the research of George Hendricks.

The first book that Mody C. Boatright assisted Dobie in editing was STRAIGHT TEXAS. He continued as assistant editor until becoming editor-in-chief in 1943.

The republication of STRAIGHT TEXAS brings us nearer the day when it will be possible for new members and anyone else interested in folklore to obtain a complete set of the Society's books without undertaking a tedious and expensive search.

WILSON M. HUDSON
Secretary-Editor
Texas Folklore Society

Austin, Texas
May 31, 1966

TAKING IT STRAIGHT

(Dedicated to Ab Blocker)

"I'll take it straight," the old-timer said.
   "Jes' let me have 'er out o' the jug.
These here mixtures and swaller-fork doin's
   Are no more'n a hat-tip to an armful hug."

The jug it gurgled, and the old-timer did too;
   His handlebar moustaches he wiped with his palm;
He rolled a cigarette in thick brown paper
   And blowed his smoke to add to the calm.

"I ain't never tasted bad whiskey,"
   He remarked in a final and sober way,
"Nor seen a woman that's ugly—
   I'm making my jedgments in the light of day."

Now, when a man thinks and feels like that
   And looks benignant and free,
What is the sense of amplifying,
   Or analyzing what might be?

The old-timer glanced at the jug again,
   And then he made a kind of bow:
"I'll give you the only toast I know
   Besides the old 'Here's how!'"

Nobody expected him to be poetical,
   But everybody knowed he'd mean what he said,
For straight he lived, just like he drank,
   Warm in the heart, but solemn of head.

He took off his hat and mopped the sweat.
   A body'd a thought he was a-going to pray.
"My pa was straight Texas," he kinder explained,
   "And this was how he used to say:

"We come into this world all naked and bare,
   We go out of this world we don't know where,
But if we've been good *hombres* here,
   We need not fear what will be there."

                        —J. F. D.

CONTENTS

	PAGE
STORIES IN TEXAS PLACE NAMES *J. Frank Dobie*	1
THE LOBO GIRL OF DEVIL'S RIVER *L. D. Bertillion*	79
ANECDOTES FROM THE BRAZOS BOTTOMS *A. W. Eddins*	86
THE ADVENTURES OF LITTLE AUDREY *Cornelia Chambers*	106
ROY BEAN: LAW WEST OF THE PECOS *Myron W. Tracy*	111
MEXICAN SPOOKS FROM EL PASO *Charles L. Sonnichsen*	120
WALK AROUND MY BEDSIDE *Martha Emmons*	130
I'SE SHO' NUFF LUCKY *Aylett Royal*	137
THE HUMAN COMEDY IN FOLK SUPERSTITIONS *Tressa Turner*	146
WITCHING FOR WATER WITH THE BIBLE *David Hall*	176
THE BLACK CAT OF COLE'S PLANTATION *Julia Beazley*	182
IRISH FAIRIES IN TEXAS *Louise von Blittersdorf Moses*	185

CONTENTS (Cont'd)

	PAGE
PIONEER FOLK WAYS	190
Afton Wynn	
WISE SAWS FROM TEXAS	239
Mrs. Morgan Smith and A. W. Eddins	
COLLOQUIALISMS ALONG THE SABINE	245
Trueman E. O'Quinn	
"OLD OBADIAH" AND "MY JUANITA"	250
Alice Atkinson Neighbors	
SILVER DREAMS AND COPPER PLATES	258
Mae Featherstone	
THE ALABAMA INDIANS AND THEIR MUSIC	270
Frances Densmore	
TWO TALES FROM THE ALABAMAS	294
Elma Heard	
HOW THE ALABAMAS CAME SOUTHWARD	298
G. T. Bludworth	
THE PLAY PARTY IN VICTORIA COUNTY	300
Helen Ashworth Moore	
CONTRIBUTORS	337
INDEX	341

STRAIGHT TEXAS

STORIES IN TEXAS PLACE NAMES

By J. FRANK DOBIE

I. THE WHATS IN A NAME

Inevitably the younger generation supplants the older, but not so is it with names. Many of the old ones may be erased, but some of them continue alongside the new. The Indians are driven back or annihilated, but their lovely names for rivers, like the Susquehanna, the Wichita, and the Washita, live on to delight the ear and to bear witness of people who possessed the land before ever a ship plowed into the western seas.

To wander about the streets of San Antonio with an eye on the name plates is to review the history of Texas. Milam Square and Alamo Plaza, the streets of Soledad (Solitude), Flores (Flowers), Alazan (Sorrel-colored), Santa Rosa, and Dolorosa (Sorrowful, so called, it is said, because a señorita who had seen her lover shot to death walked the length of it sobbing and then stabbed herself)—these names are an essential part of the city and go far toward making it one of the three or four cities of the United States with individuality and picturesqueness. When, a few years ago, some of its "progressive" citizens petitioned to change the name of the street called Zarzamora to Aviation Boulevard, the old cobble-blocks of mesquite on Alamo Plaza themselves joined in the protest; and the lovely and time-chanting name of Zarzamora yet remains. *Zarza* means *thorny bramble,* and *mora* means *mulberry.* The Franciscan padres found a new kind of fruiting bramble, the wild dewberry, growing along the bottoms of San Pedro Creek and the San Antonio River. They called it "thorny mulberry" and then named a street for it.

The map of Texas is covered with names that tell stories, reveal character, betray sentiments, call up events, express facts. Indeed, it would be impossible to find one that does not tell something, though nothing more than the inanity of the person responsible for it. I have no idea of making a full treatment of these names, for a very large book, much of it dull and full of repetitions, entailing many years of work, would be required for such an undertaking. It would constitute a biographical dictionary connected with Texas history, for thousands of towns and other places are named after men both significant and insignificant, honorable men and politicians, conventional dullards and vivid individuals.

It would constitute also something of an inquiry into the exceedingly broad fields of Texas flora and fauna. A few names of zoological import culled out of many suggest the variety of wild life represented in nomenclature: Hog Marsh, near the Concho River—so named because of the mussel shells early Spaniards observed in it; Tecolote (Owl) Ranch and Rancho de las Grullas, the translated name of which appears in Crane Canyon; Crow Flats, Buzzard Roost, Eagle Mountains, Turkey creeks in every section, Arroyo de las Gallinas (Prairie Chickens), Garcitas (Little Herons) Creek, where La Salle first landed in Texas, and Paisano Pass, named for the most interesting bird of the state, known also as *roadrunner* and *chaparral cock;* Panther Canyon, Coyote Ridge, Lobo, Bear Gulch, Beaver Lake, Buffalo Gap, Antelope Draw, Polecat Creek, Prairie Dog Town Fork of Red River, Burro Mesa, Rattlesnake Cave, Lagarto (Alligator) Waterhole, Oyster Bay, Doe Run and White Deer—probably connected with an albino deer supposed to have a madstone in its stomach.

Expressive of the plant life, a few samples are Tulip Bend, Pepper Creek Camp—named for the little native

STORIES IN TEXAS PLACE NAMES

red pepper called by the Indians *chiltipiquin*—a word perverted into Chiltipin Creek; scores of Cottonwood creeks, but, after all, but one Alamo; Onion Creek, along which early settlers saw the wild onions growing but which Spanish explorers in 1709 named Garrapatas Creek because at a camp on it *ticks* bothered them; Grapeland, Cedar Hill, Big Caney, and Carrizo, which also means *cane;* Oakville, where beside the forsaken court house the live oak tree from which men were hanged can still be seen; Dagger Flats, out in the land of the stiletto-pointed lechuguilla; Peach Point on the Brazos, forever associated with the Father of Texas, whose colonists picked for richness the soil "where the wild peach grows;" Sycamore Heights, Yucca Siding, Post Oak Point, Mesquite, Tule Canyon, Peyote, Nopal, Buttercup, and the astounding Palo Duro Canyon, named for its *hard wood* from which Indians used to make arrow-shafts.

A full treatment of Texas place names would involve consideration of geology as well as of botany and zoology. Granite Mountains, Marble Falls, the creeks named Gyp, Fossil, Iron Ore, Kaolin and Alum, Chalk Draw, Mineral Wells, Isinglass Canyon and Sal de Rey (Salt of the King)—a lake from which subjects of the King of Spain used to haul salt—are a few instances.

The action of the elements on soil is reflected in physiographical names like Powderhorn Bayou and Comal River, the lovely valley of which resembles the saucerlike *comal* on which Mexicans bake *tortillas;* like Demijohn Bend in the Guadalupe River, Gooseneck Bend in the Brazos, and Horseshoe Bend in the Colorado, all the result of shifting water currents; like Casket, Cathedral, Haystack, Hump, Smoothing Iron and Butter Bowl mountains, along with Tepee Butte and Nipple Peak. Climate and weather are reflected in the ironic name of Zephyr, derived from a cyclone, several Hurricane creeks, the wind-shifted Sand Hills of Ward County, and Polvo (Dust) near El Paso.

More human in their associations, a numerous category of names gives a kind of review of the industrial occupations both present and obsolete in which men on Texas soil have engaged. Ferries, stage coaches, overland freighting to Mexico, often with wagons timbered by home blacksmiths, the cheerful sound of a mill grinding coffee before daylight, Indian missions and trading posts, cattle trailing, home-made lye soap, and the wild and free life of the mustanger are all past; but Mustang Pens, Soap Creek, the Chisholm Trail, Trading House Creek, Mission River, Coffee Mill Creek, Wagon Timber Creek, Colbert's Ferry, and the Chihuahua Trail—all these remain yet as names. Lariat, Bronco, Spur, Roundup Creek, Straddlebug Mountain, which takes its name from the fantastic "Straddlebug" brand, Seven Heart Gap, called after another brand, and Sheep Ranch Hollow belong as naturally as grass to a ranching country. Sawlog Creek, Oilery, Quarry, Farmersville, Cottondale, Corn Hill, Alfalfa, Hay Hollow, Sorgum Flats, Sandia, which, true to its name, sends out *watermelons* by the train load, Padre Mine Canyon, Slag, Coaldale, and Tanyard Branch are just as plain in what they say of other industries.

A linguistic study of the native tribes, a knowledge of the six flags—especially of that borne by Spanish explorers—that have waved over Texas, and a tracing of the emigrants who have made up the heterogeneous population of the state would all be requisite to a thorough exposition of its place names. Newcomers always bring with them memories of the homes they have left, and many a name baldly tells where the people who gave it came from. A group of Swedes in Bosque County called their community Norse, and a band of visionary exiles from England who settled not far away betrayed alike their hopes and homesickness in naming "the City of Kent." Germans may have left their fatherland to escape the tyranny of Prussian princes, but nevertheless they called their new home Fredericksburg. It takes no research to know whence migrated the settlers of Tennessee Colony. Had the Irishmen who founded San Patricio not been so near the Mexican border, they would doubtless have named it plain Saint Patrick.

Indeed, the place names of Texas infer an encyclopediac history of the land. All I propose here is to treat of some of the names having a folk origin, whether that origin be legendary or otherwise, and to set down certain pertinent narratives savored with the folk element.

II. SPANISH-MEXICAN TRAILS

The names that have stuck to the major features of Texas topography were nearly all given by the Spaniards. Some of these exploring namers were spontaneous and realistic, others were merely pious in a literal way. Alarcón, for example, on the 8th of May, 1718, named a creek to the east of San Antonio Salsipuedes—Get-out-if-you-can—"because it is located in a thick wood." After a great deal of trouble he got out of the bottom and into one worse. This creek he named Entraaverlo—Enter-to-see-it—"because near it are two other creeks, very deep and miry, and the wood is so thick that in order to extricate oneself from the entanglement of very high trees, grapevines and cocolmecates [a vine 'twisted like a rope'] one calls loudly for a knife."[1]

On the other hand, the priggish Terán, who directed an expedition, 1691-1692, was unable to pass any stream, no matter how well named it already was, without rechristening it after some saint. "We reached the banks of a river," he says, "which had been named Nueces on preceding trips . . . . I named it San Diego." Borne thence northward, "the royal standard halted on the banks of another arroyo that, at various points, on previous trips, had been called the Medina." Terán named it San Luis Beltrán. It is still the Medina, and the Trinidad is still the Trinity, although Terán felt impelled to replace even this holy name by La Encarnación del Verbo—The Incarnation of the Word. With him

[1] *Diary of the Alarcón Expedition into Texas, 1718-1719*, by Fray Francisco Céliz, translated and annotated by Fritz Leo Hoffmann. The Quivira Society, Los Angeles, California, 1935, p. 50.

was the noted Fray Damián Mansanet, who also kept a diary, and on the return trip to Mexico this friar upon reaching the Nueces River, so called "on account of the many pecans there, . . . named it San Norbeto, because it was his [Saint Norbeto's] day. The Indians call it Chotilapacquen"[2]—a name as unknown to the river now as either of the saint names that Terán and Mansanet tried to foist upon it.

Applying to a stream the name of the saint on whose day it was discovered or reached was very common. Such names have little to tell; nor have those which the outposters of Spain gave in memory of their homeland. Mexicans, except those arriving at an education or nursing political ambitions, are less pompous and less self-conscious than the Spanish conquerors were. Those of the class called "lower" have generally been happier and more picturesque in name-giving than were the vice-regents of God riding around with the never-sleeping idea that it was their duty to baptize everything in a country with the names of saints. San Marcos, San Diego, San José, Santa María, Santa Gertrudís, San Felipe de Austin, La Navidad (River of the Nativity), Arroyo de las Benditas Ánimas (Creek of the Blessed Souls), Espíritu Santo (Holy Spirit) Bay—beautiful names they are, but they can become monotonous, and they don't tell stories. In the region between San Antonio and the Rio Grande, where Mexicans perform a large part of the labor and where the traditions of the Spanish tongue still thrive, almost every hill, thicket, draw and flat has its name. There are plenty of Sans and Santas, but there are plenty of other names that have arisen from circumstances of the land as naturally as mesquite beans grow. From a few personal experiences I shall illustrate the Mexican genius for giving names.

In the winter of 1920 I went from Los Olmos (The Elms) Ranch on the Nueces River in LaSalle County to receive at the Casa Blanca Ranch in Duval County a

---

[2] *The Expedition of Don Domingo Terán de los Ríos into Texas*, translated by Mattie Austin Hatcher. In *Preliminary Studies of the Texas Catholic Historical Society*, Austin, 1932, pp. 13, 14, 20, 52.

herd of steers bought by my uncle J. M. Dobie from a rancher who had promised to give him a horse for a *pilón;* a *pilón* is something extra, a lagniappe. After the steers had been counted, about a thousand head, the rancher told me to pick any horse I chose out of his remuda. I picked a big, smooth, blaze-faced sorrel—one of the most powerful brush-knocking-down horses I have ever ridden. That night I heard some of the Olmos vaqueros talking about Pilón, the name they had spontaneously given the newly acquired horse.

A ranch that was leased and run in connection with Los Olmos bears the name of Camarón, *crawfish* being characteristic of the sacahuiste (salt grass) draws of that region. At the Camarón tank stock watered from three or four pastures, one of them a "trap" (a small pasture) of about 2000 acres called El Wiley—for while Wiley Seego was ranch manager he had fenced it. The wagon road leading from the Camarón to the Coma Pasture— in which *coma* brush abounds—went past another tank called Las Carpas; the men who built it lived under stretched tents *(carpas).*

One day the *caporal* (boss) of the vaqueros took his men to work in the Coma Pasture, instructing the cook to follow and prepare dinner on a certain hill at which the road from the Camarón intersected a *sendero* (path cut through brush) running east from the Piedra (Rock) tank. From the Camarón to this hill is close to ten miles. After the cook had arrived at the designated spot, he found that he had forgotten to bring flour for bread. The hill received a name, Loma de Harina (Hill of Flour)—because there wasn't any flour. The name suggests the primal French name for St. Louis, Pain Court (Short of Bread).

While the Mexicans were strengthening the dam to a tank in the Cañada Verde (Green Branch) Pasture, a mule tied to a tree set back and choked herself down. After that the tank was called La Mula. I told the *caporal* of the tanking outfit to throw a small dam across a shallow draw. "How long shall I work here?"

he asked. "Oh, about three days," I replied. The next time I saw him he told me that the Presa de Tres Dias (Tank of Three Days) would catch plenty of water when it rained.

I will quote from the diary of an observant and melancholy Mexican, who journeyed across Texas in 1828: "April 18 . . . . We halted at a place which, because it had no name, the general called Loma Grande [Big Hill]. . . . April 19 and 20 . . . We crossed the creek called La Baca [The Cow, now spelled as one word, Lavaca], and at about three leagues from this place the wheels of one of the instrument wagons broke, making it necessary to stay in a beautiful meadow. We pitched camp on the edge of the woods, and gave this place the name of Campo de la Rueda [Camp of the Wheel]. We remained at this place all the following day to repair the wheel. . . . April 22 . . . We had to halt because the fifth wheel of the instrument wagon broke; so we pitched camp near a small creek. Not knowing what to call this stopping place and seeing how unattractive it was, I suggested that it be named after me, and from then on it was, for us, Campo de Sánchez."

People who live next to the soil and for whom the soil has a deep meaning name the features of it as naturally as they name their children. They belong to the earth, and the earth belongs to them. For them the soil holds memories, and names are not merely for designation, like the numbers worn by convicts or 222nd Street. On the 20th of March, 1836, on a prairie about eight miles east of Goliad, Colonel James W. Fannin surrendered himself and something under 300 Texans to Mexican forces. As all the world knows, these prisoners were taken back to Goliad, held for a week, and then on Palm Sunday marched out and shot down. The Goliad country is a country of live oaks, many of them festooned with long Spanish moss. *Encino* is the Spanish word for *oak; encinal* means a grove of oaks. I do not know when the particular prairie, in that land of lovely live oaks, on which Fannin surrendered was named by the Mexicans;

STORIES IN TEXAS PLACE NAMES

it may have been the day after the surrender. A traveler passing that way only a few years afterwards considered it worthy of note that the fateful plain was called Encinal del Perdido—the Live Oak Grove of the Lost.

Rising in Zavala County—a name memorializing a Spanish-Mexican who stood with the Texans in their revolt—is a dry arroyo set down on maps as Yo-lo-digo. One dark night after a heavy rain, the *gente* tell, two Mexicans were walking along single file. Suddenly the man behind heard a splash. *"Es agua?"* (Is it water?) he exclaimed. *"Yo lo digo!"* (I say it is), the man who was still splashing replied. Yo-lo-digo Creek tells its own story.

Southwest of what is now Eagle Pass is a motte of pecan trees on a creek near the old Mexican settlement of Fuentes. To the north of Eagle Pass, on the Texas side, is another motte of pecans, mixed with elms, on Elm Creek. Before a house was built on the Rio Grande between these two locations the mottes were noted nesting and roosting places for Mexican eagles. Between sundown and dark every evening and between daylight and sunup every morning they used to fly in great numbers from one rendezvous to another. The creatures of the air have their roadways as well as deer and other wild land-dwellers, and the flight of the eagles always led over the Rio Grande about where Eagle Pass now stands. The Indians called the ford here, in their language, Place of the Passage of Eagles. When the Spaniards came, they translated the term into Paso de Aguila. No flight of eagles now marks the place, but the name Eagle Pass recalls their "tracks in the sky."

One of the most famous old Mexican ranches in Texas is the Randado, in Jim Hogg County. It is told that the tank here was made by hauling dirt out of the basin on cowhides hitched to the horns of saddles. The ample stockade of high, thick stone walls built as a protection against Indians and *bandidos* still stands. The land, a Spanish grant of 60,000 acres, on which unbranded horses ran by the thousands, was acquired in

1856, so the chronicle goes, by Don Hipolito Garcia at the price of twenty cents an acre. Then he built the ranch quarters and settled there with his family. It is not conceivable that the place did not already have a name, but it got another. One day Don Hipolito's children saw a peddler coming up with a pack mule, lace and ribbons floating from the pack. *"Mira al randado!"* they cried. "Look at the belaced one!" And from the peddler with laces El Randado took its name.

Another of the old and noted ranches of the brush country is Las Ánimas, in Duval County. The house was once a fort as well as residence; it is of stone, the flat roof palisaded by a rock wall behind which a man could be protected while shooting at an enemy. Literally *ánima* means *soul*, but popularly it often means *lost soul*. El Rancho de las Ánimas, then, is the Ranch of Lost Souls. Tradition explains the name.

While the country between the Nueces River and the Rio Grande was still nothing but a "mustang desert," a certain *hidalgo* came to claim a grant issued by the King of Spain. The first water he found on his land was a *charco*—a pool in a dry creek—fenced around with mesquite brush. A fence of any kind away out in that solitary region was extraordinary, but what the corral enclosed was more extraordinary. There lay the bleached skeletons of three or four men and of as many horses. Presumably the human bones were of mustangers who had built the pen to trap wild horses and had then been surprised and killed by Indians.

The *rancheros* camped by the corralled waterhole. They never forgot that night. Almost as soon as darkness came they began hearing groans as of dying men and shrieks as of horses in the agonies of death. Some saw or thought they saw *espectros* crouching by the brushy fence. There was little sleep for anybody. On the morrow the *hidalgo* found another watering place and there ordered the erection of a house. His lands embraced the waterhole of the skeletons, and after these dead ones the ranch was named Las Ánimas.

STORIES IN TEXAS PLACE NAMES 11

When Espantosa Lake got its name, I know not. It lies not far from Carrizo Springs, on the old Spanish and Mexican road between Presidio del Rio Grande and San Antonio. The Nueces River probably flowed through it at one time, but it now receives its waters from creeks that drain a big country of hills and thorned brush. A division of Santa Anna's army on its way to besiege the Alamo passed this way, and one of the many popular tales centering around the lake has to do with a cannon that these troops stuffed full of money and left in the security of the waters.

Things have happened to human beings beside Espantosa Lake to give it the reputation its name implies. One night in the seventies McNelly's rangers surprised a band of desperate outlaws camped by it, killed three of them outright and put five bullets into the fourth. In the dense thickets around the lake maverick bulls used to bellow, to be answered by the bellows of great alligators, and here the cries of the screech owl, the hoot owl, the coyote, and the panther still sound on the night air. Many people have seen will-o'-the-wisp lights at the edge of its waters, but *Espantosa* came from a particular incident.

The word means *frightful, phantasmal.* Away back in early times, as the story goes, some families from Mexico on their way to San Antonio camped here for several days in order to recruit their horses. One evening while a woman was washing clothes at the water's edge, no doubt squatted and rubbing them on a rock, men in camp heard a wild and horrifying cry. They rushed down, but all they saw was a streak of blood and the slash of a great scaled tail. *"Dios, es un lagarto!* (God, it is an alligator!)" one exclaimed. The next morning they erected a cross at the spot where the woman had disappeared. Some of them claimed to hear the cries again the next dusk. They left the place, and they left the lake with its name, Espantosa. It afforded one of the few waterings for a great distance on the old Camino Real, but in years that followed many a Spanish-speaking traveler would inconvenience himself in order not to camp by it. Among the Mexicans stories grew up concerning fierce and enormous animals in the lake that resembled bulls.

The Spanish names in Texas around which legend has most widely played are, I suppose, Los Brazos de Dios and the Llano Estacado.

III. THE ARMS OF GOD

The Brazos is the longest and most important river in Texas. On its lower reaches settled the first English-speaking colonists; the first Spanish expedition north of Mexico, Coronado's, which traversed the Staked Plains in 1541, must have camped on its headwaters. During the era of exploration it received various names, and for a long time it and the Colorado were confused with each other in nomenclature.

Brazo means *arm*. The full name of the great river was Los Brazos de Dios—The Arms of God. Even in a land where Body of Christ (Corpus Christi) and Name of God (Nombre de Dios) are to be found on the map, the name is remarkable; in attempting to explain its origin legend has been no less remarkable. Why *The Arms of God?* The earliest English-speaking comers to Texas asked the question. They received varying answers, all agreeing, however, that at one time—usually in a miraculous manner—the great river acted as a saviour to man.

A trip through Texas made in 1831 brought the noted Albert Pike to both the river and its legend. "We encamped," he says, "by the side of a pond, which is the head of one of the chief branches of the Colorado, or, [as it is now called], the Brazos de Dios River. . . . The reason given me for the change in name is this: Some years ago there was a drouth in Texas; the short river (Brazos) became dry, and the only water came down in the long river (or the Colorado). The pious Spaniards accordingly changed names, and called the long river the Brazos de Dios (or the Arms of God), on account of the special care which it took of them, and of the benefits which they received from it."

A tradition more specific that Governor Sul Ross used to tell has it that Coronado's men while wandering on the Staked Plains were perishing from thirst when some Indians found them and guided them to water in one of the forks of the long river. And because it had saved them, Coronado's men named the stream Los Brazos de Dios.

As might be expected, the tradition at the mouth of the river is very different. A long time ago, so it goes, a Spanish ship in the Gulf of Mexico ran out of drinking water. The crew were parched with thirst. They could see no land. They were lost and knew not where the coast might lie. Then a sailor noticed a muddy streak reaching out into the clear blue of the salt waters. The ship followed this streak, a current, to the mouth of a wide river; it was on a great rise and so was throwing its dirt-hued waters far out to sea. The ship sailed up the river far to get beyond the tidal mixture of salt. The sailor-men drank of the fresh waters and were saved and in gratitude christened the unknown stream Los Brazos de Dios.

But the story of drouth and saving waters that I like best connects with the famous Lost Bowie Mine on the San Saba. It came down to me, indirectly, from an old-time rancher named White, who got it a long time ago from an ancient Mexican driving two burros to a wooden-wheeled cart in the San Saba country. He was sick; White befriended him, and when he was on his feet again he showed his benefactor a parchment dated about 1760. He was looking for two dugouts, he said, somewhere between the old San Saba Mission and the site of the Waco Indian village—located where the city of Waco now stands, on the Brazos River. As the parchment read, thirty-six jack-loads of silver bullion lay buried in the two dugouts. The silver came to be stored thus:

It was a time of terrible drouth. The drouth had lasted two years, and the little colony of Spaniards on the

San Saba had gone on mining with their captive Indians and their peons until the Indians had deserted, the peons had died, and there was absolutely no water left in the river or springs. Every night the Spaniards hoped that the next change of the moon would bring rain, but no rain came, and they knew that in the nearly always dry region toward Mexico, the drouth must be even worse. So, instead of going south toward San Antonio as they would normally have gone, the Spaniards set out eastward toward the village of the Waco Indians. They had often heard of a great river flowing by the Wacos' camp, and there they hoped to find water. They left not a soul or a hoof behind, but packed on the burros their little store of provisions and what bullion they had accumulated, well knowing that they could not return until the drouth was broken.

At Las Chanas (the Llano), they found a dry bed; the Colorado was as dry as the top of a rock. Arrived at the Lampasas Springs, they found a little water, a great deal of mud, and dead buffaloes covering the ground. They pulled some of the dead buffaloes out of the bog, got a little stinking water, and slowly moved on. But the burros were poor from want of grass and starved from want of water. To carry the heavy bullion much farther was impossible. The provisions had to be taken at any price. So two small dugouts were made in the side of a hill, the bullion was buried therein, and after the captain of the band had called on all to witness the marks of the place, the cavalcade moved on.

The trail eastward was marked by dead beasts and dead men, but at last the remnant arrived at the village of the Wacos. There they found a great river flowing clear and fresh, and when they had drunk and had seen their beasts drink, they knelt down to give God thanks, and the *padre* with them blessed the stream and called it Los Brazos de Dios—the Arms of God.

The Spanish built a stockade and waited. The drouth kept on for three more years. Los Brazos still flowed clear and sweet, and memories of the rich mines and the silver bars left behind grew dim like the details of a lost dream. But at last it rained. Then the grass and weeds sprang from the earth with a great rush. The grass grew so quickly that a powerful and fierce tribe of Indians was down upon the Spaniards before they could leave. Their little settlement was annihilated. Only one man lived to get back to Mexico, and that years later, when he was so feeble and broken that he had no desire ever again to come into the region of the terrible drouth. But a while before he died he outlined on a piece of parchment that search across the desert for water, the directions, as well as he could give them, to the buried bullion, and the final disasters on the river called Los Brazos de Dios. The hidden dugouts with their wealth have never been found, and the records in the archives of Spain say nothing of a Spanish settlement at Waco beside The Arms of God.

But the waters of the Brazos, in tradition at least, have saved *cristianos* from savage foes as well as from deadly thirst. It is a matter of record that in 1758 a great horde of Comanches descended upon the Spanish mission on the San Saba River and killed two priests besides other persons. What follows is not of record, but "all the old Mexicans about San Antonio" used to believe in it.

When the Comanches made their assault, the soldiers of the presidio—the remains of which are yet to be seen near Menard—were absent. The savages had little trouble in killing the unarmed laborers in the mines. One of the priests fled toward the river, which was in flood, followed by a horde of yelling warriors. Then came the miracle. The waters opened, the priest passed safely across, and while his murderous pursuers were following in the lane made by Providence, the flood resumed its sweep and carried them to death. A few days later the priest appeared at the San Juan Mission near San Antonio and told of what had happened. Soldiers who went to the San Saba found the banks, below the passageway made by the waters for the *padre,* strewn with the bodies of drowned Comanches. Thereupon they changed the name of the San Saba River to Los Brazos de Dios. This stream is a branch of the Colorado River, but, as has already been noted, the names of the present Brazos and Colorado rivers were in early times interchanged.

This old story of opening waters has descended in another form from the "first three hundred" of Austin's colonists. It has to do with a mission on the Brazos proper,—then called the Tockonhono—a mission not recorded in history. The tale is quoted here from Mollie E. Moore Davis's novel *Under the Man-Fig*, 1895.

"The bed of the river is very deep; and the color of the water—when it creeps sluggishly along between its banks, so shallow in places that the blue heron may wade it without wetting his knees—is the color of tarnished brass. But when it comes roaring down from the faraway Redlands, a solid foam-crested wall, leaping upward a foot a minute, and spreading death and destruction into the outlying lowlands, then it is as red as spilled blood.

"On its banks, more than a century and a half ago, a handful of barefoot Franciscan friars, who had prayed and fought their way across the country from Mexico, founded the Presidio of St. Jago, and corralled within the boundary walls a flock of *Indios reducidos*.

"There were the stately church, cloistered and towered and rose-windowed—a curious flower of architecture abloom in the savage wilderness—and the blockhouse with its narrow loopholes, and the hut into which the Indian women were thrust at night under lock and key.

"The mighty forest and open prairies around teemed with *Indios bravos*, who hated the burly, cassocked, fighting monks, and their own Christianized tribesmen.

"These came, in number like the leaves of the live oak, to hurl themselves against the presidio. After many days of hard fighting, the single friar who remained alive turned his eyes away from the demolished church, and, under cover of smoke from the burning blockhouse, led the remnant of *Indios reducidos* (who because they had learned to pray had not forgotten how to fight) out of the enclosure to a little postern-gate, and down the steep bank to the yellow thread of the river below.

"Midway of the stream—thridding the ankle-deep water—they were before the red devils above discovered their flight. The demoniac yell from a thousand throats pushed them like a battering ram up the opposite bank, whence, looking back, they saw the bed of the River Tockonhono swarming with their foes. Then the *Indios reducidos* opened their lips and began to chant the death-song of the Nainis; and the friar, lifting his hand, commended their souls and his own to the God who gives and who takes away.

"But, lo, a miracle!

"Even as the waves of the Red Sea—opened by the rod of Moses for the passage of his people—closed upon Pharaoh and his host, so, with the hoarse roar of a wild beast springing upon his prey, the foam-crested wall of water fell upon the *Indios bravos,* and not a warrior of them all came forth from the river bed but as a bruised and beaten corpse.

"So the friar, falling on his knees, gave thanks. And the river, which was the Tockonhono, became from that day Los Brazos de Dios, which is to say, The Arms of God."

IV. THE STAKED PLAINS

For generations the very openness of the Staked Plains made them the Great Unknown in American geography—a part of "the great American desert." A chronicler of S. H. Long's expedition (1819) had "little apprehension of giving too unfavorable an account" of these "dreary plains." Any traveler, he says, "who shall at any time have traversed its desolate sands will, we think, join us in the wish that this desolate region may forever remain the unmolested haunt of the native hunter, the bison and the jackal [coyote]." To Josiah Gregg, whose exceedingly interesting and informing *Commerce of the Prairies* appeared in 1844, "the fearful Llano Estacado" appeared "fitted only for the haunts of the mustang, the buffalo, the antelope and their migratory lord, the prairie Indian." A few years later Randolph B. Marcy, who was sent by the United States Government to explore "those vast and inhospitable plains," reported them uncultivatable and destined to continue merely as "the abode of wandering savages."

Although the desert idea was disproved long ago, yarns about the winds and sandstorms that sweep the plains insure their remaining the subject of folk-lore. To aid popular wind-jamming, government reports treat of plans for turning bleak prairies into forests; at the same time geologists speculate on how the combined action of plow and wind will eventually cause the soil to blow away. In other words, the plow, which proved the plains to be not a desert, will, according to the prophets, turn them into one.

The Staked Plains are still a mystery, their name itself the subject of legend. The first white men in history to look upon their vastness were the Spaniards of Coronado's Expedition seeking a place where the common folk drank water from pitchers of solid gold and their king took his afternoon nap "under a tall spreading tree decorated with an infinitude of little golden bells." They did not find riches, but they found strangeness.

The chief chronicler of Coronado's Expedition was Castañeda. "Who could believe," he exclaims, "that 1000 horses and 500 of our [domestic] cows and more than 5000 rams and ewes and more than 1500 friendly Indians and servants"—for with such massed *impedimenta* did Coronado proceed—"in traveling over these plains would leave no more trace where they had passed than if nothing had been there—nothing—so that it was necessary to make piles of [buffalo] bones and cow-dung [the buffalo chips dried on top of the grass] now and then, so that the rear guard could follow the army. The grass never failed to become erect after it had been trodden down, and although it was short, it was as fresh and straight as before."

Seemingly limited only by the forever unapproachable horizon and in their levelness varied only by monotonous depressions and the curvature of the earth, the plains inspired an awe in these first lone penetrators that called for some sort of markers. "I could not find their limit anywhere I went," reported Coronado. "There were no more landmarks than if we had been swallowed up in the sea." If one of his men went off but half a league to hunt buffalo, he became lost. The country the buffalo bulls "traveled over was so level and smooth that if a man looked at them, the sky could be seen between their legs; if some of them were at a distance, they looked like smooth-trunked pines whose tops joined, and if there was only one bull it looked as if there were four pines. When one was near them, it was impossible to see the ground on the other side of them."

According to the great scholar Bandelier, Coronado upon setting out in quest of the Gran Quivira left instructions that he could be followed by means of wooden crosses he intended to erect along his route. No matter what Coronado's intentions were, we may be sure that after he got well out on the plains he had no wood either holy or unholy to put up as a sign. And, despite talk about markers, if Coronado's men named this region the Llano Estacado, history says nothing about the matter. *Llano* means *plain,* and *estacado* means *staked, enclosed with stakes, palisaded.* Nor do the chronicles say anything about *estacas* (stakes). On account of the great herds of buffaloes—the only *vacas* (cows) native to America—the Spaniards called the country "The Plains of the Cows," Llanos de las Vacas. Just when it took the name of Llano Estacado I do not know; nor do I know either when in the English tongue it came to be commonly known as the Staked Plains. Corrupting the word *llano,* the buffalo hunters and early plainsmen often called it "the *yarner.*"

But from a very early day the origin of the term *estacado,* or *staked,* became a subject for speculation. Why was the great plain called *staked?* Where and what were the "'stakes"?

As one explanation, I have quoted Castañeda's account of how a trail was marked off by piles of bones and dried buffalo chips. When American chroniclers and explorers, about a century ago, took up the subject, they all seem to have heard that either the Spaniards or New Mexicans had literally staked off a route across the great plain. "I have been assured by Mexican hunters and Indians," wrote Josiah Gregg, "that from Santa Fe southeastward, there is but one route upon which this plain can be safely traveled during the dry season; and even some of the watering places on this are at intervals of fifty to eighty miles and hard to find. Hence the Mexican traders and hunters, that they might not lose their way and perish from thirst, once staked out this route across the plains; whence it has received the name of El Llano Estacado, or the Staked Plain."

With and without variations, this explanation of Gregg's was repeated many times by writers and explorers who followed him. How a party of travelers from Santa Fe to San Antonio could have carried enough pickets with them to leave a line of visible stakes across hundreds of miles of naked plains nobody seems to have enquired. If the stakes were to loom out as guide posts and were to stand up against the tramplings of buffaloes, they would have to be fairly long and heavy and a very great number of them would be required. Of course a few stakes at some point might have given a name to the whole region, but this is not likely. One account I have heard goes that the Spaniards just stuck stobs in the ground and capped each with the skull of a buffalo.

But there are other theories as to the derivation of the name. Early explorers, one rumor goes, found out upon the plains stumps of a forest that had been destroyed by fire, those stumps affording the stakes for a name. Again it is surmised that the stalks sent up by bear grass or other varieties of yucca were the original stakes. Indians of the Plains, who needed no compass or guide posts any more than wild geese need them, have even been credited with a line of stakes capped by buffalo skulls. To me the most plausible of all explanations is that suggested by Thomas Falconer, who accompanied the Santa Fe Expedition, 1841, and kept a diary, from which I quote:

"We commenced the ascent to the grand prairie—the Llano Estacado of the New Mexicans. This was the great plain spoken of at San Antonio as too extensive to travel over, where we should be without timber, without water, and where many of our horses would perish. At all the points where our exploring parties had previously touched it, its sides were rugged, looking, as the name denotes, as if staked from the lower ground, and as if boldly lifted up, or else as if the ground about it had at some former time sunk around it."

In other words, the palisades which bound the high plains at many places on its eastern side might well be the "stakes" of the Llano Estacado. These extraordinary escarpments have led some people to believe that the original Spanish name was not Llano Estacado but Llano Escarpado; old maps do not bear out this theory. Nor is the translation, "Stockaded Plain," as suggested by an eminent authority, convincing to me. *Estacada* is a noun meaning *palisade; estacado* is the past participle of the verb *estacar,* in the masculine form to agree with the noun *llano.* A correct translation of the name Llano Estacado would then be Palisaded Plain. If the Spaniards meant to name the plains after their palisaded eastern rim, then the theories of a century have been based on merely a popular mistranslation. Yet the connotations of the mere name, "the Great Staked Plains," are so stirring to the imagination that I should never wish to see it supplanted by "Palisaded Plains."

V. CABEZA DE VACA AND HORSEHEAD

In view of how Texas was later to become seamed by the trails of multiplied millions of Spanish cattle, ranged over by countless mustangs of Spanish blood, and dominated by men of cows and horses, it was fitting that the very first civilized human being to traverse it should have borne the name of Cabeza de Vaca. The family name was originally Alhaja, but in 1212 one of Cabeza's ancestors, a peasant, informed the King of Navarre how a mountain pass could be used to circumvent the Moors, and marked the entrance to it with the skull of a cow. The infidels were by this means defeated, and Alhaja was ennobled, granted a coat-of-arms, and dubbed Cabeza de Vaca (Cow's Head).

The bleached skull of a cow or horse makes a signal marker, whether hung on bush or tree or laid on bare ground. One of the old roads of Texas was called Cow Head Road. It was marked in the forties between Corsicana and Waco by placing the dried skulls of cattle along the route—signs more visible than tree blazes after their freshness has dimmed. This manner of marking a route, begun in Texas by Coronado, must not have been unusual. It is said that the first road—a trail—used by freighters between Houston and Dallas was along its upper windings "blazed by heaps of buffalo bones that could be seen for miles."[3]

Ox Skull Hill rises a few miles south of Sabinal, just off the old "upper road" between San Antonio and Eagle Pass. Here, a tradition of the country goes, three freighters passing with empty wagons were beset by Indians. In order to take advantage of the ground they goaded their oxen to the top of the hill and went into corral formation. But the Indians were too many to hold out against. They killed the freighters, killed their oxen, and burned the wagons. For years the bleached ox skulls lay on the hill to give it a name and a story.

Because a creek is named Cow or Bull or Beef—and there are many such in Texas—does not of course mean that more cattle ranged on it than on the next creek. Maybe something happened to a "cow brute" here— like the roping and beefing of a ferocious old mossy-horned outlaw brindled steer on the creek now called Brindle in Brewster County—and maybe it didn't. A creek in Montana named Sage, says Granville Stuart, is so called "because there is not so much as one sage bush

---

[3] John Caton, quoted in *Parade of the Pioneers*, by Otho Ann Hanscom, Dallas, 1935, p. 118.

on it." For long I have tried to find out if ever a single live oak tree grew in the vicinity of Encinal (Live Oak Grove) in Webb County. Nevertheless, we may be sure that maverick cattle were "twined" on every one of various Maverick creeks, and while the range was still all open a particular band of "mustang" cattle, black and sharp of horn, ran on Cow Bayou, McLennan County. A man who hunted them hung a bull hide high on a limb to dry; it shrank and there, black and odoriferous, tantalized coyotes and marked the spot for years, thus giving Bullhide Creek its name.

Cowhouse Creek, in the same region, got its name while Texas still had "more cows and less milk than any other country on earth"—and no sheds for milk cows at all. Under the limestone bluffs along the Cowhouse are many shelters, and therein cows that it would have taken a dog to catch and a cowboy with two ropes to tie for milking used to den up against the northers of winter and the suns of summer.

Along the coast, cattle by the hundreds of thousands were skinned for their hides and boiled for their tallow, the meat being cast away to buzzards, coyotes and fishes. The cattle were hardly worth driving off, but the Skinning War was fought against men who rode the range killing them in order to peel their hides. On a creek in De Witt County cattle that bogged, or perhaps were cunningly killed near the bog holes so that their carcasses would not appear suspicious, furnished so many hides that the stream acquired the name of Cuero (Hide). The town of Cuero took its name from this creek.

The name Pecos seems to be a corruption of Puerco (Hog), Spaniards probably having seen some javelinas, "Mexican hogs," on the river. It is one of the most singular streams in America. Ages ago its lower reaches, before disgorging into the Rio Grande, cut an impassable canyon through solid rock. Higher up, its writhings for hundreds of miles resemble a great canal rather than a river, not a bush or tree along the banks of saline and alkaline soil to mark its course, no valley to distinguish its presence, bleak prairies and naked breaks on either side of it. The traveler across the trackless land of early days did not know that he was near the Pecos until he stood on the brink. Then he saw far below him a sullen stream of dark water, in time of drought often so bitter that no animal will drink it, flowing between perpendicular banks—a gulch as impassable as the deepest moat ever trenched around a medieval castle.

There was one crossing on this Pecos that became continent-famous. It is no longer used, but it will always be remembered. Remote now from any road and to be gained only by traversing bleak and solitary land that will never be plowed up, it is still Horsehead Crossing. What white man first discovered it or who marked it or named it will probably never be known. Two historic routes blended on the left bank of the river and crossed here: the old Chihuahua Trail from San Antonio and the Butterfield Stage Road, to California, from Jefferson Barracks on the Missouri River. The crossing became the most noted, the most desired and the most dreaded mark on the Goodnight-Loving Cattle Trail. Here bands of Comanches or Apaches lay in wait to rob and kill travelers and herdsmen; here grew up a little graveyard, untended and uncherished, for no habitation of the living—excepting a lone and temporary stage station—was ever erected at Horsehead Crossing, and no camper tarried here longer than necessary, such a dreary, forsaken place it was.

Whether the Spanish ever used Horsehead Crossing is doubtful. One old story has it that Indians—Apaches or Comanches—placed the skulls of mustangs at the crossing as a sign for some of their tribesmen who were following. When Judge O. W. Williams, of Fort Stockton, reached the trans-Pecos country in 1884, he heard how away back in the forties a small detachment of soldiers or rangers who had captured a herd of ponies from Indians near the Pecos and found them an impediment, killed the animals at the crossing, then unnamed and little known. Some time later the skulls were so placed as to mark the ford.

Corroborative of this account is the entry made by John R. Bartlett in his journal for October 30, 1850, upon reaching the Pecos River. "After our fatiguing march of two days and one night without rest . . . I examined the river. . . . Found the water at the Horse-head Crossing, which was a quarter of a mile from our encampment, to afford the greatest facilities. Here there was a bank about half the height of the main bank, to which there was an easy descent, and one equally so to the water. It is the place where other parties seem to have crossed, and hence rendered easy of access. *I noticed a long line of horse or mule skulls placed along the bank, which probably gave* [the crossing] *the name it bears.*"

There is a Horsehead Canyon in Erath County, although before 1861 it was known to the few frontiersmen acquainted with it as Mulberry Canyon. In that year a posse of settlers whose horses had been raided followed the Indian raiders into the canyon. During the fight that followed many horses were killed and for years their bones lay on the ground. Hence Horsehead Canyon.

Mustang Bayou, Mustang Island, **Mustang Pens,** Wild Horse Mesa, Horse Thief Canyon, Dead Horse Canyon, Caballo (Horse) Pass, Laguna de Caballo, Horse Pen Creek and Horse Pen Bayou, Arroyo Potranca (Filly Creek), and Yegua (Mare) Creek—these names, like those "certain dank gardens" Stevenson speaks of, "cry aloud" for a story. There are dozens of Mustang, Horse, and Wild Horse Creeks. Many of these names are no doubt general, yet many also must have been prompted by particular horses or particular experiences with horses.

Years before the Civil War, Joe Tumlinson got together a large number of rawhide riatas to build mustang pens with. His idea was to use the ropes successively for pens in several places, for it was hard to drive a band of mustangs off their own range. How successful he was with his pens is not remembered. The rawhide probably held, in accordance with the old saying that Texas was held together with rawhide. The name of Rope Pen Creek in De Witt County commemorates Joe Tumlinson's enterprise.

Early in this century John Dinn established a ranch in the Hebbronville country at a lake far better known than its impermanent waters would warrant in a less arid country. According to Mexican tradition, an Indian once stole a horse from the Santa Niña (Holy Child) Ranch near by and led him off. At the lake he tried to ride the horse, mounting three times to be thrown each time. In anger he shot the horse and killed him and went *pa' alla*. Ever since then the lake has been known as Laguna de Caballo, and the ranch is "Horse Lake" too.

About 1880 a considerable party of surveyors under the direction of General Geno of the United States Army was making its way down the Rio Grande above the mouth of the Pecos River. The country became so rough and canyon-cut that they could proceed no farther with horses. They could leave the river and make a great detour by way of Fort Stockton, or they could make rafts and float down the river. They decided to abandon their horses and take to rafts. In order to prevent their horses from falling into the hands of Apaches, who were yet marauding back and forth across the Rio Grande, they shot them down, thirty or forty head. That is how the deep gorge of the Rio Grande for a long distance above Del Rio got the name of Dead Horse Canyon.

"A mare is a horse but a horse is not a mare, and a mule is neither," as my father used to say. There are plenty of Mule creeks in Texas, and there is at least one White Mule Creek, which might have been named either for the white colored scion of a mare and a jack—an animal supposed never to die, for "whoever saw a dead *white mule?*"—or for that liquid known as "tarantula juice" and "mountain dew" as well as "white mule." The ultimate of stubbornness was as the saying went, to be "as stubborn as a government mule." One of these government mules, branded U S, ran with mustangs in what is now Haskell County. Always on the alert, a sentinel impossible to slip up on, he was warier and fleeter than the wariest and fleetest of the wild horses he had joined. He gave more than one mustanger a run for his money, but he was worth sure enough money, and finally he was captured on a creek—Mule Creek now, of course.

The word *stampede* connotes cattle or horses. In 1839 Major George Erath led the pursuit west of the Brazos River after some Indians that were back-trailing following a raid into Milam County. "On their way down," Erath says, "the Indians had driven the buffalo before them, killing large numbers, so that the whole country was covered with their carcasses. The stench of these bodies, together with that of the bodies of the dead Indians"—for there had been a "sharp brush" with the marauders—"terrified our horses at night and caused them to stampede. This occurrence gave the name Stampede to the creek where it took place." The horses were recovered on another creek—Horse Creek thenceforth.

VI. INDIAN SIGN

In Mexico, where the bulk of the population is Indian—assimilated and unassimilated,—Indian names by the thousands are yet attached to the soil; in Texas, where Indian and Spaniard remained alien to each other, the Christian never getting far enough along to enslave the native and pick up his language, the conquerors adopted but few of the aboriginal place names. The English-speaking frontiersmen, while readily taking over Spanish names, were even more indifferent to those of Indian origin than had been their predecessors. Original Indian names for places, like Waxahachie, Anahuac, Quitaque, Copano, and Tahoka, are now comparatively rare. They are hardly as common as native names for plant life, like *juajilla, huisache, mesquite, sacahuiste* (salt grass), *anacahua* ("knock-away," as the folk call it), *quamash* (much to be preferred to the synonymous "false hyacinth"), *yaupon,* and the "all-thorn" *junco.*

Anglo-Americans made virtually no attempt in Texas to Christianize the Indians, their single purpose being to get rid of them. Numerous tribal names—like Alabama Village, Seminole and Comanche, Kickapoo Springs, Cherokee County, Lipan Flats, Karankawa Bay, Ayish Bayou, Tonkawa Bottom and Tonk Valley, the creeks of Bedias, Choctaw, Kiowa, Keechi, Delaware and Shawnee, Caddo Lake and Tehuacana Hills—attest in a general way that certain tribesmen were here or there. Tepee Draw in Irion County, Mound Prairie on the old Kickapoo Road east of Palestine, Scalp Creek, self-explanatory, and Blanket Creek, on which some "blanket Indians" had a camp, are but name-signs put up by the vanquishers of the red man to mark his trail of retreat. They are signatures, traced by proxies, marking his having been here and his vanishment—signatures hardly so veracious as the hand-prints which tribesmen from the dawn of history have left in rock shelters. (Some of these prints, red from the ochre in which the hand was dipped, on the walls of a gorge in San Saba County are responsible for the name of Bloody Hand Print Canyon.)

Yet behind any generalized tribal names may lie some specific incident, as the following account, probably apocryphal, will illustrate. Long before Fort Stockton was established, the springs at which it is located were known as Comanche Springs. Here one night some hunters, to whom the country was all unknown, camped. After dark they heard wolf barks all around them and dimly saw wolfish forms skulking out beyond the fire. One of the hunters shot at a bulk that came into fair view and seemingly hit it. At daylight he found that his target instead of being a veritable lobo was a Comanche, dead as Hector's pup, in a wolf skin. From this incident the springs were thereafter called Comanche Springs.

A definite squaw, too, obscure as in life, probably lurks behind the name of each of several Squaw creeks. On the one in Hood County the squaw was found lost, some say; according to others, she was here killed by warriors from an enemy tribe, the act bringing on a fight between her own band and the slayers.

Frontiersmen did attach the names of a few individual Indians to sites in some way connected with them, like Victoria Peak, named after the Apache chief who was chased all through the mountains of West Texas, and Quanah, after Quanah Parker, the Comanche chieftain who was the son of tragic Cynthia Ann. Luce's Bayou, according to legend, was named after a girl, half-Indian and half-Negro, that a party of settlers from Louisiana brought along as a slave. After nooning on a stream that empties into San Jacinto Bayou, the movers missed the slave girl. Then they "cut for sign" and out on a prairie found her track. It was pointed back east. The men followed it and finally sighted the girl, but she ran like an antelope. After a two-day chase they captured her, almost all her clothes and much of her skin torn away by thorns. The prairie on which Luce's track was picked up became known as Lost Prairie and the bayou from which she slipped away took her name.

History bears out the tradition that the Angelina River is named after an Indian maiden whom Spanish missionaries about 1690 found living in a village on that stream and who proved to be so "modest and amiable" and eager for knowledge—particularly of the Christian doctrine—that they educated her. She became a fluent interpreter, and on more than one occasion she befriended Spaniards and Frenchmen against the hostilities both of her kinsmen and of the wilderness.

To the Indian, the trail of his retreat is "the Trail of Tears"; to the average white man, who lumps all tribes and all kinds of tribesmen together as Indian, it is a trail of blood. And blood let by Indians has given name to more than one place along the trail. In 1868 a band of Comanches found six or eight women and children alone in a picket house in Llano County. After scalping one woman and leaving her for dead, although she subsequently recovered, they made the children and the other women captive and hurriedly retreated. A posse made up to follow them found the head of a child fixed on a jagged stump that had been shattered by lightning; some accounts say on a rock. The rock or stump, whichever it may have been, was on a low mountain, and Baby Head Mountain it was named. Rain that falls on its slopes sheds into Babyhead Creek, and Baby Head is the name of a small community that grew up not far away.

Popher Creek, in Angelina County, remembers an Indian in a different way. As a legend of the country runs, Chief Popher had a wayward young son named Jim who killed a pair of peddlers for their calico and hand mirrors. White settlers captured him and sentenced him to be shot.

Then the aged chief plead that he might be executed in his son's place. He himself, he reasoned, had lived out his time of usefulness and would soon die anyway; the boy would repent and become a good man. The settlers agreed to this proposal and even allowed Chief Popher to set the time of his execution and pick the place where he was to die.

He chose the slope of a little creek along which he had killed many a deer. At the hour set he appeared, without guard, dressed in a robe of calico with long sleeves and ruffles falling below his hands. He knelt, gave the tribal war-whoop, and twelve men fired. Only one of the twelve guns had a ball in it, however, the other eleven being loaded with blanks, no one of the twelve executioners knowing what was in his gun.

With a bullet through his heart Chief Popher fell dead and was buried where he fell. Popher Creek the little stream draining by the place of execution and burial was thereafter called.

Indian Bend and Indian Creek, Indian Gap and Indio Ranch, Indiahoma and Los Indios Junction—the word Indian is attached to some place in nearly every part of the country. Perhaps an old Mexican will tell you that here the Indios roped a goat herder and dragged him through the prickly pear; or an old-timer will tell how his pa and another man once killed a Comanche out on that creek and cut a razor "strop" from his back. "Yes, it shore would make a razor sharp." On another creek the Indians could not remove from a horse the steel hobbles that a smart settler had got in order to circumvent thieves—and so they cut off the horse's feet. That's how that Indian Creek got its name. There is a longish legend about Indian Bluff on the Canadian River, near the Oklahoma boundary line.

"See that tall rocky cliff over there?" the old hunter known as "Doctor" Barton gestured. "Well, seems like during early days there was a man and his family a-living here on this side the river. He had a mighty purty little baby girl, besides some other young 'uns, and then of course there was their ma. Over beyant the river a lot of Indians hung out. Some of them lived in the caves, they say. They was friendly enough. One old yaller-belly in pertickler. He used to climb down the cliff and get in his bull-hide boat and come acrost to visit the family. The little girl baby took to him mighty friendly. She'd play with a medicine bag he had hung round his neck, and he got to taking her for rides in his boat. It was mighty queer that her pappy and ma would let her go that-a-way, but they done it.

"One day the Indian and the white man had a rucus. I don't exactly recollect all the details, but it seems the white man wanted the Indian to chop wood or do something like that, and the Indian renigged. Then the white man picked up a stick and hit him over the head. The Indian left in a fury and didn't come back for a long time. The white man got scared now lest he'd started sure-'nough trouble. Maybe, too, he felt sorry for flying off the handle that-a-way.

"Anyhow, when he looked out one day and seen the old Indian coming acrost the river, he was glad. The Indian acted like nothing had ever happened and the little girl was friendlier than ever. She wanted to go riding. Her ma was against it and her pappy was too, but the little thing pitched and cried around so much that they finally gave in.

"The old buck began paddling straight acrost. Then on the other side he climbed out with the baby in his arms. He'd never landed her on that side before, and naturally the family was alarmed, but they couldn't do nothing. The river is wide here, as you can see, and the white man dassent shoot for fear of hitting the baby. He called out for the Indian to come back, but the Indian just kinder dangled the baby up in front of himself. He kept going and began climbing the cliff. When he got to the top, he stood still on the edge a minute or so, waved his hand to the folks on the other side, and then let out a war-whoop and with the baby still in his arms jumped over the cliff to the rocks and water below.

"That's all there is to the story. Indian and baby were both killed. Now you know why folks call this place Indian Bluff."

In what was once the great buffalo—and therefore Comanche and Kiowa—range between Pease River and the Red in Hardeman County, stands a line of four rounded hills called Medicine Mounds. They are extraordinarily conspicuous, the cones rising about 350 feet above the surrounding plain. Flanking them to the west is the gully-washed scar of an ancient buffalo trail. Round about are yet to be picked up Indian arrowheads of flint. The gypsum waters of a spring at the base of one mound was drunk by sick Indians as a physic. To the mounds pertains a legend common in the country.

On top of the highest of the four is a flat cap-rock—a protector against erosion. It was, the Indians believed, the dwelling place of a powerful and benevolent spirit. Here the spirit could view the country for miles and miles on all sides, and from this lofty point of vantage he was wont to direct the arrows of hunters to the vitals of buffaloes and to deflect those of enemies shot at his wards, the Comanches.

One time a band of Comanches that came to hunt in the wide range of the good spirit included, as almost every such band included, a medicine man. Women were along to cure the meat, prepare the hides for robes, and do other services. But there was one woman who could do no work. She was the daughter of the medicine man, and she was young and beautiful, and she lay sick with a fever, every day growing weaker.

Her father had sucked worms and evil spirits out of many a brave and many a squaw, had chanted away the pains from many a girl, and smoked the weakness forth from many a boy, but he could not cure his own daughter. He had rattled his gourd all night long while he prayed and chanted. From his medicine bundle of herbs, the tails of deer, the gristle of a bear snout, the dried maw of a buffalo, eagle claws, and other medicaments he had prepared cures while the moon was dark and while it was full. He had mixed his simples in every way that inherited tradition or individual originality could suggest. He had consulted other medicine men. All had been in vain.

One morning he came out of the tepee utterly hopeless. Looking vacantly into the distance, he suddenly saw a meaning in the rock-capped peak of the great mound. He must, something told him, put all trust in the spirit dwelling there. He had eaten frugally for days. Now, without touching water or food, he went apart to pray and fast until the spirit should send him a revelation. At length it came. It was that he take his medicines to the high rock and mix them there so that the power of the good spirit should enter into them.

Hours later when he returned, he found his daughter very quiet—too quiet perhaps; when he felt her face, it was not so hot as it had been. He gave her the medicine mixed on the rock. Then again he went outside and prayed to the mound spirit—prayed with the patience of those who live under the sun, and watch shadows, and note day by day the greening and the browning of grass. At length he heard the voice of his daughter. He bounded within. Her eye was bright, her color almost healthy. She had slept deeply, she said. From that hour she mended steadily and was soon able to skin buffaloes and pack in loads of buffalo chips.

Thereafter this medicine man, and other medicine men too who learned of the source of his powers, paid seasonal visits to the spirit on the high mound, offering tribute. Today the name of the four extraordinary hills lined against the ancient buffalo trail that runs down to Pease River remains as a testimonial of the associations they had for the native people that lived by and vanished with the buffaloes—Medicine Mounds.

VII. DOWNRIGHT CIRCUMSTANTIAL EVIDENCE

On January 1, 1822, Abner Kuykendall and Thomas Boatright, who had moved out about ten miles west from the Brazos River, settled in the rich bottom of a creek. They called it New Year's Creek. That is plain enough; so is Sunday Creek, a tributary to the Palo Duro Canyon, on which a surveying party spent the Sabbath Day in 1887. Had plain old Abner and Tom Boatright been Spaniards, they would probably have named the creek after an Italian saint pertaining to New Year's Day; but they could not possibly have been Spaniards. They represent a race downright and direct, the members of which sometimes celebrate their own birthdays but never in the circuitous manner of calling it after some saint of the Middle Ages to whom centuries ago a certain day of the year was assigned. The Anglo-Saxon people can be picturesque, for picturesqueness is sublimated reality; when not conventionalized and standardized, they speak a homely language.

Generalized distinctions between races and languages can, however, be very treacherous. As has been seen, Spanish-speaking folk often named a feature of the country from some circumstance arising in connection with it or for some salient characteristic. Anglo-American pioneers who followed them gave names in pretty much the same way, though their names are generally more homely and downright, often more rough and ready—

especially more rough, euphony hardly being regarded at all.[4]

The entries for September 5 and 6, 1824, from a diary kept by Stephen F. Austin will further illustrate the frontier principle of naming. "Found at this encampment the bones of two men which had been cut up and boiled—buried them—and called the creek Cannibal Creek." Austin's party was at the time campaigning against the cannibalistic Karankawa Indians. Again, "Country on this creek very brushy and generally poor land—between it and Cannibal Creek poor wet boggy prairie with Islands of brush and small oaks—nooned [at] the crossing on this creek and called it Chapparo from the quantity of brush on it." The word *chaparro,* misspelled by Austin, means *brush,* and here is an illustration of the tendency of English-speaking men in a Spanish or Mexican country to give names in the Spanish language.

"When the first three families, Saner, Milstead and Odem, came to Bandera County in 1852," says the chronicle of that region, "they moved in wagons drawn by oxen. They crossed a little stream which they named Red Bluff Creek because of the reddish color of its steep bank. . . . They journeyed forward and came to another gurgling brooklet where the prospect was so

[4] California, in which rough-and-ready pioneer names sprang up to supplant or live beside Spanish names, affords a parallel for the principles of nomenclature in Texas. The editor of the San Francisco *Herald* wrote, in 1853, a vehement editorial on the subject. "Some of our people in the interior," he complained, "have a most ordinary taste in nomenclature. The recent election has brought to light such delectable localities as Whisky Creek, Jackass Gulch, Humbug City, One Horse Town, One Mule Town, Drunkard's Bar, Murderer's Bar, Shirt-tail Cañon, Lower Humbug, Negro Hill, Fiddletown, Coon Hollow, Jay Hawk, Condemned Bar, Mule Cañon, Greenhorn, Mugginsville, Mad Muletown, Sucker's Flat, Rattlesnake Bar, Yankee Jim's, Peppermint Bar, Mad Cañon, Humbug Cañon, Rough and Ready, French Corral, etc. For the love of posterity reform your nomenclature, good people, before it is too late. Unlike the settlers of most of the other new states, our people have retained very few of the Indian names for localities. Most of the rivers and counties in the state, and many of the settlements south of Sacramento, are still known by the euphonious Spanish titles given them by the early Californians. They were a very devout people, and sprinkled the names of their favorite saints all over the country. Thus we have San Francisco, San Joaquin, San Diego, Santa Clara, Santa Cruz, Santa Barbara, San Bernardino, Santa Ysabel, San Luis Obispo, San Andres, San José, San Antonio, San Rafael, San Leandro, Santa Tuez, San Gabriel, San Miguel, and a whole calendar of Sans and Santas. Of their unecclesiastical names, what more euphonious than Mendocino, Mariposa, Alameda, Nevada, Bolinas, Sacramento, Alviso, Salines, Sonoma, Sierra, Sancelito, Vallecito, Martínez, and Petaluma?"—Quoted in the *New York Weekly Herald,* October 15, 1853.

pleasing [that Odem remarked] he would lay his preemption there with the privilege of lifting it if they found better land to preempt farther along. That stream was thenceforth called Privilege Creek. Milstead killed a doe on a little branch, and it was named Doe Creek. . . . They camped on another little stream, and while there Odem lost his pipe. Since that time that stream has been called Pipe Creek."

Tradition, however, varies considerably the circumstance from which Pipe Creek took its name. As the anecdote goes, three pioneers riding horseback one day heard the Comanche yell behind them, and, looking back, saw a large band of the "painted savages" in pursuit. The only sensible thing for them to do was to make tracks. They spurred and quirted and were gaining well on the Comanches when they came to a creek. Here one of them—perhaps it was Odem—dropped his pipe, which he had been smoking. He halted. The other two men yelled for him to come on. "I'm going to get this pipe," he answered, and he got it and got away. Bandera County, in which Pipe Creek flows, took its name from Bandera Pass. *Bandera* is Spanish for *flag*, and the pass is said to have been named from the fact that in it a detachment of Spanish soldiers flying a flag had a fight with Indians.

Pipe Creek suggests Butcher Knife Creek, in Brewster County. One day, the story goes, a man riding southward from Alpine camped at a certain spring on a mountain creek. At the next camping place he discovered that he had left his butcher knife. He met another man and referred to "the spring where I lost my butcher knife." Some time later a man traveling north camped at this spring and found the knife. He later referred to it as "the spring where I found a butcher knife." Butcher Knife Spring on Butcher Knife Creek it became.

It was not a watch lost or found that gave Watch Mountain its name. Watch was an old hound belonging to Tate Moss, in Llano County. The year the Civil War started Watch became so intent on chasing a bear that he lost his footing and fell into a deep narrow fissure in the mountain side. Moss and his men, it is said, tried every conceivable way to extricate him, but without success. For days they tossed food to the dog, but he grew weaker, his whines and barkings thinner. Finally a bullet put him out of his misery.

A trapper out in the Big Bend once left his dog to watch camp, which was on a canyon, while he went to town for provisions. Circumstances, mixed with whiskey, delayed his return for many days. When he got back to camp he found his dog still on guard, but dead—starved to death. The dog's name has been forgotten, but that of Dog Canyon remembers his faithfulness.

Many of the topographic features of Texas were named by land surveyors. Perhaps the best known of these was that useful and just frontiersman, Major George B. Erath, for whom Erath County is named. Speaking of his work in McLennan County, Erath says in his *Memoirs*, "One of my men discovered a wasp nest and mistook it for a bee hive, and Wasp Creek received its name from that circumstance." Another early-day surveyor named Coryell was killed by Indians on a certain creek, and now both creek and county bear his name. In the same general region are two localities named Turnover and Pulltite; during the days of freighting by teams a wagon was turned over at the first named place, and it was a "tight pull" to get to the other.

These jumped-up names always have a savor. One day years ago "Uncle" Jim Norton was taking a "snort" with some men among whom was a hail-fellow-well-met stranger. "Where is it you are from, Uncle Jim?" he asked.

"By gatlins," the old frontierman replied, "I'm from Fort Spunky. The further up the creek you go, the worse they get, and Fort Spunky is at the head of it."

Uncle Jim Norton's settlement had been needing a name. It is on the map now of Hood County as Fort Spunky.

While the Saint Louis and Brownsville Railway Company was projecting a line to skirt the Texas coast, somebody asked John Pierce, across whose ranch the railroad was to build, what he thought of a station and shipping pens in the country. "Thank God," he bellowed. Then he added, "It would be a blessing." Right then he proposed the name for his station—"Thank God." Railroad officials considered that irreverent, but accepted "Blessing."

"The boys," says the autobiography of that old-time Texas cowhand who turned preacher, W. S. James, "had been [working cattle] for some weeks and run out of bread, the man they sent for supplies having been delayed on account of rain and swollen streams. Besides, he had to go sixty miles. We were camped on a little spring branch and had been living on beef straight for several days when our man came driving in with plenty of grub. The little hollow was ever afterwards called Happy Hollow."

Starvation Creek got its name in much the same way. Along in the late seventies six outlaws raided down on a cow outfit camped on a creek emptying into the Canadian River, got the drop on all hands, took all their horses and all their chuck, and made for New Mexico. One of the cowboys footed it sixty miles to Fort Elliott to give the alarm and get horses and food. While his waiting comrades lived on beef and water, they named their creek Starvation Creek. This anecdote does not ring true to the character of either cowboys or the bad men of the range, but I am following "they say" evidence.

Four of the most characteristic things in the Texas tradition are exceedingly sudden; the pull of his six-shooter by an accomplished gunman, the coming of a norther, a stampede, and the rush of flood waters down a mountain canyon. I don't know how Sixshooter Creek, in Stephens County, got its name, but there was a reason, and men remember when a place notorious for killings, like Hempstead, was commonly referred to as "Six-shooter Junction." There should be a Norther Prairie where John Custer's cow horses froze to death standing up one blizzardly night, and out towards the head of the Concho is a place yet known to some as Edgar's Boneyard, where in the year 1866 Captain James Edgar's wagon train camped storm-bound for ten days, sleet and snow covering the grass so that in the end sixty bunched-up mules were found frozen and starved to death. The story of Stampede Mesa has been told in another place. Back in early days a man and his wife made camp one evening in the bed of a tributary to Maravilla Canyon in the broken country of the Big Bend. When word reached Murphysville (now Alpine) that the couple had been swept under and down by a night flood from a cloudburst, someone exclaimed, "What a calamity!" Calamity Creek was named.

In 1850, as the old ranger Jeff Maltby has recalled, the team driven by Major Thomas, who was leading a reconnaisance party into West Texas, stopped, played out, at a spot about half a day's travel from Phantom Hill. The site was not favorable, but the major ordered camp struck. When asked why, he replied, "It was a military necessity." Camp Necessity became rather well known during buffalo days.

Disputes over the origin of the name of Fort Phantom Hill have waxed hotter than any fire ever directed upon or from "The Post on the Clear Fork of the Brazos," as the site was usually termed in military dispatches. In truth, there wasn't any such fire, although when the fort was abandoned in 1854, having been occupied only three years, it was feloniously burned. Indians called it Phantom, says one chronicler with a heroic disregard for Comanche accomplishments in the English language, "because the fort was so ghostly looking." One of the soldiers quartered at the post saw a white object on the hill about dusk, says another authority, and exclaimed, "A phantom on the hill," thus giving the fort its name. After it was abandoned it became a stage stand on the Butterfield route, and when Albert D. Richardson, the noted "Western correspondent," passed that way in 1859 he reported its name to have come "from the white ghostly chimneys of the burned fort."

All these explainers have had the cart before the horse. Before the chimneys were erected, the hill on which they still loom ghostly was named Phantom. From the northeast, this hill, it is said, appears in the distance to be a loftly elevation that gradually, as the traveler nears it, sinks almost to the level of the surrounding country. The commander of the reconnaisance party that gave Camp Necessity its name experienced this optical illusion and in selecting the site for the fort named the hill Phantom.

There is no basis for the common belief that General Robert E. Lee was stationed at the fort for a time and gave it its name. The "legend" that Larry Chittenden, "cowboy poet," who ranched in the region, wove into his ballad of "Old Fort Phantom Hill" was doubtlessly invented by him; the ballad is trite and not comparable to that author's genial and life-portraying "Cowboys' Christmas Ball."

Chinquapin trees grow in East Texas, their nuts being for some reason as lowly in connotation as "goober peas." Long before the Spaniards came to America, tradition goes, an Indian chief called his two sons, bade one of them walk east for a certain length of time and the other walk west for the same time and each establish an encampment. The one who went east called his village Natchitoches, in what is now Louisiana; the other called his Nacogdoches, both names meaning, it is said, "Chinquapin Eater."

About two miles out from Nacogdoches, the old road running east crosses what was once known as Chinquapin Creek. Here, tradition continues, travelers were in the habit of stopping to take a swig of whiskey from bottles commonly carried in saddle pockets and then to wash it down with the branch water. But circumstances alter names as well as cases.

In 1826 Hayden Edwards, who as empresario had brought his thirteen children, his brothers and numerous other people to the old Spanish-Indian town of Nacogdoches, declared the Republic of Fredonia independent of Mexico. Stephen F. Austin and Mexican troops soon quelled this premature revolt, and the Fredonians fled east. In time the Mexican troops withdrew, and on Christmas Day following their expulsion—to leave history and resume legend—some of the Fredonians reached Chinquapin Creek on their way back to Nacogdoches. There were a few women in the party and of course there was some corn whiskey. Where the eggs came from is not told, but the returners, in honor of the day and in honor of their home-coming, decided that they should not merely take the customary swig but celebrate with an egg-nog. The women mixed it, everybody drank it, and thereafter the Chinquapin became Egg-Nog Branch.

Not so common a drink as whiskey, but known to the pioneers, was metheglin. It is an old English beverage, which, for me at least, will always connote Thomas Hardy's story of "The Three Strangers." It is made by boiling honey and water together, allowing the mixture to ferment and then spicing to suit. In Bell County is an inconsequential creek bearing the name of Metheglin—probably the only creek in the world so called. How the name originated is a matter of local history, not legend.

An early settler on this creek, then unnamed, was a character by the name of Morrison. Like many other good citizens of the time, he was fond of a dram. He made and drank metheglin and he made and drank whiskey. Whiskey was cheap, selling for four-bits a gallon, but Morrison was such a good patron of his own product that he never had any to sell. His wife always called him Honey.

One day when Honey was about "three sheets in the wind," his wife gave him the bucket and told him to go down to the creek and fetch her some water. He managed to walk to the spring, but when he bent over to dip up the water he fell into it. He let out a yell and his wife lit out a-running. At the same moment a neighbor rode up. He saw there was no danger of Honey's drowning. "I'll declare!" he laughed. "Honey in water. Call your creek Metheglin now." And Metheglin Creek it has been ever since. I suspect that the corn juice from which Whiskey Creek in Young County took its name was undiluted.

It is a fact that now and then on the frontier buffaloes captured as calves were trained to be work-oxen. Living out on a creek south of Corsicana, was an individual who had great faith in his powers of mesmerism and who wanted to gentle some buffaloes. He had built a pen, and now he conceived the idea of going out and staying around a bunch of buffaloes until they were used to him, "hazing" them into the pen, and then mesmerizing them into a state of docility. He was very sure that once the buffaloes were in his pen he could mesmerise the cows so that they would allow him to milk them and the bulls so that they would pull plow or wagon.

In the manner of mustangers who "walked" wild horses down, he got a considerable number of buffaloes inside the corral. But it was they who did the mesmerising. They mesmerised that log pen until nothing was left of it but scattered firewood. Long after the creek on which it was built came to be known as Mesmeriser's Creek, some of the poles could yet be picked up.

One Eye Creek, in Cherokee County, is said to be named after a Cherokee chief who lived on it before Christian charity shot out his other eye and appropriated his homestead. One Eye serves to bring us to Hog Eye, not an uncommon old-time country name, likely to mean considerably more than meets the ear. Its implications may be akin to those of the once popular phrase, "in a pig's eye," which was a contemptuous synonym for "nix." "I could go to old Gold Horseshoes tonight and ask him for Betty, and along with her he'd deed me a thousand acres of muskeet grass, well, windmill and rock house on it, and a hundred two-year-old heifers, all cut for color besides," the boaster might say. "Yes, in a pig's eye," the bladder-puncturer would retort.

Along in the fifties a settlement with ambitions

sprang up close to the line between Jack and Wise counties. A doctor named Shelton and a cowman named Earhart each wished to have it called after himself. The population took sides. After a bitter contest, the Shelton faction won. But the cow people were in the saddle, and, the grapes having turned sour, they dubbed the place Hog Eye. It has never outgrown the name. There's another Hog Eye in Gregg County.

One day before the Civil War a strolling fiddler stopped at the Lytton home, near Lytton Springs, in Caldwell County. He met with a reception as hearty as that found by Sam Galloway in O. Henry's "The Last of the Troubadours." Word went over the grapevine telegraph that music was in the air, and by nightfall of the second day people from miles around were coming in to dance. It was soon discovered that, despite his lengthy tuning up, his sweeping flourishes and his way of emphasizing time with bobbing head and patting foot, the fiddler could really play but one tune. That one, though, he could certainly make ramble. He called it "Hog Eye," and he played it with so many variations and so much persistence that the dance did not break up until morning. The fiddler went on his way, but for a long time afterwards "Hog Eye" was a kind of byword in the neighborhood. It was fastened on the Lytton home, and the old place is still known as Hog Eye.

Away back in the days when Mr. Fishback of the Sulphurs raced so hard and so close against a blue norther that his nag came into the barn with her hindquarters frozen and her forequarters foamy with sweat, a fiddler was making a different tune famous all over Hopkins County. Yet he was not a fiddler of just that one tune. He could play "Hog Eye" too. He could play anything he had ever heard, and he had heard everything. "Hell among the Yearlings," "Sally Goodin," "Nigger in the Woodpile," "Cotton-eyed Joe," "Leather Breeches," "Natchez under the Hill," "Turkey in the Straw," "Soapsuds under the Fence," "Hogs in the Corn," "Money in Both Pockets," "Kitty O'Neal," "Dinah Had a

Wooden Leg," "Saddle Old Spike," "Mollie, Put the Kettle On," "Little Black Bull Came Down the Mountain," "Eighth of January," "Sandy Land," "Money Musk," "Tommie, Don't Go," and "Come into My Bower"—he played them all and about "forty-'leven" others.

But his favorite was "Blackjack Grove." When he tuned up for that and sang out, "Partners to your puncheons," and then began his calls:

"Hands in your pockets, backs to the wall,
Take a chew o' terbaccer and balance all"—

certainly "it wus gettin' lively." The puncheon floor would fairly rock, and the dust rise so thick that a fellow in the corner might steal a kiss without being seen. Some say the fiddler made this tune up and named it after the blackjack timber in the country. Anyhow, the town that grew up around him took the name of Blackjack Grove. It was a center to which freight wagons came from hundreds of miles away for supplies; the hum of its commerce was as lively as the fiddler's tune. Then along in the eighties Blackjack Grove was shortened to Blackjack; the commercial importance of the town was shortened even more. Finally it ceased to be even Blackjack and became just Cumby.

It would be strange if a land on which so much blood has been spilled as the soil of Texas did not reflect in some of its place names the starkness of violent death. When I was a boy in Live Oak County, a short drainage course between some hills of black chaparral and juajilla called Dead Man's Hollow made a vivid impression on my mind. The story was that a horse thief finally paid for his horses by swinging until he rotted down from the limb of a live oak growing in the hollow.

In Lampasas County a young man whose horse walked out from under him while he remained spurring at the air, one end of his stake-rope around the limb of a Spanish oak and the other end around his neck, gave a comparatively mild name to the locality. Scary Lane runs close to the tree from which he was hanged. Contrary to expectation on the part of some, the limb of the tree did not die immediately after it had been used as a gallows.

Back in the early 70's when there were no fences to control the range and cattle were too cheap to make stealing them and driving them away very profitable, hides found a ready sale and hide thieves rode brazenly throughout Southwest Texas. Their activities brought on what is remembered as the Skinning War. They went armed with prong-bladed, or forked, knives mounted on long handles. Upon finding a bunch of cattle, one of these range butchers would dash up behind a cow or steer and shove his knife against the tendon on the animal's hind leg, hamstringing it. A single rider might disable several head of cattle out of a bunch; then he would kill them and skin them.

The depredations became so blatant that cattlemen of McMullen and adjoining counties got together to put a stop to the business. They found that a Mexican ranch on the dividing line between Duval and McMullen counties was headquarters for skinners of the region. Early one morning they surrounded the ranch *jacales*. After fifteen Mexicans had been hanged they counted about the premises over three hundred hides bearing brands of the vigilante cattlemen. Dead Man's Ranch the place came to be called, and it goes by that name to this day.

I don't know whether it still goes by the name or not, but along in the eighties a sheepman named Stedman owned Dead Man's Ranch, near Dead Man's Crossing, on Devil's River. According to the story, a pack of dogs bayed a wildcat in a thicket near the crossing, which up to that time had no name. In getting to the wildcat some cowboys found the bones of a man, only a few rotten rags left of his clothing. About one of the finger bones was a diamond ring, and in a pocket that still held together were some gold and silver coins together with a wad of bills decayed beyond value.

Murderer's Creek, Muerto Creek, Dead Nigger Creek, Dead Man's Canyon, Dead Man's Island, Dead Man's Hole, numerous creeks called Dead Man, and Boothill Cemetery, wherein men killed about old Tascosa were buried with their boots on—all suggest stories of violence. Many a name innocent in sound has blood behind it. For instance, in Clarksville there stood—and likely stands yet—a tree known up and down the Red River country as Page's Tree. One day in the forties a traveler named Page fell in with a settler whose saddlebags gave out a rattling that he took to be from gold and silver. The fact that it was made by a chain, which the settler was carrying to a log-rolling, did not save him from being murdered. The murderer was overtaken, brought to Clarksville, and hanged from the tree. Again, a man wearing "copperas pants" (green colored) was found dead in a grove of trees in Coryell County. Copperas Grove got its name.

Gamble Gully, in Live Oak County, should have a story, but it is merely named for a man named Gamble who is not remembered as a gambler. Off the coast of Chambers County is a small island called Vingt Un — Twenty-one. Tradition has it that Lafitte's pirates used to play the game of cards known as *vingt-et-un* here, and left the name. The name of Concan, a picturesque location and a few houses, on the Frio River in Uvalde County, seems to be derived either from "coon can," which is a game that Negroes play with both dice and cards, or from the Mexican card game of *con quien* (with who), which is a derivative of the Portuguese *con quian*. There must have been a game that was not freeze-out poker at Concan sometime. A Bret Harte might have made any of these places as famous as the California mining camp was made by "The Outcasts of Poker Flats." Incidentally, the word "flats" as applied to apartment houses seems to be passing out of usage; "apartments" does sound more respectable—but there is a building of several floors and several rented compartments in the vicinity of the University of Texas that still

STORIES IN TEXAS PLACE NAMES 47

goes by the name, won somehow years ago, of "Poker Flats."

A sense of respectability, connected with the ancient and enduring patronization of country plainness by urban puppets, has been the death of many a homely rustic name. The substitute is usually an attempt at elegance; yet not always is it accepted. A few years ago there was a movement among some of the inhabitants of Muleshoe—named after the Muleshoe Ranch, its brand a mule shoe—to change the name of their town to Roseborough! Wild geese used to honk over the feed in every creek in the coastal country. One of these creeks in Harris County was appropriately named Goose Creek. A village on the creek took the same name. Years later a very rich oil field gave the vicinity publicity, the village population, and Ross Sterling wealth. Numerous ambitious inhabitants then voted to change the name to Ross City, Sea Gate, or something else more elegant than Goose Creek. But Goose Creek still remains the name. Geese can no longer feed on the oil-fouled stream, but the name has memories. Before the discovery of oil in Eastland County, what is now Desdemona—named, presumably, for Othello's wife—was known as Hog Creek. Should oil or some other enterprise ever bring the village of Bigfoot into popular interest, citizens with lots to sell would no doubt undertake to get the name changed —probably to Cinderella. The community was named for that rough-hewn and highly flavored old frontiersman, Indian fighter, and Texian individual, Big Foot Wallace, who built his cabin in the vicinity.

The classic tradition belongs in any educational program, but let it not lay hands on those rural schools named Greasy Neck, Mud Dig, Mud, Way Back, Big Lump, and Allseeing Eye! Steal Easy Mountain, Tallow Face Mountain, Yearling Head, Hog Skin, Sodville, Peg Leg Crossing, Smuggler's Gap, Sixshooter Draw, and the creeks of Sparerib, Toewash, Troublesome, Wall Eye, Squabble, Skinout, and Gunsight, so named either because an Indian shot the front sight off a gun with which a teamster was drawing a bead on him or because in the vicinity a hill and a gap line up like the sights of a gun—these may not be lovely names, but they are honest.

Hide Town was all right for a name as long as the place served as a supply camp for buffalo hunters, though doubtless Henry David Thoreau, who found Jackass Flat in California too "unphilosophical" for a name, would not have approved of it. When the smell of buffalo hides was no longer detectable, the people sniffed and called their town Snyder; they missed a chance for downrightness—but perhaps not for respectability—when they neglected to call it Pete Snyder, after the rawhide character who set up the trading post.

While it was still Hide Town, a freighter with a thirst that called for something not cooling drove up to a "holler" not far distant. It had been raining pitchforks and bob-tailed heifer yearlings, and the usually dry gully was on a tear. The mule-skinner could not wait for it to run down. He slashed in. The flood washed his wagon against a tree and drowned his team. He floundered out, walked to Pete Snyder's "place," and reported, "That's the hell-roaringest little holler I ever see." Hell Roaring Hollow it was named.

"Cursed be he that removeth his neighbor's landmark," is a passage out of the Scriptures that has been ejaculated to juries by many a lawyer for the defense. On the Brazos River up in Palo Pinto County at a place known as Possum Kingdom the government is building a dam; in honor of the senator who milked the federal cow to get juice to build it, the name Morris Sheppard Dam was proposed by political sycophants, but the senator refused to allow it. On the Colorado River in Burnet County, near the mouth of French John Creek, another federal dam is being built, and it is to bear the name of another political milker—Buchanan Dam. I don't know who French John was and the character of the king of Possum Kingdom will always be sealed to me, but French John Creek and Possum Kingdom say something fresh and honest and earthy that names meant to flatter ephemeral politicians could never attain to.

Another good name that politics obsoleted was Dog Town, on the Frio River. The cattle of the half dozen ranchers comprising its population were so wild and the brush in which they ran was so thick and thorny that the cowmen kept dogs and more dogs of a mongrel breed to chase them with. In 1876 while McMullen County was getting organized and the minds of the brush-poppers were being directed toward a suitable name for their county seat and post office, Samuel Tilden was running for the presidency of the United States on the Democratic ticket. As ardent Democrats the owners of the cow-dogs voted to substitute the name of Tilden for Dog Town.

When the Santa Fe Railroad built across the XIT Ranch it put in at a certain place a switch for unloading cottonseed—at that time a staple cattle feed. Located in the vicinity was a bunch of "pet" Hereford bulls imported from Missouri. They knew well the food value of cottonseed and haunted the grounds where it was unloaded, in order to pick up the generous spillings. The tracks were not fenced, and the bulls habitually lay down on them. As the train approached, the engineer might ring his bell and blow his whistle frantically, but the mild-eyed, full-bellied bulls kept on chewing their cuds and keeping their beds. Invariably the train had to stop while a brakeman prodded the bulls clear. The switch had no name and the conductor in reporting his shipments referred to it as Bull Town. But this was too vulgar for railroad men in the offices, and they in making a map changed it to Bovina, the name of the village that now marks the place where taurine lords bullied the mechanical world.

In pioneer days nearly all meat was fried in a skillet; then gravy, well thickened with flour burned brown, was made in the grease. A boy might sop the skillet with a biscuit or a hound might lick it. Expressive of these culinary processes, a community in Grayson County called itself Lick Skillet. With the advent of broiled steaks it became self-conscious and assumed the name of Pilot Grove—not a bad name either, for the grove of trees that marked the place was a landmark, like Pilot Knobs, by which travelers steered their course. Why Rake Pocket, in Rusk County, was so called I do not know, but I can imagine why the inhabitants changed its name to Pine Hill.

Among the first colonists down the Brazos River was a man known as "Popcorn" Robinson. He won his title by raising popcorn. Then a settlement was made on or beside his field. At first it was called Popcorn Patch; soon, however, it was named Brazoria, a derivative of Brazos.

Of course a name can become too ridiculous to be tolerated. O'naga means nothing to me, but it meant a joke to people in Denton County, and they took to calling the villagers "O'niggers." This was not to be endured. O'naga called a town meeting. Every citizen who had an inspiration wrote a name on a slip of paper and placed it in a hat. Then the school teacher, supposed always to be intellectually honest, reached, blindfolded, into the hat and drew out a slip. The name on it was Aubrey, the name of the village now. This was before Little Audrey "laughed and laughed" so much.

The United States Post Office Department, which has to approve all names for post offices, is even more respectability-minded than the populace. During the Civil War John Chisum, of the Jinglebob ear-mark, the Fence Rail brand, and Billy the Kid fame, moved his cattle into what is now Coleman County and in time opened a store. Bill Franks ran it, selling over the counter "conversation juice" as well as frijoles. He was a practical joker, and occasionally refilled an empty bottle with plain water and set it among the liquor bottles. Then he would, when a customer called for "White Mule" or some other such brand, pull down the bottle of water and deliver it. The trick was appreciated—by everybody but the man tricked. In honor of it the cowboys selected Trick 'em as a name for the proposed post office. The postal officials, however, did not consider that dignified enough and registered Trickham.

Pinhook is not a name to be chosen above great riches; its successor, the neat little city of Paris, might as well, however, have been named Prague or Petersburg or Philadelphia. The apish appropriators of the names of famous cities forget that most of the names they appropriate were originally expressive of something and as much in place as they are out of place when applied elsewhere. Texas, not satisfied with one Boston, has Old Boston and New Boston as well.

Yet, "Call me Ishmael" opens the most powerful novel in American literature. An old and far-away foreign name may be evoked to say exactly the right thing about a place as well as about a person. The yarn goes that about 1834 a group of colonists east of the Colorado River, in what is now Wharton County, raised a bountiful corn crop while planters elsewhere raised none. That fall from the Navidad, the Lavaca, the Brazos and the San Bernard they came to buy corn from the well-stored cribs on the Colorado. Generally well read in the Bible, these colonists knew the story of how Joseph's brethren found corn in Pharaoh's land, and they called the place of the corn crop amid the wilderness of Texas—Egypt.

The man on horseback—the *caballero*—has always looked down upon the man afoot—the *peon;* and cowboys in the days when they lived in and slept upon the saddle usually had mingled contempt and pity for clodhoppers. About the time nesters began plowing up a valley south of Midland, it happened to rain; then the frogs "hollered." A pair of cowboys riding by spoke to one of the nesters about the deliciousness of frog-legs, particularly the legs of the particular variety of frogs inhabiting this particular draw. The nester wanted to know how the frogs were caught. "Why, you just build you a loop," the most brazen of the cowboys answered, "and when you find a toad asleep or maybe waiting quiet to catch a gnat, you throw the loop over him. He can't jump out, and there you have him." Whether the nesters or the cowboys gave the draw its name is not recorded, but Toad-loop Draw it is. When another group of family men took up state land in Childress County, cowboys, certain that not even the most expert of dry-farmers could plow a living out of that soil, condemned the settlement as Poverty Flat. The plowmen survived though and asked for a postoffice. The Postoffice Department, which has been responsible for thousands of characterless names, assigned Tell for the new name. Why not William Tell, I cannot tell.

There has been more than one Bucksnort in Texas. "Father had a tussle with a wounded deer—a very large buck—one morning, and the deer gave a peculiar whistle or snort, so common to them. The little hollow [on which the tussle took place] was, and is until this day, called Buck Snort." There was a Buck Snort in Shelby County too, but the inhabitants all left it to live in Timpson, brought into existence by a railroad. The sensitive dwellers in Buck Snort of Marion County could not move so readily, and so they moved to change the name of their community to Buena Vista (Good View), the first word in which name they pronounce Boo-nah. Buck Den in Real County is a good name for that hill country so plentiful of deer. Buckhorn, Austin County, no doubt goes back to some colonial incident connected with a buck. Double Horn Creek, which empties into the Colorado River, derived its name from the interlocked antlers of two buck deer that died in combat on it.

David Crockett "despised this way of spelling contrary to nature"; his school held the same philosophy towards pronouncing foreign words. It was according to nature that the creek which French traders had named Isle d'Bois, in Denton County, became Zilly Boy. Many Spanish names, even though the original spelling be retained, have suffered just as radically in pronunciation. There are several Cibola or Cibolo creeks in Texas, *cíbolo* being the Spanish for *buffalo;* they are all pronounced Sea-Willow. *Yegua* means *mare,* and is prop-

STORIES IN TEXAS PLACE NAMES   53

erly pronounced with the accent on the first syllable; but Yegua Creek is the Yea-Waugh.

Sometimes spelling as well as pronunciation of Spanish names takes on corruption, as exampled in Ladonia, a debasement of La Doña—The Madam—the place being named for a decisive woman. Again the name of Itasca is a descendant of Atasca (It Sticks)—a reference to the black-waxy soil on which the village is situated. Similarly, Tascosa—the name of a dead town of frontier days made notorious by its Boothill graveyard—is descended from Atascosa (Boggy), expressive of the quicksands of the Canadian River, which it overlooked. But in the border country, where gringos as well as Mexicans speak Spanish, Atascosa as the name of a river, a town and a county has kept its purity.

Now and then in the history of Texas a plain, carefree name has supplanted one of smoother sound. After having ridden far across barren, rough, arid country, Captain Jack Hays of the Texas rangers, as an old story goes, came to a forbidding gorge at the bottom of which he could see water. He asked a Mexican conveniently near what the stream was named. "Señor," replied the Mexican, "it is called the San Pedro." "Saint Peter, hell!" the Texan ejaculated. "It looks like the devil's river to me." And Devil's River it became.

Thrifty, dime-valuing German Wends of Lee County within reach of Brown's Mill used to leave their letters with a dime in a box at the mill. Then when enough dimes had accumulated to pay a man for a trip, a volunteer mail carrier would take the letters to a postoffice. In time the people asked for an office of their own; they got it under the name of Dime Box. A community in Lamar County asked for a postoffice to be called Lake View; the Postoffice Department refused to accept the name and asked for a substitute. One of the citizens who had just noticed the picture of a razor on a tin tag fastened to a plug of chewing tobacco suggested Razor. Razor the name was and is.

Even in names coined for real estate exploitation there has at times been something naive and natural. "We passed some very amusing cities," wrote an English emigrant a half century ago—"Log City and Larietta City. They were both in the middle of the prairie, and all the city was a small pile of logs thrown on the ground and a sign-board; not a house or an animal, or a human being anywhere within ten miles."

When the Southern Pacific Railroad Company was building across the dry uninhabited land between Del Rio and El Paso, officials had to give names of some sort to various section houses, switches, and pump stations: some literary-minded individual consulted the alphabet of New England poets and named two switches for Emerson and Longfellow; then he switched to the English poets and selected Dryden. The manner of name selection here was much like that pursued by the legislature of Texas on occasion, as when it named about the drouthiest and most waterless county in the state Moore, after the Commodore of the Texas navy.

The Southern Pacific Railroad calls itself the "Sunset Route." A pump station in Brewster County bears the anomalous name of Tesnus, which may suggest tetanus but which is the word "sunset" spelled backwards. A man named Gilmer put up some sawmills in Jasper County and wanted to name the sawmill town for himself. Learning that Texas already had one Gilmer, he spelled his own name backwards and got Remlig. The name is no doubt an accurate expression of his sense of beauty, and it must have been very flattering to his ego— as flattering as Gibtown was to Mr. Hardware Merchant Gibbins, or as Tin Rag, on the Cotton Belt Railroad, was to Mr. Garnit, his name spelled backwards.

VIII. PROLONGED SHADOWS

"History," said Carlyle, "is the prolonged shadows of a few individuals." The names of virtually all the men who had anything outstanding—and of many who had nothing—to do with the history of Texas are listed in the state atlas. From the names of counties, towns, cities and other localities a Texan dictionary of biography might be compiled. Naming some place for a man in general, however, does not—can not—produce a personal relationship between him and it. The act of a legislature or a chamber of commerce that compliments an individual by giving his name to a highway or a street is one thing; a man's intimate experience with some physical feature of the earth that makes it take his name, as if it were his own child, is another. S. Rhoads Fisher, Secretary of the Texas Navy, never made a track in the three-fourths arid county that, named after him, was not organized until he had been dead half a century; the relationship between the man Fisher and Fisher County is purely accidental, extraneous. On the other hand, Henry Castro brought families from France to found the town of Castroville, brought it into being; it is something as personal to him as a book that he might have written or a tree that he might have planted. His name belongs to it; it is a part of him and he is a part of it; his shadow will always be on its rock.

Down in Brazoria County, where Austin's "first three hundred" colonists settled, is a stretch of ground known as Bailey's Prairie. Nobody knows where Brit Bailey is buried or just where his cabin stood, but everybody knows that old Brit was on that prairie even before Stephen F. Austin arrived and that the prairie belonged to Brit. Austin, it is said, tried to put him off and had to back off himself. Then when the old frontiersman came to die, he gave directions for his burial. "Bury me standing up," he ordered, "facing westward. I have never yet looked up to any living man, and when I am dead I don't want folks saying, 'Here *lies* Brit Bailey'."

On military maps of the Big Bend of Texas is noted down a watering place under the name of Indian Well. This is not what the leathery-skinned riders of that vast and desolate region know it by. Cotera Wells, they call it, and an extract from the memoirs of a frontiersman named Augustus C. Cotera will convince any reader that the name belongs. "It was in July, 1880," he wrote, "that the detachment of cavalry I was with set out from Mexican Springs for the Rio Grande to locate the mouth of San Francisco Creek. My business was to make a survey of the route, taking bearings and measuring the distance. Eight or ten cavalrymen were detailed to assist me. The main command soon outdistanced us. The day was terribly hot, and the dry air and blazing sun sapped all the moisture out of our bodies. Before noon our canteens were empty and both men and horses were suffering for water.

"We were following along an old Indian trail when I saw in it a bag of soda crackers and a tin of corned beef, already opened, together with a note from a lieutenant with the advance party saying that here was my lunch. I was too thirsty to eat such dry food and went riding on with my head down. Then presently I noticed a small dark hole amid rocks a little to the right of the trail. At the same time my horse became very restless, and I got down to investigate. Kneeling and peering into the hole, I saw the glint of water about two feet below the surface of the ground.

"I called for the men to help uncover it. We all got hold of a stone slab about three inches thick and full five feet long by four feet wide. It covered a fine cistern full of clear, cold water—a *tinaja*, as the Mexicans call it. The horses were fighting to get to it. I put a man down in the hole, his feet braced against the sides, and we started a chain of hats out of which the horses were watered. Then after we had drunk all we wanted and filled our canteens, we started on after the cavalry troop.

"At San Francisco Creek we found several details of men digging out cobble stones in the dry bed, searching for water. I reported to Captain Livermore—for whom Livermore Mountain is named—how I had found a good well. He immediately ordered his men to saddle, repack and back trail. Then we made camp at the *tinaja*. After all the animals and all the men had drunk, the level of the water was still where it had been at the beginning, showing that the cistern was supplied by an underground spring.

"During the evening the men gathered rocks and piled them up into a column eighteen or twenty feet high. Then on top of the column they placed the big stone that had covered the well. With some red ochre procured from the vicinity they wrote on the rock, 'Cotera's Well.'"

Perryman Thicket is in Coryell County. Before barbed wire, as Bigfoot Wallace used to say, "played hell with Texas," Judge Perryman was riding along alone one day looking through his cattle that grazed out from Stampede Creek. He was on a good horse that had, however, been pretty well ridden down. Hung from his saddle horn was a morral containing his lunch of biscuits and jerked beef. He wore a six-shooter, but something was wrong with it and it would not shoot. Then he saw a bunch of Indians and saw that they had spied him. He put out for the creek, meaning to cross it and get into brush edging the opposite bank. The creek was boggy and his horse floundered. One of the Indians was approaching at a dead run. Perryman did not take time to extricate his horse; he quit him and got into the thicket. There, well hidden, he paused to see what the Indian would do. He saw the Indian discover the morral of victuals, sit down, and devour them. Then he watched the Indian work the horse out of the bog and gallop off with him to rejoin his brothers. Judge Perryman got back home and to safety all right, but his name stayed with the thicket.

Fort Darnell in Jack County, never anything more than a motte of trees, marks another fiasco. Passengers in a stage coach passing near here saw mounted men in the distance. "Indians!" they said, and took refuge in the motte. Before it was discovered that the horsemen were peaceable cowboys, a young fellow crazed with fright took out down the road afoot. The daughter of a Colonel Darnell, then stationed at Jacksboro, took after him, halted him, disarmed him, and more or less brought him back to his senses. After that the motte amid which the stage coach had halted was known at Fort Darnell.

Some names seem to say that a character out of reality was there. Sallie Keaton Slough, Jim Ned Creek, Jim Nail Branch, Coffee's Station (a trading post in Preston's Bend on Red River), Goacher's Trace—named for that old frontiersman who had a secret lead mine that is still a secret,—and Jernigan's Thicket imply, by sound at least, characters that "belong in a book." I never see the name of Colbert's Ferry but that I yearn to know what manner of man it was who ferried so many immigrants to Texas across Red River. One time, a story goes, a young fellow from Missouri whom Colbert was ferrying over confessed that he was timid about going to Texas, he had heard so much concerning the desperate men there. "Bud," the ferryman assured him, "don't bother any more about that. As soon as we butt against the other bank, get down off your horse, drink yourself full of this Red River water, and you'll be able to hold your own with any of them." The youngster took the advice literally and drank until he was swelled up like a poisoned pup. Then he bounded into the saddle and started off. "Hold on!" Colbert cried. "You did not pay your ferriage." "Now see here," the youth answered back, "I'm not a-going to pay it. I've done tanked up on Red River water." All Colbert could say was, "Well, it has taken effect remarkably soon."

As long as the tradition of trail driving lives, Doan's Crossing on Red River, where millions of Texas longhorns passed headed northward, and Doan's Store hard by, where Texas outfits bought coffee, lard, flour and sixshooter cartridges to last them until they reached Dodge City, Cowboy Capitol of the world, will keep green the name and memory of C. F. Doan. The creditor of all cowmen and deliverer of love letters to cowboys who had been "moseying along" at the rate of ten to fifteen miles a day from the ranches on the Nueces without receiving a word from home, he was known from the

Canadian Rockies to the Rio Grande as the friend of trail drivers.

One of the big cowmen was Shanghai Pierce. When he was afoot he stood six feet four. Whether he was a good rider or not, his employer down against Matagorda Bay used to say, "Put Shang on the bad horses. Don't risk the niggers. They're worth a thousand dollars apiece." His voice was like a fog-horn sounding on top of a mountain in the frosty morning. A railroad put up a station and shipping pens a mile or more from his house; they say that Shanghai used to stand on the gallery at home and bellow out exceedingly audible orders to men working in the pens; when he went to San Antonio and greeted his friends sitting in the shade in front of the old Menger Hotel, people on Military Plaza six or eight blocks away could hear him. He was a character "if God A'mighty ever made one," and he was as egotistical as he was individual. He had a life-sized statue executed and erected of himself on his land, and imposed his name on two railway stations—Shanghai and Pierce. He is a tradition, a legend all over southern Texas, and many an anecdote that passes current is hinged on those names.

There should be something in the same region named for Charlie Siringo, who in that rollickiest of all range narratives, *A Texas Cow Boy, or Fifteen Years on the Hurricane Deck of a Spanish Cow Pony*, went a good way towards immortalizing "old Shanghai" by the left-hand road. When I get to a place that holds memories of a man, I like to find his name. The "Raven Cafe" in Huntsville, where Sam Houston lived and died, does not have much about it suggestive of the hero of San Jacinto, but it is pleasant to find the name anyhow. The Stephen F. Austin Hotel in the capital of Texas, named after the Father of Texas, is like hundreds of other standardized hotels over the nation, its solitary claim to individuality being its name, but that is something. It is a pity that it could not have been built to express the character of the man it is named after, as the Driskill Hotel across the street, with its great lobby, its vast rooms, its noble furniture, and the busts of its founders, Robert Driskill, and his two sons Bob and Tobe, high up outside resting on the heads of longhorn bulls, expresses the amplitude and solidity of Texas cowmen and trail drivers.

Padre Nicolás Baille was another cowman. The long narrow island off the coast of Texas that the king of Spain granted to him—Padre Island—keeps his name green. He ran hundreds of cattle on it, but the Texians drove them away following the battle of San Jacinto, that being the time when Texas cowboys got their start. Since 1879 the island has been owned and stocked by Pat Dunn, "Don Patricio." Now the fine causeway bringing the island to the mainland is called the Don Patricio Causeway.

Naturally the men who came on the scene first had the lead over all others in fixing their names to the land. Also they had within themselves more than the average share of individuality. The trails they made, even though no longer traveled, are still plain by name. Charles Goodnight was the first white man to establish a ranch in the Panhandle of Texas; he drove 10,000 head of buffaloes out of the Palo Duro Canyon, locating his herd behind them. Later he built a house where the village of Goodnight now stands. Before that he and Oliver Loving had broken what all people familiar with range lore know as the Goodnight-Loving Trail. On this trip Loving received from Indian arrows a wound that caused his death. The place where he received it on the Pecos River is named Loving's Bend; his old ranch, on the Brazos River in Palo Pinto County, is circled by Loving's Bend also. All the names of Goodnight and Loving that the land bears were—"if blood be the price"—like England's admiralty, "bought fair."

The most famous shot in Plains history, I suppose, was that made by Billy Dixon during the Adobe Walls fight in 1874, when with a buffalo gun he killed an Indian on horseback three-quarters of a mile away. After that climax in his shooting career Billy Dixon took up two sections of land and settled down to grow up with the country. Buffalo hunter, rancher, trader, the first postmaster in Hutchinson County, the first married settler too, he belongs to that part of the plains as mud belongs in the adobe bricks of a "stick and mud chimney." The written story of his life, *The Life and Adventures of Billy Dixon*, is a kind of bible to people along the Canadian. A little creek, only that, is named for him, while the county through which it runs is called after a Mississippian who had merely an accidental adventure in Texas. Dixon County would be right, like Kendall County, where, after he had written the enduringly interesting *Narrative of the Texan Santa Fe Expedition*, George W. Kendall settled down to raise sheep and be at home on the soil he loved.

J. Wright Mooar was at the Adobe Walls fight, too; he killed the white buffalo and got a sack of flour from Billy the Kid—and Mooar's Draw belongs to him. It belongs in the manner that Haley's Peak, in the Big Bend, belongs to Lawrence Haley, who while ranching for years beneath it would hardly allow a woman to enter his range and who specified in his will that a cow, a cowhorse, and a sheep be graved on his tombstone. It belongs as essentially as the Bloys Camp Meeting Grounds, in the same country, belong to that pioneer circuit rider "Brother Bloys," who made this camp meeting one of the traditions of the West.

One of the old names of Texas that rings like a ballad in the ears is Groce's Retreat. Its name has nothing to do with a military movement. Jared E. Groce came to Texas in 1827, bringing close to a hundred slaves, cattle, sheep, hogs, horse-stock and a caravan of fifty wagons provided with farming implements, pontoon bridges, provisions, looms, spinning wheels, furniture—all the materials for setting up a vast plantation. At Bernardo, as he called this plantation on the Brazos, he erected perhaps the first cotton gin in Texas. While the colonists were still harmonious with Mexico, the plantation fed a Mexican army; during the revolution it supplied Sam Houston's army with corn, beef, and other provisions, and turned the "Big House" into a hospital. But the air—and mosquitoes—on the Brazos were malarial to Groce, and he had another home built out on Wallace Prairie in what is now Grimes County; it was his "retreat." Hardly a vestige of Groce's Retreat can be found now, but a community in the vicinity retains the name, and like one of the old bells calling his hands in for bountiful food and deep rest, it seems to call back the plantations and grand ways of Jared E. Groce.

IX. FOLK ETYMOLOGY

One class of stories to explain certain names is based on folk etymology. Thus *nogal* means *walnut;* the plural of the word is *nogales*. There can be little doubt that a certain prairie in Trinity County now known locally as Nogalus Prairie was originally called Nogales, like the border town of Arizona, from the walnut trees in its vicinity. Corrupt pronunciation could easily change the word into Nogalus—and Nogalus had to be explained.

According to the story, one day during the Civil War a band of States Rights men appeared in the community to hunt for renegades; after considerable search they found seven hiding in the woods. They took them to a big oak tree on the edge of the prairie, hanged them all, and rode away. Later some old men found the bodies and with the aid of a few Negroes buried them. Then, as the story goes on, the locality became known as No-Gallows Prairie, because the seven had been hanged without benefit of gallows. No-Gallows in time became abbreviated and corrupted into Nogalus. But, according to another version of the same story, no man of the seven who were hanged wore a pair of galluses, or suspenders. This lack, unusual for the masculine costume of the time, inspired a new name—No-Gallus Prairie; then the two words were run into one, just as the two Spanish words, La Mesa became Lamesa, in Dawson County, or as the name of Lu Ling, a Chinaman who fed a bridge crew on Plum Creek in Caldwell County, became Luling.

All stories like this attempt to be humorous. The Navasota River was named early in the history of Texas.

Probably Indian, its meaning has not been satisfactorily explained, but folk etymology is never at a loss. The old-timey way of pronouncing Navasota is something like Nav-a-sot, with the accent on the last syllable and the suggestion of an *r* at the end of it. One day, as the popular explainers of the word tell, some land surveyors stopped at the cabin of a settler who had "located" on the Navasota River, as yet unnamed. After a good dinner of cornbread, fried bacon and turnip greens—with plenty of pot likker—the surveyors sat picking their teeth on the front gallery. One of them noticed a numerous and thrifty brood of chickens following a hen that was scratching about in the front yard.

"You must have had mighty good luck when you set that hen," he said.

"No, stranger, we nev'r sot her a-tall," the settler replied. "She sot herself out in the woods there, and one day she just come up with that covey of chickens."

The settler's phrase, "nev'r sot her," gave the strangers a name for the stream they were surveying along—and the Navasota it has been ever since.

Galveston took its name from one, or perhaps both, of the viceroys of Mexico named Galvez. Its bathing beaches are as famous as its hurricanes, and its chamber of commerce seeks annually to make even more famous an exhibition of "bathing beauties"—a "gal show." Thence, by popular etymology very modern, Galveston is a name derived from "Gal-with-a-vest-on."

The name of Texas has been variously explained by this phonetic method. A version of the story said to have come down from Gail Borden, of condensed milk fame, publisher of one of the earliest newspapers in Texas, has it that refugees from justice found their way to Galveston Island while Lafitte was yet there. He received them as brothers. Joyously they chorused, "When all other states forsake us, this one takes us." The words *takes us* ran themselves into *Texas,* and the land of hospitality to thieves was named.

This explanation of the name of Texas, rather popular at one time in a jocular way, is not much more absurd than some of the more serious explanations that have been made. The *Telegraph and Texas Register,* printed an account, July 24, 1839, to the effect that after a body of Comanche warriors had gone south to overcome the Aztecs and met defeat, the remnant upon crossing the Rio Grande and getting a wide view of their native land, exclaimed, "Tejas," later spelled Texas and meaning "Happy Hunting Grounds." Another version of the same myth attributed to Sam Houston has it that a few Aztecs fled north from the Spaniards when they were conquering Montezuma and after crossing the Rio Grande and reaching the coastal plain called out in thankfulness, "Tejas," their word for "Paradise."

Much has been written on the origin of the word Texas. The pueblo Indians of New Mexico, who have lived in houses for centuries, yet speak of themselves as *techados,* "roofed," in contradistinction to the nomadic and houseless tribes. Some writers have contended that Texas comes from *techo,* meaning roof, or from *teja,* the covering of a building, allusive to the huts in which the domiciled Texas Indians dwelt. Both Hodge and Bolton have long and full treatments of the word based on the testimony of the earliest Spanish discoverers of the Texas Indians and lands. One is surprised and delighted at the ways in which Texas was spelled by the Spanish chroniclers; no doubt other spellings than the following could be adduced, but they are sufficient to demonstrate variety: *texias, teijas, teixas, thecas, techan, teyas, tehas, teysas, techas, tejas, teisa.* The sound—whatever it was—was uttered by certain Indians, often in greeting, to mean *friends* or *allies.* These aboriginal users of the term were Indians of Hasinai stock inhabiting the upper valleys of the Angelina and Neches rivers. Spaniards designated them as the Tejas, Tehas, Texas, etc. Indians. Then the territory to which they were restricted was called Texas. The geographic term was very early extended to include territory east of the Trinity River. When San

STORIES IN TEXAS PLACE NAMES 65

Antonio was settled, the "Province of Texas" was extended westward to the Medina River, and then gradually to all the territory included within the present state of Texas. To Mexicans the Texans are still *Tejanos*.

Incidentally, the early English-speaking settlers in Texas called themselves Texians—not Texans; Texican was also used.[5] Men of the old breed yet say "Texian." There are still a good many Texians in Texas; the remainder of the population is about equally divided between Texans and people who merely live in Texas.

Elgin, Texas, might suggest the place in Illinois where watches are made, or the Elgin marbles, expressive of immortal art, in the Birtish Museum. But there is nothing Hellenic about the folk yarn of how this little town at the crossing of two railroads got its name.

When the first railroad arrived, no town existed and only a few settlers lived in the neighborhood. Whether Mr. Miles was a settler or not, he "operated" in the country, heading the "Miles gang." The Miles gang did not want a railroad, and they announced that they would not have one. The track pushed forward anyway; once or twice they tore gaps in it; the gaps were repaired. At length the first train was announced. The Miles gang swore they would "shoot the lights out it." They had probably had more experience in "shooting the lights out" of a man and "shooting daylight into" him than they had had in any way with trains.

Now this first train, like many trains to follow it, was slow running. By the time it got into the neck of the woods over which the Miles gang were so jealous, darkness had fallen; the engineer had lit the headlight of his engine and the brakeman had lit the lanterns swinging from the roof of the passenger coach. The Miles gang were waiting, and when the train thundered by— it was a good deal more like thunder than lightning—they blazed loose. They shot out several lights, including the

---

[5] For a discussion of the right of "Texian" over "Texan" see *The Encyclopedia of the New West*, by John Henry Brown and William S. Speer, Marshall, Texas, 1881, pp. 472-473; also *Texian* (Annual), edited by William Neal Ramey, Austin, 1886, Vol. II, No. 17, p. 285.

headlight. The darkness and the post oak thickets swallowed them into security. The next evening they were on hand to shoot again. The trainmen got to saying to each other just before they reached the place of the shooting, "Look out! We're going to have Hell again!" The shooting became so regular that in expectation of it the conductor would warn all passengers to "lay low," adding, "We're in for Hell again." Time went on and the shooting stopped, but the spot of the shooting was known up and down the railroad as "Hell Again," commonly pronounced "Hell 'gin."

Then a little station was built at the place. It was already named, but "Hell 'gin" would not attract purchasers for town lots. The station agent was a man both ready and considerate. Out of consideration for tradition he was loath to throw away the old name so rich in connotations; his ready wit found a way for it both to be and not to be. He further apocopated the corruption. The new town was called Elgin.

This is the story, though the editor of the Elgin *Courier* avers that his town was called after a Scotchman named Elgin. It must be admitted that the folk explanation does not have a ring of authenticity comparable to that of Checkup in Cherokee County. One day a passenger told the train conductor that he wanted to get off at a certain place on the line. "You needn't stop the train," he said. "Just check up." A short time afterwards some farmer put up at this place a shack for selling sardines and crackers, and the place was called Checkup.

The Wichita River, like the Wichita Mountains across Red River in Oklahoma, was obviously named for the Wichita Indians. "Their name," say the scholars, is of "uncertain origin and etymology." But where grave research falters the folk-tellers stride forward with assurance.

There are no falls now in the Wichita River anywhere near the city of Wichita Falls; in fact it is hard sometimes to find the water in the river at all. Yet just below the place where a wagon road crossed the stream to enter the village there was a fall of a foot or so, which debris from a flood-smashed dam obliterated. Before wagon ruts ever marked out a road or a house was built on the site, Indians used the ford here.

One time, the story goes, the Wichitas had been out on the plains hunting buffaloes and were returning to the camp grounds in the mountains that now bear their name. When they came to the river, they found it on a rise. They wanted to cross but did not know how deep it was. As a compliment to a certain maiden, the chief of this band designated her to test the depth. She had little trouble in holding up her skirt, and as she progressed into the mud-thickened waters she kept calling out, like a leadsman, the depths. Of course she spoke in her tribal tongue, "Ankle-deep," "calf-deep," "thigh-deep,"—and then, as she reached the deepest part of the water and was about to step where it was more shallow, "wichita," or, in English, "waist deep." "Wichita" ever afterwards the Indians called this ford, and the white buffalo hunters learned the name from them and added the word Falls. Waist-deep Falls, then.

The same story has been told to explain the name of the Washita River in Oklahoma; it is also told concerning the town of Waukarusa (now Lawrence, Kansas), located near what was then known as the Waukarusa River. The first Kansas settlers were pleased with the name. But soon they dropped it, "because they learned the following legend of the name. Long before the time of white settlers an Indian girl on horseback came to the stream while it was up from a big rain. Her steed"—probably a runty calico pony—"went in deeper and deeper, until as she sat upon him she was half immersed. Surprised and affrighted, she ejaculated, 'Wau-ka-ru-sa! (Hip-deep!)' She finally crossed in safety, but after the invariable custom of the savages, they commemorated her adventure by renaming both her and the stream Waukarusa."

X. ORIGINS OF PLACES

Among legends reputed to be of Indian derivation, numerous ones account for the origin of rivers, lakes, mountains, etc. Almost without exception they are puerile and sentimental. The ground now covered by Sour Lake was, for example, once a great mound. It erupted, and sank, and the depression was filled with "sour water," the medicinal properties of which were discovered by native tribes long before the advent of the white man. Caddo Lake had its origin in a "chill" that cracked the earth and left a basin. The springs of the San Marcos River originated through the tears of a Mexican maiden slain by Indians, etc., etc.

In the time of the most primitive Greeks, before anything was known of geology or the laws of nature, such myths had an interest; and because they were sincerely believed in and came fresh from a childlike imagination they still have a kind of interest. But diluted imitations of such as applied to the modern world are too much like the skimmed milk called "blue john" to please the taste of an intelligent person.

Another class of origin myths hark back to miracles wrought by mission padres. The padres were much more real than some of the stories fastened on them that have come down. Foremost among them in miracle-working was Fray Antonio Margil de Jesús.

Through him the berries on the wild sarsaparilla, or coral vine, became red for the first Christmas celebration in a mission at San Antonio, and the *gente* of that region still call it the Margil vine. Before this, at a night camp on the road from Nacogdoches to San Antonio a "tiger" —a jaguar or a panther—killed one of Margil's pack mules. In the morning the venerable padre made the ferocious beast come and kneel before him. Then a servant put the dead mule's pack on the animal, which carried it docilely all the way to Bexar, where it received a pardon for its offense and was sent back into the wilderness. Just before the travelers got to San Antonio, however, they were threatened by a band of ferocious savages: with a short prayer Father Margil transformed them into peaceful deer. Finally, at the very moment of his death, which was in the City of Mexico, August 2, 1726, all the mission bells in Texas rang out of their own accord, untouched by hands. But it was as a Moses with an Aaron's rod, striking water from the very rocks, that Father Margil became most famous.

History gives 1716 as the date when he set up the mission of Our Lady of Guadalupe at Nacogdoches. The town, recorded a Mexican traveler one hundred and twelve years later, "is watered by two creeks of clear water that run on the east and west sides, the first known as La Nana [The Mammy] and the second as El Bañito [The Little Bath]. On the west bank of La Nana there are a few boulders from which two small springs of cold and clear water flow and keep two circular basins . . . always full. These two springs are known as *los ojos del Padre Margil* [the eyes (springs) of Father Margil]." When, a few years after this observation, Shephen F. Austin recorded in his diary the legendary account of the origin of the *ojos*, the story must have been a century old.

Austin was at Queretaro, Mexico, when he made the following entry: "In the orchard there are many very pretty cypress trees. I collected seeds from them to carry to Texas. They showed me some of these trees planted by the hands of the Rev. father Morfit [Father Margil], who had been a monk in this convent, & a missionary at Nacogdoches in Texas. . . . At Nacogdoches all the springs went dry, & he went out with the . . . necessary apparatus to perform miracles. He struck a blow with a rod of iron on a rock, which stands on the bank of the creek La Nana, & immediately a stream of water gushed out, sufficient to supply the inhabitants with water to drink."

At San Antonio the potent padre ran into another drought. Overcome by heat and thirst, he and his company of monks and soldiers stopped in a valley where there was grass for the horses but not one drop of water for man or beast. There was nothing to do but pray, and while all the religious prayed, Father Margil's eyes perceived a ripe cluster of mustang grapes just above him. With praises to God, he began climbing for the juicy fruit; he did not know how astringent it is. He had to reach far out for it, and in reaching he fell. He swung to the grapevine, however—swung with such force that he somehow jerked its roots out of the ground. Then from the hole made by the extirpation a plenteous and refreshing spring of water gushed out. Thus originated what is now called the San Antonio River.

SOURCES

GENERAL SOURCE: The fullest lists of the place names of Texas are to be found, without discussion, in Rand McNally's *Indexed Pocket Map* of Texas, issued periodically, and *Gazetteer of Streams of Texas,* prepared under the direction of Glenn A. Gray, issued through the Department of Interior, Washington, D. C., 1919. Many names not listed in either of these sources are found on the topographic maps issued by the United States Geological Survey, Department of the Interior, Washington, though not more than a fifth of the territory of Texas has been covered by these excellent maps. Some names not listed in the two main sources are found on the county maps in the Land Office of the State of Texas.

The History and Geography of Texas as Told in County Names, by Z. T. Fulmore, 1915 (reprinted at Austin, 1936), gives, not without some errors, the history of Texas county names. *Texas Towns,* by Fred I. Massengill, published by the author at Terrell, Texas, 1936, contains succinct information on the name-history of more than 2000 post offices. A commendable beginning toward tracing the origins of town names is found in a fifty-page essay that prefaces *Texas Ballads,* by Paul Morgan, Dallas, 1934. The *Texas Almanac,* issued by the Dallas *News,* for 1926 has a considerable list of town names with explanations of their sources. *Animals and Streams: A Contribution to the Study of Texas Folk*

Names, by John K. Strecker, a bulletin issued by Baylor University, 1929, is a discussional and alphabetical treatment of stream names derived from those of Texas fauna.

PARTICULAR SOURCES. Instead of cluttering my text with footnotes, I have alphabetized place names treated of, giving the sources of my information so far as I think those sources may be of any value to students. For thirteen years or more I have been gathering data on the subject. A good deal of it has come from conversation that I see no use of annotating.

Sources concerning particular names:

ANGELINA RIVER. *Romance and Tragedy of Texas History,* by S. H. Dixon, Houston, 1924, pp. 15-19.

BABY HEAD MOUNTAIN. W. S. Adair in Dallas *News,* Nov. 26, 1922; Houston *Post,* Jan. 19, 1930; theme by Freda Dabbs, Univ. of Texas.

BLESSING. Martin O'Connor, Victoria, Texas.

BOVINA. *The X I T Ranch of Texas,* by J. Evetts Haley, Chicago, 1929, pp. 148-149.

BRAZORIA. See Popcorn Patch.

BRAZOS RIVER. Albert Pike, "Narrative of a Journey in the Prairie," *Publications of the Arkansas Historical Ass'n.,* Conway, Arkansas, 1917, Vol. IV, pp. 110-111; Elizabeth Williams, Waco, Texas, a descendant of the Ross family; J. Frank Dobie, *Legends of Texas;* George W. Bonnell, *Topographical Description of Texas,* Austin, 1840, pp. 82-83; Mollie E. Moore Davis, *Under the Man-Fig,* Boston, 1895, pp. 1-3; "The Arms of God," by C. M. Girardeau, in *The Texas Magazine,* Houston, May, 1897, pp. 431-434; Mayne Reid, *Odd People,* New York, 1889, pp. 284-285; *Texas,* by William Kennedy, London, 1841, pp. 167-168.

BUCK SNORT. Beeville *Picayune,* Jan. 9, 1931; James, W. S., *Cowboy Life in Texas,* Chicago, 1893, p. 87.

BULLHIDE CREEK. "History of McLennan County," by George B. Erath, *Texas Pioneer Magazine*, Austin, 1879, Vol. V, No. 1.

BUTCHER KNIFE CREEK. "Local Place Names," by Freda Gibson, *Publications No .I of West Texas Historical and Scientific Society*, Alpine, 1926, p. 41.

CALAMITY CREEK. Victor Smith, Alpine, Texas.

CAMP NECESSITY. *Captain Jeff*, by J. W. Maltby, Colorado, Texas, 1906, p. 129.

CAMPO DE LA RUEDA. See Loma Grande.

CANNIBAL CREEK. *Austin Papers*, ed. by Barker, Vol, I. p. 886.

CHAPPARO CREEK. Austin Papers, ed. by Barker, Vol. I, p. 886.

COMANCHE SPRINGS. *Reid's Tramp*, by John C. Reid, Selma, Ala., 1858, p. 118.

COPPERAS GROVE. *Seventy Years in Texas*, by J. M. Franks, Gatesville, Texas, 1924, p. 74.

CORYELL CREEK. *History and Geography of Texas as Told in County Names*, by Z. T. Fulmore.

COTERA WELL. Ms. of Augustus C. Cotera.

COW BAYOU. See Wasp Creek.

COW HEAD ROAD. *History of Navarro County*, by Annie Love Carpenter, Dallas, 1933, p. 76.

COWHOUSE CREEK. Frank E. Simmons, Oglesby, Texas.

CUERO. Houston *Chronicle*, Jan. 19, 1930; letter from Geo. H. Carter, Austin, Texas.

DEAD HORSE CANYON. Victor Smith in *Legends of Texas*, published by Texas Folk-Lore Society, Austin, 1924; Freda Gibson in *Sul Ross Skyline*, Alpine, Texas, June 20, 1924.

DEAD MAN'S CROSSING AND RANCH ON DEVIL'S RIVER. *Stories and Poems of Western Texas*, by William Averitt, New York, 1890, pp. 25-26.

DEAD MAN'S RANCH. "Still Had Ten Minutes Left," by O. W. Nolen, Cotulla, Texas, *Record*, Feb. 5, 1937.

DEVIL'S RIVER. Paul Morgan, San Marcos, Texas; also floating traditions.

DIME BOX. Dallas *News,* June 1, 1924.

DOE CREEK. *See* Pipe Creek.

DOG CANYON. Victor Smith, Alpine, Texas.

DOLORES STREET. San Antonio *Light,* Aug. 22, 1925.

EAGLE PASS. *Life of Jesse Sumpter,* by Harry Warren, 1902. Ms. owned by Frost Woodhull, San Antonio.

EDGAR'S BONEYARD. Carl Raht, *The Romance of Davis Mountains and the Big Bed Country,* El Paso, Texas, 1919, p. 237.

EGG-NOG BRANCH. Henry C. Fuller in Houston *Chronicle,* Feb. 4, 1923; Vivian Richardson in Dallas *New,* June 21, 1931.

ELGIN. *Texas Ballads,* by Paul Morgan, Dallas ,1934, p. 50, and from floating tradition.

ENCINAL DEL PERDIDO. *Prairiedom,* "by a Suthron" [F. B. Page], New York, 1845, p. 142.

FORT DARNELL. *History of Jack County,* by Thomas F. Horton, Jacksboro, Texas, *circum* 1935, p. 136.

FORT PHANTOM HILL. "Historical Sketch of Jones County," by Hybernia Grace, *West Texas Hist. Ass'n Year Book,* Abilene, Texas, 1927, Vol. III, pp. 32-38; "Western Frontier Forts of Texas," by Arrie Barrett, *ibid.,* 1931, Vol. VII, pp. 128-129; "The History of Jones County," by Thelma Thomas, Dallas *News,* June 29, 1924; *Hunter's Magazine,* Ozona, Texas, May, 1911, p. 21; *Captain Jeff,* by W. J. Maltby, Colorado, Texas, 1906, pp. 124-126; also p. 74; *Beyond the Mississippi,* by Albert D. Richardson, Hartford, Conn., 1867, p. 228.

FORT SPUNKY. Houston *Chronicle,* Jan. 27, 1930.

GIBTOWN. T. F. Horton, Jack County, Texas.

HAPPY HOLLOW. James, W. S., *Cowboy Life in Texas,* Chicago, 1893, p. 87.

HEIFER CREEK. *Some History of Van Zandt County,* by Wentworth Manning, 1919, pp. 178-179.

Hell Roaring Hollow. *See* Hide Town.

Hide Town. "Lore of the Llano Estacado," by J. Evetts Haley, in *Texas and Southwestern Lore,* Austin, 1927, p. 82.

Hog Eye. *History of Jack County,* by Thomas F. Horton, Jacksboro, Texas; also a letter from the author.

Horsehead Canyon. *Frontier Times,* Bandera, Texas, Feb., 1926, pp. 41-43.

Horsehead Crossing. O. W. Williams, Fort Stockton, Texas; John Russell Bartlett, *Personal Narrative,* New York, 1854, Vol. I, p. 96; "The Cienega Fight," by Donald F. McCarthy, in *Frontier Times,* Bandera, Texas, Dec., 1926, p. 4.

Indian Bluff. L. W. Payne, Jr., in *Legends of Texas,* Texas Folk-Lore Society, Austin, 1924.

Kent, the City of. Dorothy W. Renick in *Southwestern Historical Quarterly,* Vol. XIX, pp. 51-65.

Larietta City. Thomas Hughes, *Gone to Texas,* New York, 1884, p. 7.

Lickskillet. *The Annals of Elder Horn,* by J. W. Bowyer and C. H. Thurman, New York, 1930, p. 8.

Llano Estacado. *See* Staked Plains.

Log City. *See* Larietta City.

Loma Grande. "A Trip to Texas in 1828: José María Sánchez," tr. by Carlos E. Castañeda, *Southwestern Historical Quarterly,* Vol. XXIX, p. 268.

Luce's Bayou. G. T. Bludworth, Fort Worth.

Luling. Gates Thomas, San Marcos, Texas.

Margil, Springs of and other legends connected with. "The Prison Journal of Stephen F. Austin," *Quarterly* of the Texas State Historical Association, Vol. II, p. 185; "A Trip to Texas in 1828: José María Sánchez," translated by Carlos E. Castañeda, *Southwestern Historical Quarterly,* Vol. XXIX, pp. 282-283; *Legends of Texas,* pp. 204-205; *History and Legends of the Alamo and*

Other Missions, by Adina de Zavala, San Antonio, 1917, pp. 65-68, 150; *Combats and Conquests of Immortal Heroes,* by Charles Merritt Barnes, San Antonio, 1910, pp. 76-89; *San Antonio de Bexar,* by Mrs. S. J. Wright, Austin, Texas, 1916, pp. 121-122.

MEDICINE MOUNDS. L. W. Payne, Jr., in *Legends of Texas,* Texas Folk-Lore Society *Publications,* Austin, 1924.

MESMERISER'S CREEK. *History of Navarro County,* by Annie C. Love, Dallas, 1933, p. 87.

METHEGLIN CREEK. Alex Dienst in *Legends of Texas,* Texas Folk-Lore Society, Austin, 1924; E. W. Winkler, Univ. of Texas.

NACOGDOCHES. "The Birth of Justice in Texas," by Alice L. Perkins in *The Texas History Teachers' Bulletin* (Univ. of Texas Bulletin No. 2546, Dec. 8, 1925), p. 38.

NAVASOTA. Mary Jourdan Atkinson, "Pioneer Folk Tales," *Pub. No. VII,* of the Texas Folk-Lore Society, Austin, 1928, p. 76.

NEW YEAR'S CREEK. "Reminiscences of Early Texans," by J. H. Kuykendall, *Quarterly* of the Texas State Historical Association, Vol. VII, p. 29.

O'NAGA. Paul Morgan, San Marcos, Texas.

PAGE'S TREE. Folio on Red River County, Archives, Univ. of Texas.

PERRYMAN THICKET. *Seventy Years in Texas,* by J. M. Franks, Gatesville, Texas, 1924, p. 63.

PIPE CREEK. *Pioneer History of Bandera County,* by J. Marvin Hunter, Bandera, Texas, 1922, p. 228.

POPCORN PATCH. "Early Texas Nomenclature," by Noah Smithwick, *Quarterly* of the Texas State Historical Ass'n., Vol. II, p. 174.

POPHER CREEK. Elma Heard, Lufkin, Texas.

PRIVILEGE CREEK. *See* Pipe Creek.

PULLTITE. Frank E. Simmons, Oglesby, Texas.

RAKE POCKET. Beeville *Picayune,* Jan. 9, 1931.

Randado. J. Will Falvella in San Antonio *Express,* Aug. 12, 1923.
Razor. Dallas *News,* June 1, 1924.
Scary Lane. Paul Morgan, San Marcos, Texas.
Snyder. See Hide Town.
Sour Lake. Houston *Post,* July 2, 1903.
Squaw Creek. *History of Hood County,* by Thomas T. Ewell, Granbury, Texas, 1895, pp. 20-21.
Staked Plains. *Early Western Travels,* edited by Reuben G. Twaites, Vol. XIV, p. 20; *Thirty Years of Army Life on the Border,* by R. B. Marcy, New York, 1866, p. 27; Castañeda's *Narrative of the Expedition of Coronado,* Winship's translation, Pt. I, Chap. XIX, Pt. III, Chap. VIII; *The Gilded Man,* by A. F. Bandelier, New York, 1893, p. 220; *Commerce of the Prairies,* by Josiah Gregg, New York, 1844, Vol. II, p. 181; *Exploration of the Red River of Louisiana in the Year 1852,* by R. B. Marcy, Washington, 1854, p. 100; report of Captain John Pope to the Sec. of War on *A Route for the Pacific Railroad . . . from Red River to the Rio Grande,* Washington, D. C., 1854, Chap. II; *Notes through Unexplored Texas . . . 1854,* by W. B. Parker, Philadelphia, 1856, p. 161; *Texas,* by Jacob de Cordova, Philadelphia, 1858, pp. 43-44; *Beyond the Mississippi,* by Albert D. Richardson, Hartford, Conn., 1867, p. 232; *Letters from the Frontiers,* by George A. McCall, Philadelphia, 1868, p. 430; *Texas Rural Register and Immigrants' Handbook,* Houston, Texas, 1875, p. 34; *A Pictorial History of Texas,* by Homer S. Thrall, St. Louis, 1878, p. 40; "Report on the Geography . . . of Llano Estacado or Staked Plains," by W. F. Cummins, in *Third Annual Report of the Geological Survey of Texas,* 1891, Austin, Texas, 1892, pp. 129-131; *A Standard History of Oklahoma,* by Joseph B. Thoburn, 1916, Vol. I, p. 18; *Buffalo Days,* by Homer D. Wheeler, Indianapolis, 1925, p. 237; *Letters and*

Notes on the Texan Santa Fé Expedition, by Thomas Falconer, ed. by F. W. Hodge, New York, 1930, p. 110; Robert T. Hill in *A Guide to the South Plains,* Lubbock, Texas, 1935; "The Peculiarities of the Llano Estacado," by Fannie G. Iglehart, in *Year Book for Texas, 1901,* by C. W. Raines, Austin, 1902, pp. 235-237.

STARVATION CREEK. *Frontier Times,* Bandera, Texas, Nov., 1926, pp. 44-45.

SUNDAY CREEK. J. C. Tolman, in *The Texaco Star,* Houston, Texas, Dec., 1925.

TELL. Dallas *News,* Jan. 1, 1924.

TEXAS. Hodge's *Handbook of American Indians;* "The Native Tribes about the East Texas Missions," by Herbert E. Bolton in *Texas Historical Association Quarterly,* Vol. XI, pp. 249-276, which treats very fully of the name "Texas"; *The Telegraph and Texas Register,* July 24, 1839; floating traditions; clippings, undated, in Bishop Gregg papers, Archives of Univ. of Texas; *Roemer's Texas,* tr. by Oswald Mueller, San Antonio, 1935, pp. 280-281.

TOADLOOP DRAW. J. Evetts Haley, "Lore of the Llano Estacado," in *Texas and Southwestern Lore,* Austin, 1927, pp. 86-87.

TRICKHAM. Gay, Beatrice Grady, *Into the Setting Sun: A History of Coleman County,* Santa Anna, Texas, 1936, pp. 16-17.

TURNOVER. Frank E. Simmons, Oglesby, Texas.

WASP CREEK. "History of McLennan County, by George B. Erath, in *Texas Pioneer Magazine,* Austin, 1879, Vol. V, No. 1.

WATCH MT. Houston *Chronicle,* Jan. 19, 1935.

WAUKARUSA. *Beyond the Mississippi,* by Albert D. Richardson, Hartford, Conn., 1867, pp. 36-37.

WICHITA FALLS. Ms. by Paul Morgan, San Marcos, Texas; and *The History of Wichita Falls,* by Jonnie R. Morgan, Wichita Falls, Texas, 1931, p. 12; "History of Wichita County," by Lucile

Disicre, *Texas History Teachers' Bulletin,* Univ. of Texas, 1925, p. 81; Dallas *News,* Sept. 30, 1923.

YO-LO-DIGO. Interview from J. H. Walker, by Dawson Duncan, Houston *Chronicle,* May 18, 1930.

ZARZAMORA STREET. San Antonio *Express,* Dec. 25, 1929.

THE LOBO GIRL OF DEVIL'S RIVER

By L. D. BERTILLION

In the fall of 1830 John Dent and Will Marlo went in partners to trap fur along the headwaters of Chickamauga River in Georgia. Pelts were plentiful, and they got along harmoniously enough until the spring of 1833, when they fell out over a division of the winter's catch.

A woman was at the bottom of the quarrel. She was Mollie Pertul, daughter of a mountaineer. While trapping in the vicinity of the Pertul cabin, John Dent had fallen in love with her and the two had engaged to be married. In forming their partnership the two trappers had agreed to sell jointly all pelts they took and to divide the money equally. Through two seasons this agreement they had carried out, but now Dent insisted on taking half the hides and disposing of them in his own way. He had a notion that he could get more money, to start married life on, by selling his fur separately.

After a bitter quarrel the division was made as Dent wanted it. Immediately almost, Marlo began telling around that he had been cheated. The quarrel went on for about two weeks; then there was a fight in which Dent stabbed Marlo to death. Public opinion was against him, and there was nothing for him to do but skip the country. Before leaving, however, he managed to see his love and tell her that he was going to locate a place in which they could live together and that he would return and steal her away.

Months passed by and people began to lose interest in the matter. During all this time, presumably, Mollie Pertul heard nothing from her murderer lover. Then a little after sundown on April 13, 1834—just a year to the day after Marlo was stabbed—the mountaineer girl went to the cow lot to milk as was her daily custom. After she had been absent from the house an unusually long time, her parents decided to investigate and see if anything had gone wrong. They found the cows unmilked and in the empty milk pail a Bowie knife with dried blood caked about the hilt. It had a staghorn handle of peculiar design that made it easily identified, next day, as the knife with which Dent had killed Marlo.

In the darkness of the night the parents called and searched for Mollie, but in vain. As soon as daylight showed, a few mountaineers who had been summoned began looking for sign. They struck the tracks of a man and woman leading to the Chickamauga River. There they found in the bank a freshly driven stob to which, apparently, a small canoe had recently been moored. Mollie Pertul was gone without a word of explanation and without a moment's preparation. All she took with her were the clothes on her back.

Six months passed. Then old Mrs. Pertul received a letter postmarked Galveston, Texas. It read:

"Dear Mother,
"The Devil has a river in Texas that is all his own and it is made only for those who are grown.
"Yours with love—
"Mollie."

In those days the people of Georgia were not familiar with the streams of Texas and their names. Indeed, very few people in Texas itself knew anything about Devil's River, far to the west of San Antonio, the outpost of all settlements, its inhabitants almost exclusively Spanish-speaking. Mrs. Pertul and her husband and neighbors merely considered that somewhere in Texas

THE LOBO GIRL OF DEVIL'S RIVER   81

Dent had to himself a river on which to trap. They knew that Dent was a devil all right, though maybe they were a little surprised at Mollie's admitting it.

Now, one of the little known chapters in Texas history is of a small colony of English people who in 1834 settled on Devil's River, calling their settlement Dolores. It was short-lived. Indians killed most of the settlers. A few of them drifted into Mexico. The remainder, fourteen adults and three children, in attempting to get back east were attacked at Espantosa Lake, near what is now Carrizo Springs. After killing them all, the Comanches threw their bodies and the carts in which they were traveling into the lake. That is why to this day Mexicans consider the lake haunted, the name Espantosa meaning "frightful."

Dent and his bride had joined this English colony. Devil's River had plenty of beaver; so did the Rio Grande both above and below where Devil's River empties into it. We may be sure that Dent did not live in the group of Englishmen, but, like the lone wolf he was, off to one side. He, no doubt, had an agreement with the Indians. A considerable ride westward two or three Mexican families, more Indianized than anything else, raised a few goats on the Pecos Canyon.

About noon one day in May of the year 1835, a rider on a reeling horse drew up at one of these goat ranches. He told the Mexican *ranchero* and his wife that he was camped where Dry Creek runs into Devil's River. He said that his wife was giving birth to a baby and that they must have help. The Mexican woman agreed to go with her husband, who at once began saddling the horses. Meantime, one of those black electricity-charged clouds for which that part of the country is noted was coming up. A bolt of lightning struck the messenger dead.

This delayed the Mexicans considerably in getting off. From the description of his camp site given by the dead man the *ranchero* knew how to reach it, but night came on before he and his wife got over the divide to Devil's River. They did not find the camp until next morning. There, under an open brush arbor lay the woman dead, alone. Indications pointed to the fact that she had died while giving birth to a child. Yet no child was visible. No child could be found. No trace of it was evident anywhere. Tracks thick around the brush arbor made the *ranchero* suspect that lobo wolves had devoured the infant.

In the scantily furnished brush cabin the Mexicans found a letter, which they took along to show the first person they might encounter who could read English. This letter, as it later developed, had been written by Mollie Pertul Dent to her mother in Georgia several weeks before her death. It served to identify her and her husband. Thus their romance ended.

Ten years passed. A wagon road that had been laid out across the new Republic of Texas to El Paso went by San Felipe Springs (now Del Rio), where there were a few Mexicans, and on across Devil's river, only twelve miles beyond, and then across the Pecos. Occasionally armed travelers passed over the road. In the year 1845 a boy living at San Felipe Springs reported that he had seen a pack of lobo wolves attacking a herd of goats and with them a creature, long hair half covering its features, that looked like a naked girl. Some passing Americans who heard the story quizzed him. But they seemed more interested in getting his description of what a naked girl looked like than in getting information about the strange creature he reported. The story was ridiculed, but it spread back among the settlements.

Not more than a year after this a Mexican woman at San Felipe declared she had seen two big lobos and a naked girl devouring a freshly killed goat. She got close to them, she said, before they saw her. Then they all three ran. The naked girl ran at first on all-fours, but then rose up and ran on two feet, keeping in company with the wolves. The woman was positive of what she had seen. The few people in the Devil's River country began to keep a sharp lookout for the girl. They recalled the disappearance of the dead Mollie Dent's infant amid lobo tracks. Men of the camp told how female wolves carried their cubs by the scruff of the neck without injuring them. Perhaps, they said, some lobo wolf in whom the mother instinct was strong had carried the new-born to her den and raised it. Indians reported having noted in sandy places along the river barefoot tracks, sometimes accompanied by hand prints.

A hunt was organized to capture the Lobo, or Wolf, Girl of the Devil's River, as she had now come to be called. It was made up mostly of wild-riding Mexican vaqueros. These people had doubtless never heard anything of the story of the wolf-suckled Romulus and Remus who founded Rome or of wolf-nursed children in India like Kipling's Mowgli, but far out on this isolated, stark border they had been confronted with unmistakable evidence of a human being reared by and running wild with lobo wolves.

On the third day of the hunt two of the riders jumped the girl near a side canyon. She was with a big lobo that cut off from her when she dodged into a crevice. Here the vaqueros cornered her. She cowered at first like a rabbit. Then she spat and hissed like a wildcat. She fought too, clawing and biting. While the vaqueros were tying her she began to belch forth pitiful, frightful, unearthly sounds described as resembling both the scream of a woman and the howl of a lobo but being neither. As she was howling forth this awful scream, a monster he-wolf, presumably the one from whom she had become separated, suddenly appeared rushing at her captors. The fact that one of them saw it coming before it got close enough to use its powerful jaws probably saved their lives. He shot it dead with a pistol. At that the wild girl sank into a silent faint.

The captured creature was now securely tied and could be examined more carefully. She was excessively hairy, but breasts of beautiful curvature and other features showed that she was a normally formed human female. Her hands and arms were muscled in an extraordinary manner but not ill proportioned.

Having revived from her faint, she was placed on a horse and carried to the nearest ranch. There she was unbound and turned loose in an isolated room for the night. With gestures of kindness she was offered a covering for her body, food and water, but no eagle of the free air, no lion of the deep jungle, ever showed more distrust and fear of its captors than she. She backed into the darkest corner, and there she was left alone. The door to the room was closed. The only other opening was a little window across which a board had been nailed.

The ranch was but a two-roomed hovel, alone amid the desert wilderness. By dark four or five men were gathered at it, and now the wild and frantic being fastened up in the room began voicing forth the terrifying screamish howls. Through the log walls of many vents they carried far on the night air. Soon they were answered by the long drawn out, deep howls of lobos beyond. Lobos seemed to answer from all sides, and their dismal and far-carrying voices brought answers from farther and farther away. All the lobos of the western world seemed to be gathering. Rancheros who all their lives had heard lobos howl had never heard anything like this, either from such a number of wolves now assembling or in the sullen, doom-like quality of the long, deep howling. Nearer and more compactly the horde gathered. Now they would howl all in unison, a bass-throated chorus of ferocity and darkness and lost hopes such as no musician of the world ever dreamed of. Then they would be silent as if waiting for some answer, and the wild girl in the dark room there would answer back with her unearthly howling scream, a voice neither of woman nor of beast.

After a time the great pack made a rush for the corrals, attacking goats, milk cows and the saddle horses. The noises made by these domestic animals, especially the screams and neighs of the plunging, kicking horses, brought the men to the rescue. Ordinarily no man at all familiar with lobo wolves would fear one. Now these rancheros kept together, shooting in the darkness and yelling as they advanced. The wolves retreated.

THE LOBO GIRL OF DEVIL'S RIVER

Meantime, in the pandemonium, the Lobo Girl somehow wrenched the cross plank from the window and got out. It was supposed that she immediately rejoined the wolves. Hardly another howl was heard that night, and the next day not a track of the girl could be found. For a long time the sight of a wolf in that particular region was very rare.

Nothing more was heard of the Wolf Girl of Devil's River for six years. Meantime, gold had been discovered in California and travel westward had greatly increased. Along in 1852 an exploring party of frontiersmen hunting a route to El Paso that would be better watered than the Chihuahua Trail, as the road used was called, rode down to the Rio Grande at a sharp bend far above the mouth of Devil's River.

They were almost upon the water before they saw it or could be seen from its edge. There, sitting on a sand bar, two young wolf whelps tugging at her full breasts, they at close range caught clear sight of a naked young woman. In an instant she was upon her feet, a whelp under each arm, dashing into the breaks at a rate no horse could follow. The creature could have been no other than the wild Lobo Girl of Devil's River.

So far as is known she was never glimpsed by man after this, though perhaps some of the old-time Apaches might have had a tale to tell could they have been asked. What the fate of the Lobo Girl—or woman—was, nobody probably will ever know. During the war of extermination that has been waged on lobos, the most predatory of animals that stockmen of America have known, in the border country, a wolf has occasionally been found with a marked human resemblance, and for many years now "human-faced" wolves, so called, have been considered the final culmination of a Georgia murder and elopement. If man can bear the "mark of the beast," why may not beast bear the mark of the man? Speaking only for myself, I will say that despite the fact that over a century has passed since the beginning of the incidents just related, yet during the past forty years I have in the western country met more than one wolf face strongly marked with human characteristics.

ANECDOTES FROM THE BRAZOS BOTTOMS

By A. W. EDDINS

Editorial Note.—One of the most characteristic forms in which the humor and the wisdom of the American folk have found expression is the orally-transmitted anecdote. During the last century it was, as Bret Harte has observed (*Cornhill Magazine,* N.S. VII, 3), "common in the barrooms, the gatherings in the 'country store,' and finally at public meeting places in the mouths of 'stump orators.' Arguments were clinched, political principles illustrated, by a 'funny story.' It invaded even the camp meeting and the pulpit. It at last received the currency of the public press. But wherever met it was so distinctly original and novel, so individual and characteristic, that it was at once known and appreciated abroad 'as an American story.' "

Mr. Eddins has written down, "purely from memory" he says, a number of such anecdotes as those Bret Harte had in mind, and it is hoped that others may be recorded.

They are essentially comic parables, or *exempla,* the applications of which to politics, religion, and morals are obvious.

—M. C. B.

NOBODY BUT ME AND YER FATHER

A country fellow who had been elected to the office of constable was considerably elated over his new honor. When he went home, he explained to his wife and children the prerogatives of his new office and boasted at length about how important he had become.

The children, powerfully impressed by their father's talk about the importance and dignity of being a constable, said to their mother, "Mother, are we constables too?"

"Hush, you silly brats," she said with a toss of her head. "You ain't constables; jest me and yer fayther."

MORE NOISE THAN WOOL

An Irishman fresh from Dublin went to work on a Texas sheep ranch. The owner of the ranch was called away in the midst of the shearing. He told Pat to finish the work. "Shear everything on the place," he said, "and pack the wool in the barn."

When he had finished shearing all the sheep, Pat, remembering that the boss had said to shear everything, caught the old sow, and after a mighty struggle, mixed with many squeals and grunts, succeeded in shearing her.

Out of breath, discouraged, and disgusted, Pat looked first at the old sow and then at the pile of hair, and said, "By my faith, shearing a pig gives a great big noise but precious little wool."

DRIVE ON THE CART

The village scamp had gone from bad to worse. He was constantly drunk, always idle, never supporting his family. Finally he came home one night drunk, beat his wife, and abused the little children. The neighbors, who had been supporting his family, were so disgusted with his worthless conduct that, after a short discussion they decided the best thing to do would be to take him out and hang him.

They placed him in a cart and started out of town toward a convenient tree. On the way they met a prominent citizen who had been off on a trip and did not know what they were about.

He stopped the procession and asked what was the matter. They told him how this man had consistently refused to work and provide for his family, how the neighbors were tired of supporting him in addition to his family, and how they had decided to hang him to get rid of him.

"Don't do that," said the good man. "It will be too bad to hang him. I'll help to support his family and him too. I'll give a bushel of corn right now."

The culprit in the cart raised up and asked, "Is it shelled?"

"No," said the man, "it is not shelled, but you can soon shell it."

The lazy rascal sunk back down in the straw and drawled, "Then drive on the cart."

WEATHER PROPHETS

It has been said that George B. Erath, the famous German pioneer and Indian fighter, was the author of the expression: "Nobody prophesies about Texas weather except newcomers and damn fools."

For many years this has been a favorite gag in Texas social life. It was one of the sells in the old saloon days, and the unfortunate tenderfoot who fell for it always had to set up the drinks to the crowd.

One dull, slow evening when things were at an absolute standstill in the saloon, a fresh young guy with a derby hat and store-bought clothes breezed into the place, walked up to the bar, and ordered a drink. The usual crowd of loafers looked on disapprovingly but said nothing. Leisurely finishing his drink and wiping his mouth with a bright silk handkerchief, the newcomer said, "Well, I believe it's going to rain."

The golden opportunity had arrived; the whole crowd was alert and watchful. Then the older nester, the leader in all the local wars of wits, said very fatherly, "My friend, did you know that there were only two kinds of people who prophesy about Texas weather?"

"Two kinds of people who prophesy on Texas weather?" mused the stranger. "That's very queer. Who are they?"

Then the old nester, with all the contempt and sarcasm in his power, sneered, "Newcomers and damn fools."

The crowd rose with a mighty shout and gathered around the newcomer shouting, "Haw, haw, haw." "He got you that time." "You are it." "He got you good." "Set um up. Set um up." "You owe the drinks to the house." "Come on, set um up."

The young fellow stood smiling at all their hurrah. He was not the least troubled about their demands for the drinks. When the hubbub had died down and they were all properly up against the bar, he said very calmly and slowly, "You say there are only two kinds of people who prophesy about Texas weather—newcomers and damn fools. You are right. Those are the only two kinds in Texas."

THE WISE FERRYMAN

A wise old ferryman carried the immigrants across the river on the way to their new homes. Day after day these men with their families and belongings in the covered wagons were rowed across the river. The river was wide and the crossing tiresome; and as the passengers had seen few people on their long journey, they were inclined to be talkative. One fine looking man with his wife and six or seven growing boys said to the ferryman, "We certainly hated to leave our old home. The neighbors were all such good people. It was such a pleasant place to live. But the boys are all growing up, and we just had to go where we could get more land. We do hope we will find another place just as good."

The ferryman replied, "You will. There are many good people in this part of the world and you will be sure to find them."

On the next trip there was a tall, rough, dirty man with slovenly wife, quarreling children, and a bunch of snarling dogs. He too told why he was going out West.

"We were pretty well fixed up back East," he said, "but the people were so mean we couldn't get along with them. We had to sell out and leave to avoid trouble. We hope to better ourselves, but I guess it will be just as bad out West."

"I'm afraid so," replied the ferryman. "There are lots of mean people in this part of the world."

And so day by day the stream of travelers passed on, and always the ferryman could tell each one just what he would find in his new home, because he knew that people always find what they are looking for.

ALL FACE

On a cold dreary day an Indian and a white man were making a journey together. The Indian had on no clothing except a blanket, while the white man was bundled up in all the clothes he possessed. The white man continued to complain about the cold and to wonder why the Indian was not freezing. He said to the Indian, "I don't understand it. With all my clothes I am about to freeze, and you, with only a thin blanket, do not seem to be cold at all."

"Is your face cold?" asked the Indian.

"No, my face is not cold, but I'm just about to freeze everywhere else."

"Me all face," said the Indian.

NOT A DROP OF WHISKEY IN THE HOUSE

The village saloon was at its very best. It was Saturday night. All the laborers had received their pay checks, and the saloon was cashing them while everybody was "setting 'em up" to everybody else. The crowd was beginning to get mellow, and good fellowship ruled supreme.

Then one of the leading celebrators looked up the street and called out, "Look, everybody. Yonder goes that old fool Tom Smith. He's going home this early. Look at the darn fool. He's got a whole sack of flour on his shoulder, and I'll bet he ain't got a drop of whiskey in his house."

PIG OR PUPPY?

Two old Southern gentlemen were fast friends, and both were very fond of dogs. One Christmas morning one of them hoped to afford the other a pleasant surprise by giving him a fine puppy for a present. He put the puppy in a tow sack and gave it to old Mose, a very reliable negro man, with instructions to take it to his neighbor with his compliments.

On his way, Mose stopped at the village saloon to get a Christmas toddy. While he was in the saloon, some village youngsters saw the sack and took out the puppy and put a pig in its place. Mose hurried out, took up the sack, and went his way. When he reached his destination, he opened the sack and was astonished to find a pig instead of the puppy he had started with. He hurried back to explain and to find out his master's wishes. But when he came back by the saloon, he decided that he needed another toddy; so he put the sack down and went in. The boys, seeing the sack, took out the pig and put the puppy back in its place. Mose hurried out, took up the sack and hurried home. When he opened the sack to show his master the pig, there was the puppy that he had started with. Very much disgusted, Mose said, "Ober dare you'se pig. Down here you'se puppy. What is you anyway?"

THE WISE MAN

There was once a wise man who had learned, as he thought, everything in the world. As there were no more fields of knowledge for him to conquer, life had lost all its pleasure to him. He knew all there was in this world to know. There was nothing left for him to do execpt to die. Before he died he decided to take one more good smoke. He filled his pipe carefully, and told the little negro servant to bring him a light. The fire had burned low, and there was nothing left but a few live coals. The servant hesitated a moment, then reached down and filled his palm with cold ashes, brushed a live coal on top of the ashes, and came smiling to his master's pipe. The wise man looked on in astonishment and said to himself, "And I call myself a wise man, when a little negro boy knows more about lighting a pipe than I do. Wise man, nobody knows it all. Why the wisest man in the world can learn from the commonest fool."

IT PAYS TO KISS AT HOME

The richest man, leading banker, social light—the king-pin of the town—found himself in serious financial difficulties. All he owned had been swept away. He signed away all his property to his creditors and went home a pauper. There he made a clean breast of the whole matter to his good wife, but she did not seem to be greatly depressed. "Oh," she said, "don't worry. I guess we will get along somehow."

After supper she said to her husband, "Let's take a walk," and they strolled down the street together. They came to the largest department store in the city. The husband, impressed with its magnificence, said, "What a beautiful store. What a fine business this is."

And the wife replied, "Yes, it is a good business. Our last quarterly dividend was thirty per cent. You see, I own a large block of the stock."

They continued their walk, and as they passed a large flour mill the wife said, "This mill is also a good investment. I have received large dividends from it."

They crossed the street and came by a leading hotel. The wife stopped and said, "I own a half interest in this hotel and it pays us well."

In amazement the husband asked, "Where did you get all the money for these investments?"

"Don't you remember, my dear, when we were first married, and you were a rich young man and I was a poor girl, every time you kissed me you gave me a ten dollar bill. Well, I saved all those bills and invested them. Now we have plenty to live on. Aren't you glad?"

The husband looked at her with astonishment and regret. Then he spoke from the bottom of his heart, "My God, old woman, if I had only done all my kissing at home, we would have owned the whole darn town."

LESS SAID ABOUT IT

The country church was in a stir. The young people were all going to the devil and taking the church with them. With their dancing, carousing, and love-making, they were bringing shame to the church and disgrace to Christianity. Something had to be done. One of the young sisters was caught in the act of "necking" with one of the gay young sinners, and was brought before the church for discipline.

The evidence was conclusive. One of the leading sisters in "Zion" had walked behind the young couple on the way home from church and had witnessed the disgraceful love-making.

The older members thought it necessary to save the church from humiliation by putting a stop to such outrageous doings. The younger and more liberal members, while not approving the actions of the erring sister, thought that there might have been mitigating circumstances, and that the girl might not have been entirely to blame. The lovely spring weather, the bright moonlight, the shady road, and the handsome young man had all contributed to the girl's mistake, and they were rather inclined to give her another chance.

After a long and violent discussion, they all turned instinctively to the old grandmother of the church, whose Christian life was above reproach, and whose good deeds had blessed the church and community for half a century. By unanimous consent they asked her for advice in the solution of their problem. She was reluctant to express an opinion. She begged the congregation to excuse her, pleading ignorance and inexperience in such matters. But the congregation continued to insist and promised to abide by her decision whatever it might be.

Finally, she rose very slowly and reluctantly, and said, "Brethren and sisters, I am honored that you want my opinion about our dear sister, and about love-making in general. I am afraid that it is not what you would expect of me. But honestly, brethren and sisters, from the depths of my heart I really and truly believe that if there was more of it done and less said about it, the world would be better off."

AIN'T LOST

A fine city man had a brand-new buggy and a prize-winning pair of trotters that he wished to try out. He drove along the country roads, speeding a little here and walking a little there, studying the good points and admiring the beauty of his new rig. He was so delighted with the prospect that he failed to notice the road. Later on he realized that he was lost, but he hoped by driving on to find his way, or at least to meet someone who could tell him how to get back to the city.

But it was a long lonesome road. For a long time he followed the windings, hoping every hilltop would bring him within sight of some dwelling. When it was almost dark he saw in front of him a cotton patch and a good-sized country boy chopping away in the rows. He reined his tired team near the fence and called out, "Hello, boy."

"Hello yourself," the boy replied, still wielding his hoe.

"Where does this road go to?"

"Hain't never seed it go nowhars. Hit allus stays right whar hit is," said the boy, still digging away.

"How far is it to the next town?"

"Don't know; never measured it," replied the boy.

Thoroughly disgusted, the man said with some heat, "You don't know anything. You are certainly the biggest fool I ever saw."

The boy looked a long time in the man's eyes; then he said with contempt, "I knows I don't know nothing. I knows I'se a fool. But I ain't lost."

HOG-THIEVES HANGING TOGETHER

A young district attorney was trying his first case. It was a rather simple one, a clear case of hog theft with no complications. The defendant was an old-timer who lived in the back country and did not seem to be a person of any consequence.

The case was called and the defendant appeared without a lawyer and announced himself ready for trial. The young attorney explained that the state would furnish a lawyer if the defendant was not able to hire one. The defendant declined and the trial proceeded. The attorney put on his witnesses, developed his evidence, and very courteously turned his witnesses over to the defendant, who, however, did not ask a single question. The attorney closed his case and asked the defendant to put on his witnesses. The defendant had no witnesses.

Then the attorney made his argument before the jury, and the defendant was told that he might make a speech in his own behalf if he wished. The defendant said that he could not make a speech, but if the judge and attorney would permit, he would like to whisper a word or two in the ear of each of the jurymen. This request was granted, and the defendant passed to each member of the jury and whispered something in his ear. Then he sat down. The judge gave the charge and the jury retired. In a few minutes they brought in a verdict of "not guilty."

The attorney was astonished, for the verdict was clearly contrary to both the law and the evidence. The man had been proved guilty. But the jury had cleared him. The more the attorney thought about the case, the less he understood it. Finally he went to the defendant and said, "The jury has declared you not guilty. That makes you absolutely free from the charge. You can never be tried again for that offense. You won your case and I congratulate you. But I cannot understand why. I will give you ten dollars to tell me what you whispered in the ears of those jurymen."

The old man smiled, reached out for the ten, and replied, "I said, 'Now is the time for all us hog-thieves to hang together.'"

LIE HERE, DEACON

A good Baptist deacon used to freight some in early days. The roads were very bad, and the large ox teams were sometimes unruly and hard to handle. It was said that whenever the team stalled or the wagon bogged down, the deacon would be very patient and gentle with his team. He would speak softly to them and try to encourage them out of the trouble. After he had tried all the gentle means he knew, he would take off his hat, lay it very gently by the side of the road, and say regretfully, "Now, deacon, you lay right there till I cuss these damn oxen out of this bog."

He always came out of the bog.

"GOL DERN THESE BISCUITS"

The teacher was trying to teach the word *grace* to the minister's little son. The little fellow spelled slowly *g-r-a-c-e,* but he could not pronounce the word. After he had tried several times, the teacher said, "What does your father say when he sits down to breakfast?"

The child thought a minute and then replied, "He says, 'Gol dern these biscuits; they are heavy as lead.'"

THE LORD'S PRAYER ON A BET

Two senators were on their way to Washington. The roads were long and tiresome, and their horses slow. In order to make the time pass more pleasantly, they told many things about their past lives—how they were raised, how they were educated, how they got into politics, and like interesting topics. One told how, as a child, he used to walk three miles every Sunday to church, and how he became an excellent Bible student. The other recalled the particulars of his early church experiences. One thing after another led one of them to say something about the Lord's prayer. The other remarked that he had also learned it when he was a boy. Then the first one said, "I'll bet you five dollars you can't repeat it now."

"I'll bet you I can," said the other.

"All right, begin."

Then he began very reverently:

> "Now I lay me down to sleep.
> I pray the Lord my soul to keep.
> If I should die before I wake,
> I pray the Lord my soul to take."

The other handed him the money and said, "You win. By golly, I didn't think you knew it. I bet you've been studying up on it lately."

WHITE AS PEARLS

The Master and His disciples were making a long journey one hot day across the hills of Samaria. They came to a narrow place in the road. Right at the most difficult place lay a dead dog blocking the way. The dog had been dead several days and was very badly swollen and offensive.

The disciples were furious. Each one jumped over the dead dog with disgust and curses of contempt. Last came the Savior, who gathered His skirts carefully and calmly and stepped lightly over, saying as He passed, "His teeth are as white as pearls."

"ANYBODY, O LORD!"

The village spinster was getting along in years and all the available men were passing her by. It began to dawn upon her that unless she did something quickly, she was doomed to be an old maid. Greatly depressed, she went out in the woods to think it all over. She finally decided that since there seemed to be no hope in men, she would call upon God for help. She knelt down and poured out her soul to the Lord. "O Lord," she said, "hear my prayers. This day send me a man. Send me a man, O Lord, that I may not be so lonesome. O Lord, do send me a man."

Just then an old owl in the neighboring tree cried, "Who! who! who!"

She jumped to her feet and shouted with joy, "Anybody, Lord. Anybody will do."

PREDESTINATION FOR THE INDIAN

In the early days of the Republic of Texas when the Indians were especially bad, an old Primitive Baptist preacher was preparing for a long trip across the Indian country. He was especially careful in cleaning and loading the long rifle that was to accompany him. A friend, seeing his preparation and knowing his belief in predestination, said to him, "Uncle Billie, why are you so careful about your gun? If you meet the Indians and you are predestined to die at that time, why you will die anyway; so why worry about the gun? 'What is to be will be anyway,' you know."

"Yes, I know all about that," said Uncle Billie, "but it might be the Indian's time."

CONTRADICTORY DREAM REVELATIONS

It is said of this same minister that a notorious character of the community thought he would be able to take advantage of him because of his belief in mystic visions. So one morning he drove his wagon up to Uncle Billie's crib and said to him, "The Lord told me in a dream last night to come to your crib and get a load of corn."

Uncle Billie reached up over the door and took down his long rifle and said, "Yes, but the Lord must have changed His mind, for He told me this morning not to let you have it."

FAITH AND EXPECTATION

A good old sister in Zion had long been worried about the mountain that stood in front of her cabin and cut off the view of the great valley beyond. Many times she had wished that she could pick it up and lay it out of her way. At church one day the preacher discussed the power of prayer. Quoting from Scripture, he declared that if one had sufficient faith, one might say unto the mountain, " 'Be thou removed,' and straightway it would fall into the sea."

The good sister heard with great interest, and that night she prayed long and fervently that the mountain might be removed from her door. Then she slept the sleep of the righteous until the early dawn. She waked and hurried to the door to see whether the mountain were gone. But there it stood just as high and as rugged as ever. In disgust she turned away and said, "Just as I expected."

G. P. C.

The church was in an uproar. The congregation was badly divided on the question of whether or not they should grant a certain young brother, whose reputation for piety was none too good, a license to preach.

A few of the older conservative members were a little doubtful about the sudden call to the ministry, and wanted to put him off until they could be a little surer about the reality of the call. Many of the younger brethren were very enthusiastic about the wonderful conversion and vocation of the applicant. They thought a real miracle had happened, and they were anxious to see him licensed and put to work in the Lord's vineyard. They recounted with great seriousness how, according to the young man's own testimony, the Lord had appeared to him in a vision and had shown him the three letters "G. P. C." flaming in the sky, and how a still small voice had said, "Follow these." There could be no doubt about the interpretation. G. P. C. meant "Go Preach Christ." And the young man should be sent on his way.

But the old deacon was on his feet, replying, "Brethren, I do not deny the vision. I am sure that the Lord has spoken to this young man. But knowing this young man as I do, and appreciating to some degree the great wisdom of the Lord, I am sure that you all misinterpret what this vision meant. 'G. P. C.' in this case can only mean, 'Go Pick Cotton'."

PRESCRIPTIONS FOR ENTERTAINING PREACHERS

When John and Mary married, they did not amount to much either financially or socially. But they both buckled down to work, John trading in cattle and Mary planning and saving. Soon they were the up-and-coming people in the community. And when they built their new home, which was the best house in the whole community, people began to take notice.

Just then it was decided to hold a great revival meeting in the community. It was to be a union meeting and all the community was to join in. A big brush arbor was built, and all preparations were made until the question arose as to who would keep the visiting preachers. Since John and Mary had the best house, it was unanimously agreed that they should keep at least one; and after much urging they consented.

The very day the meeting was to begin, John got an urgent business call and had to leave at once. As he was making hurried preparations for his journey, Mary, in despair, asked, "What am I to do about the preacher who is to stay with us during the meeting?"

After a moment's consideration, John said that he did not think that they could afford to disappoint their friends, and they had best keep their promise.

"But what must I do? How do you entertain a preacher? I never saw a preacher in a home in my life."

John said, "Well, when he comes, invite him in, see that his horse is fed and stabled, and put him in the front room until supper. After supper he will go to church, and after church he will come back and go to bed. So you see, he will not be much trouble."

"But they are not all the same kind of preachers. Am I to treat them all just alike?" asked Mary.

John paused in his preparation long enough to say, "If they send you a Presbyterian, put the new Bible on the table, make a nice fire in the fireplace, and leave him alone. If he is a Baptist, put a pitcher of water, a sugar bowl, and a spoon on the table, and get the quart of rock and rye from the cellar and put it by the sugar bowl, and all will be well."

"But," said Mary, "suppose they send a Methodist?"

John thought a moment and said hastily, "Then send me a telegram and I will come home at once. You are too good looking a woman to trust with any Methodist preacher."

HELPING THE LORD DECIDE

The big town church called the up-and-coming village minister to be their pastor. Like all orthodox ministers, he took the matter under advisement and waited for the Lord to direct him. A day or two afterwards one of the big town deacons was passing through the village and met the pastor's son. After the usual courtesies, he asked the boy whether or not his father had decided to accept the new call. The boy answered nonchalantly, "Oh, he still has the matter under consideration, but he is packing up his books."

THE LORD SENT IT

The village widow was reduced to dire straits. Her cabin was old and cold and leaky. Throughout the summer, with what little family washings she could get and with a little help here and there from the neighbors, she managed to get along. But mid-winter found her in actual want. She was cold and hungry, and as a last resort she knelt before her fireplace with its few smoldering chunks and prayed: "O Lord, I know thou art going to take care of me, but, O Lord, I'm hungry. O Lord, do as thou seest fit with me, but send me some bread. O Lord, send me some bread; O Lord, send me some bread."

Over and over she prayed in her agony. The village wag was passing by and heard her. He thought this would be a good time to put one over on religion. So he hurried down to the village bakery and bought a dozen loaves of bread, climbed on top of the shanty, and threw the bread down the chimney.

The good woman with shouts of joy began to praise and thank the Lord.

"I knew thou wouldst not forget me, Lord; I knew thou wouldst take care of me, Lord. I thank and praise thee, Lord."

The wag, unable to contain himself longer, threw open the door and shouted, "Praise the Lord, you silly goose. Why the Lord had nothing to do with that bread. I threw it down the chimney myself. The Lord sent it! Phew, there ain't no sich animule is the Lord."

The good woman replied, "Yes, there is a Lord too. And he sent the bread in answer to my prayer. He sent it just the same, even if he did choose the devil to bring it."

THE MEASUREMENTS OF NOAH'S WIFE

In the good old days when the sermons were long and the people were very religious, the old pastor's young son, who seemed to be trying to live up to the traditional reputation of preachers' sons, found his father's Bible open on the study table, where the beloved man of God had been preparing his sermon for the next Sabbath; and in a spirit of fun, he pasted two leaves of the Bible carefully together.

On Sunday morning the minister stood and read, "And Noah took unto himself a wife." Then he carefully turned over the two pasted pages and read, "And the length thereof was three hundred cubits, the breadth of it fifty cubits and the height of it thirty cubits." He paused in surprise and read slowly and carefully again, "And Noah took unto himself a wife, and the length thereof was three hundred cubits, the breadth of it fifty cubits, and the height of it thirty cubits." Again he paused, took off his spectacles and wiped them carefully, and for the third time read, "And Noah took unto himself a wife." He then moistened his fingers and carefully turned the page and continued, "And the length thereof was three hundred cubits, the breadth of it fifty cubits, and the height of it thirty cubits."

Then after a long pause he said, "Brethren, I have been reading this Bible for fifty years. I do not remember that I ever read this passage before, but it confirms me in my faith in the works of the Lord, for, truly, brethren, we can say of Noah's wife that she was fearfully and wonderfully made."

WASPS IN THE PREACHER'S BREECHES

The minister of a very fashionable church went on a summer vacation. He had such a good time that he stayed as long as possible. He reached home just in time to preach the Sunday sermon. He hurried to the vestry, changed his clothes as quickly as possible, went directly into the pulpit, and began to read the morning's lesson. In his hurry to get to the service he put on his pants, which had been hanging in the vestry during his vacation, without noticing that the wasps had built a nest in the seat.

He began to read: "The spirit of the Lord is in my mouth."

Just then the wasps began to get busy. He threw his Bible down, slapped both hands to the seat of his pants, and continued, "And the devil is in the seat of my breeches. The congregation is dismissed, and the ladies will please retire immediately."

THE UNFINISHED CLAY MAN

One of our best old Southern families had an only son. He was a bright boy and was idolized by all who knew him. He grew up and was sent away to college. There by continuous hard work he undermined his health and finally lost his mind. He returned home a harmless and quiet, though hopeless, imbecile. He labored under the delusion that he was the Lord and could make a man. He spent long hours down by the bank of the branch making a man out of clay. The clay image was completed, except for an arm, when night came, and the poor youth was led away to supper. Later some devilish boys who were passing by stole the clay man and hid it in the bushes. For days the poor boy hunted his man but could not find him.

Sunday came, and the boy went with his family to church. The new preacher, a one-armed man, had just arrived, and a large congregation was out to hear his first sermon. After the services were dismissed, all the people crowded around to meet the new preacher. There was much shaking of hands and many exchanges of compliments. Finally the poor boy's attention was attracted to the preacher. He walked all around him and looked him up and down with a puzzled air. Suddenly a broad smile swept over his face, and he rushed up to the preacher, grabbed him by the hand and said in a loud and excited voice, "Say, what made you run off before I got you done?"

LINING THE HYMN

Long ago when many people could not read and hymn books were scarce, it was the custom for the preacher to read a line or two from the hymn-book and for the congregation to sing the lines he read. This was continued until the whole hymn was sung. This was called "lining the hymn."

The day was dark and gloomy, and the good old minister's eyes were bad. When the time came to sing, he rose, wiped his glasses, and after a long struggle gave up the attempt to read, and said,

"The room is dark, mine eyes are dim;
I cannot see to read the hymn."

The congregation began to sing at once,

"The room is dark, mine eyes are dim;
I cannot see to read the hymn."

The preacher waited patiently until they had finished singing, and said,

"I said the room is dark, mine eyes are dim;
I certainly did not mean it for a hymn."

Again the congregation sang,
>"I said the room is dark, mine eyes are dim;
>I certainly did not mean it for a hymn."

Then with considerable irritation he said,
>"Confound it, this is no hymn at all;
>The old devil must be in you all."

Again the congregation patiently sang,
>"Confound it, this is no hymn at all;
>The old devil must be in you all."

The preacher ended in disgust, "Let's pray."

THE ADVENTURES OF LITTLE AUDREY

By CORNELIA CHAMBERS

Little Audrey is a folk-lore character about whom thousands of nonsensical short tales—during the past five or six years—have been told. Sometimes Little Audrey parades as Little Emma or Little Gertrude, but she usually is recognizable by a catch phrase—"she just laughed and laughed." The amusing incident is typically a catastrophe. Little Audrey sees the humor in any situation.

A nice thing about Little Audrey is her integrity. She is no hypocrite; she does what she wants to do, says what she wants to say, and makes no bones about it. Little Audrey will never have inhibitions. Further, she is a very modern girl. She is having new adventures constantly, as indicated by the puns on floating power automobiles and the carioca dance steps. To her, irony predominates over sentiment. She has few illusions.

Little Audrey is nation-wide in distribution. In Texas she is well-known, particularly in universities and high schools. Approximately one out of ten students is a Little Audrey fan with a number of her adventures tucked away in his mind. The following are some of the stories known and collected by the author.

Little Audrey and her papa were out riding one day in their new stream-lined car. Papa was proud of the car, and he was giving it the gas; he wanted to see how much it would make. All of a sudden the road turned, but papa did not; he went straight on and into the lake. Little Audrey saw what was going to happen, and she just laughed and laughed. She knew all of the time that their car had floating power.

Once upon a time all the children in Little Audrey's neighborhood were taking lessons. It was the proper thing to do; if you did not take lessons, you simply were not in the social swim. So Little Audrey cried and cried, 'cause she was not taking lessons. After a while her mama said, "Little Audrey, if you will just stop that bawling, I'll let you take lessons." That made Little Audrey awful happy; so she sat down to think about what kind of lessons she would take. Well, after a long time she decided to take parachute lessons. So Little Audrey practiced and practiced, and after a while it was time to give her recital; you know if you take lessons you just have to give recitals.

Well, people came from far and near to see Little Audrey parachute jump. She went way up high in the airplane and got ready to jump. She looked down and saw all those peple watching her, and then she jumped out. On her way down she just laughed and laughed, 'cause she knew she was going to fool those people; she didn't have on her parachute.

Once upon a time Little Audrey got lost on a desert island. Along came a big bunch of black cannibals and kidnapped her. They tied her up to a tree and started their pot to boiling. Little Audrey knew they were going to make stew out of her; so she looked around at those lean, hungry cannibals and counted them. There were nineteen. Little Andrey just laughed and laughed, 'cause she knew she was not big enough to make enough stew to go around.

One day Little Audrey and her mother went for a walk out in the forest where some lumbermen were felling trees. Just as they came along, the men cut down a big oak, and it fell right on mother! Little Audrey just laughed and laughed, 'cause she knew all the time that Mother couldn't carioca.

That night Little Audrey and her mama and papa and her little brunette sister were sitting at the dinner table. Papa said, "Little Audrey, pass the cream, please." So Little Audrey passed the cream to her papa, and he poured some into his coffee. Then he put the pitcher down, and Little Audrey noticed that right on the tip end of the spout there was a little drop of cream all ready to fall. Little Audrey just laughed and laughed, 'cause she knew all the time that the little cream pitcher couldn't go *sniff, sniff*.

One day Little Audrey was standing on the corner just a-crying and a-crying, when along comes a cop, who said, "Little Audrey, why are you crying?" And Little Audrey said, "Oh, I've lost my papa!" The cop said, "Why, Little Audrey, I wouldn't cry about that. There's your papa right across the street leaning against that bank building." Little Audrey was overjoyed; without even looking at the traffic she started across the street. Along came a big two-ton truck that ran over Little Audrey and killed her dead. The cop just laughed and laughed. He knew all the time that that was not Little Audrey's papa leaning against the bank building.

One time Little Audrey and her little brother were inspecting a ship. They went over it from top to bottom, and then little brother decided he wanted to go way up high to the crow's nest. Little Audrey told him he better not go, but he was awful hard-headed; so up he went. When he got up there he waved to Little Audrey, lost his balance, and came tumbling down. Little Audrey looked at the remains and just laughed and laughed, 'cause she knew all the time that her brother just could not stand hard ships.

One time Little Audrey took her grandpa out walking. Little Audrey got awful hot; so she said, "Grandpa, let's go down to the old swimming hole and take a swim." But grandpa didn't much want to, 'cause he was blind. But Little Audrey begged and begged, and finally grandpa agreed to go. So they went down to the old swimming hole and put on their bathing suits. There was a big tree, growing out over the water, that the kids used as a diving board. Little Audrey told her grandpa to climb up the tree and dive off. But he didn't want to; so Little Audrey had to make him. When he jumped off, Little Audrey just laughed and laughed. She knew all the time that the swimming hole had dried up.

Little Audrey's brother was a jailbird. One time when he was up for three years he broke out of jail. The sheriff looked and looked for him, but he couldn't find him anywhere. After about a month the sheriff decided to put the bloodhounds on the trail. And that made Little Audrey just laugh and laugh, 'cause she knew all the time that her brother was anaemic.

One day Little Audrey and her mother were driving along when all of a sudden the car door flew open and Little Audrey's mother fell out. Little Audrey just laughed and laughed, 'cause she knew all the time that her mother had on her light fall suit.

The nurse was going to take Little Audrey out for a walk; but the nurse was absent-minded, and she forgot until she was outside to take Little Audrey with her. So she called up to the cook and said, "Cook, throw Little Audrey out the window, and I'll catch her on the second bounce." The cook threw Little Audrey out the window and then she just laughed and laughed. She knew all the time that Little Audrey was not a rubber ball.

One day Little Audrey's mama went to town, and while she was gone Little Audrey decided to bake a cake, 'cause she wanted to show her mama how smart she was. She got down the recipe book and mixed the cake according to directions. She sifted the flour, creamed the butter and sugar, beat the eggs, and stirred the ingredients together. Then she was ready to cook the cake; so she looked at the recipe book and it said:

"Now set in the oven for thirty minutes." So Little Audrey crawled into the oven and closed the door.

By and by Little Audrey's mama came home. She looked everywhere for Little Audrey, but she couldn't find her. All of a sudden she smelled something burning. She opened the oven door, and there was Little Audrey, burned to a crisp. Her mother just laughed and laughed. She didn't know that Little Audrey could read.

The next day Little Audrey and her grandma were standing on their front porch watching the men pave their street. There was a cement mixer, a steam roller, and all kinds of things to watch. All of sudden grandma saw a quarter out there right in the middle of the street. She dashed right out to get it, but just as she picked it up along came that old steam roller and rolled her out flatter than a sheet of theme paper. Little Audrey just laughed and laughed, 'cause she knew all the time it was only a dime.

One day Little Audrey was playing with matches. Mama said, "Ummm, you better not do that." But Little Audrey was awful hard-headed; she kept right on playing with matches, and after a while she set the house on fire, and it burned right down to the ground. Mama and Little Audrey were looking at the ashes, and mama said, "Uh huh, I told you so! Now, young lady, just wait until your papa comes home. You certainly will catch it!" Little Audrey just laughed and laughed. She knew all the time that papa had come home an hour early and had gone to bed to take a nap.

The next night Little Audrey and her date were sitting on the sofa when all of a sudden the lights went out. "Oh, said Little Audrey's boy friend, "it sure is dark in here. I can't even see my hand in front of me." Little Audrey just laughed and laughed, 'cause she knew all the time that his hand wasn't in front of him.

ROY BEAN: LAW WEST OF THE PECOS

By MYRON W. TRACY

Not many actual men of so recent a date as Roy Bean, who died in 1903, have become so completely legendary. People by the thousands who know nothing of him as a man repeat yarns—yarns ever growing wider, wilder and taller—of his bizarre decisions and arbitrary gestures. Besides numerous magazine articles, there are at least two books[1] about him; on the centennial grounds at both Dallas and Fort Worth during 1936 replicas of his combined saloon and justice of the peace office were erected. Yet, popularly, Roy Bean is not a man; he is a buffoon justice, "Law West of the Pecos." No doubt he will continue so to be; it would please him immensely could he know how his reputation, no matter what it is, has grown; I have no idea of changing it. However, while in the early 90's I was in the employ of the Southern Pacific Railroad, working in and out of Langtry, Texas, where Old Roy ran his Jersey Lily Saloon and from it administered the law as especially designed for "West of the Pecos," I came to know him well and learned at first hand some of the stories that have passed into current tradition.

---

[1] Lloyd, Everett, *Law West of the Pecos*, San Antonio, Texas, 1931; McDaniel, Ruel, *Vinegaroon: The Saga of Judge Roy Bean*, Kingsport, Tenn., 1936.

On the one hand, Roy Bean was a publicity hound that P. T. Barnum would have gloried in, often performing stunts for no other reason than to gain notoriety. On the other hand, he was an intelligent—and likable—man, shrewd in his knowledge of Mexicans and frontier character, and naturally original in his ways, though he often showed a silly over-estimation of his own importance.

He was fond of talking about his past experiences. He had in 1842, he told me, at the age of fourteen, run away from his Kentucky home, two years later driven a wagon from Independence, Missouri, over the Santa Fe Trail, and then during the Mexican War driven an ammunition wagon with General Taylor's army. He liked to recall noted Texans like Mustang Gray and Jack Hays. He did not know Jack Hays personally but he retained the tradition of a toast that had been drunk to him one night in a saloon: "Here is to Jack Hays, a man who never failed a friend or a foe, and may he never want for either." He claimed to have been in charge of a wagon train attached to the Confederate Army, and recalled experiences while freighting between San Antonio and El Paso after the Civil War. Billy Miller, his son-in-law, told me that Bean's real name way Roy Boone and that he was a member of Daniel Boone's tribe in Kentucky. I merely transmit the statement for whatever it may be worth.

Bean kept in an old trunk a lot of newspaper clippings about himself. On one occasion he brought out for me to read what Horace Bell[2] had written concerning his, Bean's, Headquarters Saloon at San Gabriel, California, in 1853. Some time prior to 1890 an intelligent man who was, I assume, wanted elsewhere had lingered around the Jersey Lily Saloon long enough to

---

[2] Bell, Horace, *Reminiscences of a Ranger*, Los Angeles, California, 1881, 92-94. In Bell's later book, *On the Old West Coast*, posthumously published, N. Y., 1930, 223-236, there are several other anecdotes about Roy Bean. Among Western chronicles there are none more delightful than these anecdotal reminiscences of genial Horace Bell.—J. F. D.

write quite a sketch of Roy Bean's life.³ In 1892 Bean gave me this sketch in manuscript, and I sent it to the Chicago *Record*, which published it the same year. When Bean saw the article and read it, he was indignant at a statement characterizing him as "very illiterate."

The best known stories about Bean's decisions and judgments as a justice of peace were current during his lifetime. He was ready to confirm virtually all of them, but when I asked him about fining a dead man for carrying a six-shooter, he said that story was not true. It was probably occasioned by the way he disposed of a Mexican who had been killed in a shooting scrape at Painted Cave. His daughters told me and Billy Miller that they were with their father when he examined the dead man, finding ten dollars in his pocket and a six-shooter, four empty cartridges in it, still in his hand. Bean appropriated both the gun and the money, remarking to the girls at the same time that, "These greasers are poor shots. They waste a lot of good ammunition. Anyhow, there's no sense in this ten dollars' going to waste."

One of the first cases he had, according to what he told me, was trying some gamblers who had won all the money a stage driver had and then his stagecoach and horses. The stage outfit no doubt belonged to somebody for whom the driver was working.

"I ordered the outfit returned to the driver," Bean said, "and the money as well. Then I dismissed the gamblers. They were sore and as they started to walk out made some sassy remarks. I ordered them back and fined them $30 each for gambling. They said they would not pay such a fine and started to leave. I called a ranger to bring them back. 'How much did I say the fine was?' I asked. 'You said $30,' one of the gamblers spoke up.

---

³ This must be the individual I heard of through Bill Easterling, an old trans-Pecos newspaper man, who had it in his memory that the man had been hired by Roy Bean to write his life and did write it. Jim Wilson, of Alpine, says that the fellow was "a tramp school teacher," that Bean boarded him for three months in the expectation of getting the biography written but that the boarder was usually too drunk to write.—J. F. D.

'Well, I guess I made a mistake. It's $50 each.' They howled like so many coyotes. 'If I hear any more about the matter from any of you,' I said, 'it will be a hundred dollars.' They shut up and paid up."

I asked Bean if he kept any record of the cases that came before him.

"No," he answered. "I have got the cleanest docket in the State of Texas. Not a scratch of a pen on it."

One time at Shumla, a station east of Langtry, I had an interesting conversation with the sheriff concerning some of his own experiences and Roy Bean's ways. The sheriff may have embroidered a little for my benefit. A body almost had to embroider when Law West of the Pecos came up as a subject.

The sheriff went on to tell how he and his men "killed and captured" a gang of train robbers just as they were about to cross the Rio Grande into Mexico.

"And what became of the captives?" I asked.

Looking at me sharply, the sheriff replied: "I guess you know as well as I do what would happen if we took some train hold-ups before Judge Bean. So what was the use?"

I agreed that it would be a waste of time and energy to take such criminals before the judge, who would order them shot or hanged and would probably criticize the sheriff for not attending to the matter without legal consultation.

The sheriff went on to cite two instances in which he took prisoners before Judge Roy Bean.

"What is the prisoner charged with?" Roy Bean asked.

"Stealing horses."

"Whose horses?"

"Mine."

"You sure about it?"

"Caught him at it."

"Who nicked his ear?"

"I did when he didn't stop."

"Poor shot, Jack, but if you had got him he would not have been properly finished as becoming a horse thief. It's my ruling that the prisoner is guilty. The rest is your business, Jack. You'd better buy him a drink before you string him up. Court is adjourned."

"The next prisoner I took before Judge Bean," said the sheriff, "was a man that everybody had for a long time known to be a rustler but that nobody had been able to pin the evidence down on.

" 'What is this galoot charged with?' asked the judge.

" 'Running stolen cattle across the Rio Grande down at Painted Cave.'

" 'Sure this is the man?'

" 'Caught him in the middle of the ford driving the cattle.'

" 'Then what did you bring him here fer when I am so busy? In a case like that always give the galoot what he deserves. Take him away and string him up.'

"Then turning to a line of men at the bar who had been listening, Roy Bean asked, 'Well, boys, what are you going to have?' "

Bean's peremptory discharging of a man who had killed a Chinaman, on the ground that he could not find a word in the "Revised Statutes" about a Chinaman; his being fooled into having his pet bear killed; his manner of divorcing couples he had married, if they wanted divorces, are all commonly known stories.

His constant rival was Jesus P. Torres, who operated the Eagle's Nest Saloon across from the Jersey Lily. One time while his own place of business was empty and free-spending patrons were making the Eagle's Nest gay, Roy Bean sent his deputy, Phil Forrest, over to arrest Torres for "disturbing the peace." Later on Torres discharged a man who had been in his employ. The man appeared before Judge Bean and entered suit against Torres for wages due and not paid. Torres demanded a jury trial. While the jurymen were making up their verdict Bean got word to them that if they wanted pay for their services they would have to find a verdict against Torres. According to the verdict they brought in, they must have wanted pay for their services.

It used to be told that the judge had suffered the indignity of an appeal from his court but once. A man charged with something somehow got his trial postponed until he could get a lawyer from San Antonio, three hundred miles away, to represent him. As soon as the lawyer, a young man, got off the train from the east Roy Bean opened court. The lawyer at once began raising objections to Bean's method of procedure. Finally he announced that he would appeal the case. Then Roy Bean placed his sixshooter on the table in front of him, the muzzle pointed towards the lawyer and his own forefinger on the trigger. "There is no appeal from this court," he stated. The young lawyer agreed and had no more objections to offer.

The story of how Roy Bean collected ten dollars for a bottle of beer has been told many times. I have a version quite different from the usual one. The passenger trains always stopped at Langtry for the engines to take on water. One hot day when the train stopped, a passenger alighted and hurried over to the Jersey Lily, the sign on which was very visible from the railroad, for a bottle of beer. He found the proprietor sleeping peacefully on a billiard table.

Raising himself lazily on his elbow, Roy Bean said, "You'll find a cold bottle behind the bar. Help yourself." Then he relapsed to the reclining posture. He heard his customer run out of the room, but he did not hear the tinkle of coin on the bar. He sat up and looked. There was no money on the bar. He was filled with wrath.

Grabbing from the pool table on which he lay his cartridge belt, with the ever reliable Colt's attached to it, he began buckling it on and making tracks for the train. As he ran up, the conductor was about to signal the engineer to go ahead. "Hold that train," the judge yelled. The conductor saw the judge still fooling with

ROY BEAN: LAW WEST OF THE PECOS 117

his belt and obeyed. "I got business on this train," old Roy hastily explained. "Hold it till I get back."

As he entered the smoking car, his gun was in a working position.. He had no trouble locating his customer. He demanded four-bits for the bottle of beer. The startled customer took one look at the gun and quickly held out a ten dollar bill. The judge jammed it into his pocket.

"Fifty cents for the beer and nine dollars and fifty for collecting," he announced. "This squares your account. You can keep the bottle. As he stepped off the car, he thanked the conductor, adding, "You can go ahead now as soon as you damn please."

Finally I'll give an illustration of how Roy Bean ran things. One night while I was talking with the telegraph operator in Shumla, his instrument began to click. After listening a while, he told me that a Mexican had been stabbed to death in a gambling quarrel at Langtry and the murderer had run across the Rio Grande, Bean's deputy, Phil Forrest, hot on his trail.

When I got back to Langtry the next day, Roy Bean's son Sam and a Mexican were just getting on their horses in front of the Jersey Lily. Old Roy was out on the little gallery, or porch, saying, "Now, Sam, if you see a Mexican within five miles of that flock of sheep, pull down on him. If you miss, then ask him what in the hell he is doing there. Get back as soon as possible. Billy Miller will be along with his train. Then we will get that greaser that got away on the other side last night—or know the reason why."

After Sam had ridden away I learned that some mutton had been sold around Langtry at a very cheap price the day before. Roy Bean was sure that a Mexican thief had been in his flock of sheep. He now called my attention to a tent on the Mexican side of the river, about a mile from it.

"That is the camp of a greaser selling tequila and mescal," he said. They are both stronger than any forty-rod. I am not going to put up with such business around here. As soon as Billy Miller's train"—a work train—"pulls in here this afternoon, I'll get some of his men and we'll get that murderer who escaped last night. He's at that camp. Phil Forrest went over there and found five or six armed men objecting to having their *compadre* brought back into Texas."

Sure enough, as soon as Billy Miller's crew came in, Roy Bean told him what he wanted, and in no time Miller had three men picked out to make the raid into Mexico. I was going with them, and the judge armed me with his old forty-four. Just as we were about to set out, we saw the tent being pulled down. "They are making tracks for the interior," Sam Bean, who had returned from the flock of sheep, yelled. The armed invasion of a foreign country was all off.

As I walked back into the Jersey Lily to return my artillery, a comely young Mexican woman rushed up to the *juez*, talking and gesticulating like a windmill in a whirlwind. The judge listened about a minute and then pointed to a bench over in the corner of the saloon, where the woman proceeded to sit down.

"Phil," he called to the deputy, who with Sam was on the gallery outside, "you will find this woman's man down near Pedro's shack dead drunk. Bring him back. Look out for his knife."

"Now, Sam, get those two chains and locks in my room."

Phil soon brought up the drunk. He was as disgusting as disorderly. Without wasting any patience on him, Roy Bean ordered him chained to an iron bar which had a swivel ring fastened in the top of it, its lower part fixed in a solid rock. The chain on the Mexican was longer than the other one, which was now fastened to the collar of a pet bear. If the Mexican stayed at the end of his chain the bear could not quite reach him. The bear did not have the aspect of being always a pet. As he slowly approached the Mexican, until he was close enough to slap him with a paw, the latter gazed stupidly. Then he went down on his face and hastily rolled to the end of his chain.

For the next half hour the Mexican was busy dodging the bear. The bear seemed to enjoy the game. At the end of that time both prisoners were released. In a sobered condition the Mexican now respectfully stood in front of the judge. His decision was that the woman should have the family burro and camping outfit, all their possessions, and that the man be out of town and on his way somewhere else within fifteen minutes.

Sam Bean told me that the iron bar was the only jail his father had and that for years it had—with the help of the bear—been used for no other purpose than to sober up drunks. The individual I saw sobered up had got "mean drunk" on tequila purchased from the bootleg tent on the other side of the Rio Grande.

MEXICAN SPOOKS FROM EL PASO[1]

By CHARLES L. SONNICHSEN

All up and down the valley near El Paso the ghosts are walking. Almost any night at the proper time and place they may be heard bewailing their sins of violence or greed, entreating the passer-by to get them out of Purgatory, or moaning over some hoard of buried gold. It is lucky for the nerves of most Americans that they are unaware of this condition; if their eyes should suddenly be opened, the Anglo-Saxon population of the valley would probably diminish rapidly. Fortunately, however, our ghosts are mostly Mexican, and as a rule they reveal themselves only to their own countrymen, who are not readily susceptible to shock.

El Paso itself has a number of ghosts, though the Chamber of Commerce has no statistics about them and the whole atmosphere of the town is anything but congenial to their kind. Perhaps because of this inhospitable atmopshere, it is next to impossible to pin an El Paso ghost down to dates and places. A story as pathetic as the one which follows makes one long for further details, but none are to be found.

THE BIRD AT HART'S MILL

An indefinite number of years ago a certain Mexican woman was living in Paso del Norte. She was a widow

---

[1] For the material in these stories I am indebted chiefly to Mrs. Pauline Polser and Miss Josefina Escajeda.

MEXICAN SPOOKS FROM EL PASO   121

with two children, but was not ambitious to continue her widowhood any longer than necessary. A lover appeared and offered her the comfort she desired, but he would not include the two children in the transaction. The poor woman could take it or leave it—she could have the man or the children, but she could not have both.

She chose the man. The children she drowned near the dam at Hart's mill. The site of this mill is marked by a monument just off the highway leading north out of El Paso; the structure itself has been gone these many years. The Mexican woman, however, still haunts the spot. She appears in the form of a bird with a plaintive voice, and can be heard at twilight calling—calling for her lost children. For until she finds them she can never be restored to human form and find peace in the grave.

Many another spot in El Paso has its familiar apparition; as for instance the house on North Oregon Street where a girl once committed suicide, and where men are still embarrassed when the girl's ghost pulls the covers off them at midnight. But for first-class ghosts with real sap in them, one has to go down the valley to the older Mexican towns, where several hundred years of simple history have prepared the mind to receive marvels. In Socorro and San Elizario the old families and the old beliefs are almost as they were before Americans entered the valley. There is no bank in either hamlet, and people still secrete their valuables as they did in the days of the Apache raids: behind a loose brick in the wall; in a hole in the ground such and such a distance from a door or window; beneath a particular tree or bush. Consequently, there is much talk of buried treasure, and it is quite possible to find people who have met the ghosts that always guard such deposits.

The Zartuche family has had intimate contact with several such *patrones* of treasure. Señora Zartuche is famous in her own district as a dealer in charms and spells, and might be expected to know about ghosts too. But her husband, poor fellow, was there ahead of her, if this story, current in Socorro, is to be trusted.

A GHOSTLY BABY SNATCHER

When Señor Zartuche was a baby, he was the victim of a malicious ghost who came every night at midnight and took him out of the house into the yard. There they would stay a few minutes; then the ghost would bring him back. Nobody knew why a spirit should behave in this eccentric manner, and nobody was able to do anything about it. The members of the family, of course, were completely terrorized, as who would not be to see a sight like this? But in spite of the cries and entreaties of the family and in spite of the kicks and squalls of the boy himself, the gloomy spectre carried out his nightly schedule.

Yes, it was hard on everybody, but particularly on the little boy. Every night he waited for the ghost, his little body shaking with terror. Day by day he grew thinner and paler, and it was quite obvious that soon there would not be any little boy for the ghost to carry out.

At last his mother was reminded of something she had once heard—that if one made himself into the shape of a cross on his bed, with arms flung out wide and face to heaven, he would be safe from witches. Perhaps the same treatment would make a ghost think twice about what he was doing. As a last resort, therefore, the mother got into bed with her child, and, as soon as she heard the ghost coming, assumed the required position.

The thing drew near, its fiery eyes fixed on the child, its claw-like hands extended to seize him. Then it saw the mother and drew back. "Now," she thought, "is the time to speak to it," for, as all Christian people know, a ghost cannot speak to a living person unless the person speaks first. She got out the right words with some difficulty:

"*En el nombre de Dios, diga lo que quiere?*"—In the name of God, what do you want?

The ghost began to talk. It told the woman of a buried treasure in that very house. She must dig in a particular spot and she would find first of all a saddle. Under the saddle were two earthen pots, one full of gold and the other of silver. Finally, pointing with a skinny forefinger, the ghost showed her where to dig.

By this time the *señora* was so frightened that she fainted away with a groan that would have wrung your heart. When she came to herself, the ghost was gone— to return no more.

Of course she wanted to find the treasure. She thought of starting to dig at once; but unfortunately, when she awoke from her fainting fit, she had forgotten in which corner the treasure was buried. She began to dig, nevertheless, since a Mexican house has only a limited number of corners and Mexican people have plenty of time. Her family helped her, but none of them found either the saddle or the gold under it. At last they gave up in despair.

Some time later, a man who had heard the story decided to try his luck. He dug a little deeper than anybody else, and there was the saddle. He pulled the rotted relic out, and beneath it were the two earthenware pots. But do not suppose there was any gold or silver in them! Of course not! Everybody knows that the person to whom the ghost points out the location of buried treasure is the only one who can find it. In this case the two earthenware pots were full of charcoal.

Everybody in Socorro has heard this tale about Señor Zartuche—even his wife; but he will not talk about it. If he sees a stranger coming he will run. His wife says he is a little crazy, and it is a subject on which one hesitates to contradict her.

If one asks whether her husband's condition may possibly be due to his unfortunate experience in childhood she will reply, *"Quien sabe?"* and tell you about another ghost, well known in Socorro, which she has seen herself.

THE GENTLEMAN FROM SPAIN

This tale goes back many years to the time a strange Spaniard came up from Mexico hunting for buried treasure. He had a map which had been bequeathed to him, in the usual manner, by a dying friend, and he went to work in a certain adobe house which has been used as a store and which can still be recognized by the words GENERAL MERCANTILE painted on one wall.

The Spanish gentleman kept very much to himself. He was handsome, wore fine clothes, and should have displayed a social personality. But he chose not to make friends or to tell people about himself, and all they could find out was that he had a daughter in a convent in New York City to whom he frequently wrote letters.

He lived on msyteriously in Socorro for some time. Then one morning, very early, a goat herder on his way out of town with his flock heard the most horrible commotion coming from the adobe house. It sounded like a man frightened out of his wits or in terrible agony. The goat herder abandoned his flock and ran to see what the howling and roaring were about. What he saw was something to set one's hair on end. In a freshly dug hole lay the Spanish gentleman, stone dead; the marks of his struggle upon him; his pick and shovel at his side. On the table was a letter to his daughter in New York, telling her that he was near the end of his quest. The treasure was almost within his grasp. If the map proved to be reliable, he would be a rich man tomorrow.

The map! It should have been there along with the pick and shovel and the melancholy remains of the ambitious Spaniard. But, search as they might, the people of Socorro could not find so much as a scrap of it. Therefore, being constitutionally disposed to accept the inevitable without distressing themselves, they put the Spanish gentleman out of their minds and thought of other things.

This, however, did not suit the Spanish gentleman at all. The family which moved into the adobe house began to report the most peculiar disturbance. They would wake up in the night with the chill of fear running up and down their spines and hear in the darkness the clanking of iron. Something would rattle like a chain. Then would come the regular click and crunch of a spade digging in the earth. Then voices—babbling and unintelligible and far away, but human voices, none the less.

This went on without too much discomfort to the people of the house until the time when a woman who lived there awoke in the middle of the night to find someone shaking her. She awoke unwillingly, as one does at such an hour, but she sat up fast enough when she saw who was disturbing her.

"El Caballero de España!" she shrieked.

Hearing himself thus addressed, the vision spoke in reply. He told her of great wealth buried beneath the house—an enormous sum in a huge chest. He told her how he himself had located it and dug to where he could plainly see the carved lid. Then two hands reached up out of the hole and seized him by the ankles. He struggled and yelled like a madman, but in spite of all his effort those two hands drew him down—down into the hole. And that was the end of him.

Then he informed her why it had been necessary for him to disturb her rest. Before he had ever left Mexico City, he had promised to pray thirty souls out of Purgatory with the proceeds of his treasure hunting. He had been unable, of course, to keep his word. Now, said he, those thirty souls turned sixty cold and dismal eyes on him every time he passed that way in the other world. Something had to be done about it, and if the woman would dig up the treasure and get those souls through Purgatory, she could keep half the treasure. Was it any wonder, he asked her, that a spirit in his situation should find it impossible to rest? Then he showed her a map which he had in his hand. He unrolled it and began to explain the exact location of the buried gold. But by this time the woman was tried beyond her strength; she fainted away before the directions were complete.

The treasure has never been recovered, but many people in Socorro have heard the sounds of digging and seen ghostly human forms in the old house. Mrs. Zartuche says she once got a good look at the apparition and recognized him as the Spanish gentleman.

Other inhabitants of Socorro have had more or less close contact with the world of spirits. Some have seen the white ox who survived two Apache massacres and used to appear when the Indians were lurking about. Joaquin Trujillo once lost a friend who had found gold on Mount Franklin and thereby earned the hatred of the old witch of the mountain. Several people have come close to the cross of white stones which marks Pancho Villa's buried treasure. And a flickering fire sometimes betrays the location of an Indian mine to the east of town near a mound called the Hill of the Virgin. A girl and boy once saw near this place two terrible figures—a ferocious dog and a half-naked man. The man said solemnly, "To him who does no harm, no harm shall come." Then man and dog disappeared. The boy and girl did likewise in the direction of their home.

But perhaps the most blood-curdling experience of all happened to two newlyweds.

GOLD BENEATH THE MIRROR

Concha and Manuel spent the first days of their married life in an adobe house owned by an old Socorro woman noted for her hard features and bad disposition. She rented this place to anybody who cared to live there, but she always came around every day to see what was going on. Every day she poked her sharp nose and sharp eyes through the door and cast her suspicious glance into every corner as if she were expecting to find something wrong. Often she never said a word—just looked around and left. Concha and Manuel didn't like it, but what could they do? After all, she owned the house.

One dark night Manuel woke up with a feeling that all was not well. He and Concha had been in bed for several hours; it must have been about midnight. He was quite sure that someone was looking at him—staring at him. He felt Concha tremble beside him and knew that she was awake and frightened too. Neither spoke a word, but both looked at the doorway.

Beside it was a woman dressed all in white. She was bending down and reaching into the ground, bringing up great handfuls of shining gold. She would pour each handful behind a mirror, and it would run down the wall, disappearing into the earth again. While this was going on, the ghost fixed a steady stare on the two shuddering figures in the bed. When it found that they were aware of what was going on, it raised a bony finger and made the gesture which says "come." Slowly, the white-clad figure walked backward out of the room, beckoning and beckoning with that bony finger.

"*Jesús, María, y José!*" exclaimed Manuel. "Concha, did you see it too?"

"*Sí,*" gasped Concha, her teeth chattering and her eyes popping out of her head.

Something pulled them out of the bed and drew them to the door. There it was, beyond the little yard, walking slowly along the bank of the *acequia,* still beckoning with that ghostly finger. It stepped into the water, still backing away, and began to sink little by little. In a few minutes they saw only a head and a long, bony arm. Then there was nothing left but the hand, still beckoning.

Naturally Manuel and Concha moved, and they didn't wait to see if there was a treasure buried under the mirror. They moved completely out of the neighborhood. But time wears out the strongest impressions, and in five years they came back to that vicinity, bringing with them David, Eduardo, and Carmelita, who had arrived meanwhile.

One day David and Carmelita were playing with some other children when an argument arose as to the ownership of some piece of juvenile property. David, who was not immediately concerned, sat down and began digging in the ground with a stick. It happened that he was in the yard of the very house where his father and mother had lived five years before.

The owner appeared at the doorway, more bent and malicious than ever.

"*Vayase,*" she screamed. "Get away from here! Quit digging in my yard! Move on, *pronto!*"

The children ran when she came after them with a stick, and David came home crying to tell his mother what had happened. Concho raised her eyebrows knowingly, and she and Manuel agreed that this was final proof of buried treasure under that house. Otherwise, why would the old woman be so excited about anyone's digging in her yard?

A few miles down the river from Socorro is San Elizario, likewise ancient and likewise full of tales. Here is one.

THE AMOROUS GHOST

Near the church in San Elizario is an old, rambling adobe house of many rooms. It was once a mansion, the property of a famous local character named Mauro Luján. Years ago this house was the scene of many a gathering of plotting politicians. During the Salt War of 1877, the bloodiest affair in Valley history, Don Mauro's house is said to have been headquarters for the leaders of the mob.

Since the old man's death, it has gone to ruin. No whitewash has touched its walls for years and no one has bothered to repair the places where the adobe has crumbled. Still Don Mauro must love it, for he has often been seen wandering from room to room saying his rosary.

Many people have lived in his house. To one pair of tenants, María de Ramirez and her husband Alejo, he revealed the location of a pot of money with which they were to have masses said for his soul. They, however, were unfaithful to his trust. They took the money across the river into Mexico, where they set up for themselves in the grocery business. They did not prosper, however, and María soon died, as one would expect.

Then an elderly pair named Maciel moved in, to whom Don Mauro was only a name. Antonio worked until late at night, leaving Bonifacia to go to bed by herself. At last the old lady went to her friend Doña Tomasa Giron and told her a strange tale.

"Every night," she said, "I go to bed by myself, because my husband is working and comes home late. And every night the ghost of an old man with a long, white beard comes and gets in bed with me. When my husband comes home and wishes to go to sleep, he has to say, 'Con su permiso,'—'with your permission'—before the old man will let him get in bed."

"Hm," said Doña Tomasa, "does he get out of bed when your husband gets in?"

"Oh, no! He just moves over."

"It sounds like Don Mauro," remarked Doña Tomasa, thoughtfully, as her mind traveled back over Don Mauro's record. "He used to be fond of the ladies," she added—"*era muy enamorado.*"

"*Y todavía es,*" said Bonifacia de Maciel, looking very wise, "*y todavía es. Me hace cariños.* He still is; he caresses me."

WALK AROUND MY BEDSIDE

By MARTHA EMMONS

"Come, an' le's talk about de Lawd, an' we'll have pallance together."

We did have parlance, Susan and I.[1] She is old and blind now, and spends much of her time to herself, meditating on the goodness of God. Failing eyesight has in no wise daunted her spirit. She declares that "Ole Satan may git de flag, but I'm gonna hol' on to de staff. I'm gonna han' it ovah to my Lawd myse'f. Yes, suh. De Lawd's been mighty good to me, an' I'm a-leanin' on Him, I tell you.

"De Lawd is so good to us. He teks keer of us whilst we's livin', an' He'll tek keer of us when we come to die, too."

Gently and quietly she rocked, then continued: "My ole frien's an' neighbors is all on 'em a-leavin' me now. One on 'em died heah a few days back. De Lawd He been tryin' to tell 'er 'bout it, I know; an' I sorto' b'lieve she know it too. She come ovah heah las' Sunday night, an' when she lef' she say, 'Well, Sis Susan,' she say, 'I may not nevah git back 'cross dis road to see you no mo',' an' sho' 'nough by Wednesday night she'uz daid an' in 'er coffin.

---

[1] The story "Walking Over Jordan," in "Dyin' Easy," of *Publications of the Texas Folk-Lore Society*, Number X, was contributed by Susan. She is fat, good-natured, and in spite of her blindness has a smile as radiant as that of Aunt Jemima.

WALK AROUND MY BEDSIDE

"An' you know, honey, dat's what I'uz tellin' you 'bout de Lawd a-helpin' us. Now, Sis' Calline's maw an' paw'd been daid foh a long time, an' she say to me dat night dat dey'd been a-spennin' all dey time wid 'er foh de las' three weeks or mo'. See, they'd jes' come back to tell 'er to come on ovah wid 'em, an' she say they talk' to 'er a pow'ful lot. She didn' allus un'erstan' what dey'uz a-tryin' to tell 'er. But dey'uz right wid 'er —plum to de ve'y las'.

"Yes, suh,—dey walk' aroun' her bedside. An' dat's jes' what I wan' de Lawd to do foh me." And she began to sing this song:

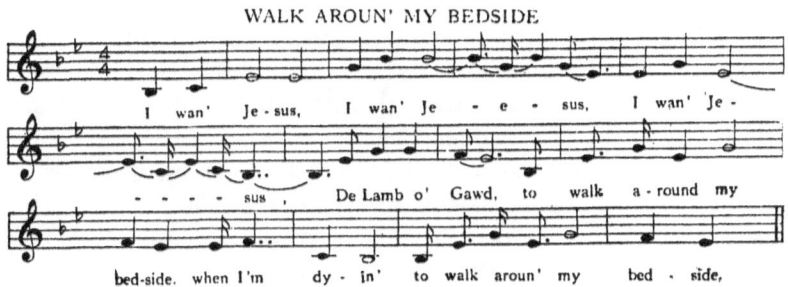

WALK AROUN' MY BEDSIDE

I wan' Je-sus, I wan' Je - e - sus, I wan' Je - - - sus, De Lamb o' Gawd, to walk a-round my bed-side. when I'm dy - in' to walk aroun' my bed - side,

    M-m-m-m, I wan' Jesus, I wan' Jesus,
        I wan' Jesus, de Lamb o' Gawd,
        To walk aroun' my bedside.

        When I'm lonesome,
        To walk aroun' my bedside.
        When I'm lonesome,
        To walk aroun' my bedside.

Refrain: I wan' Jesus, I wan' Jesus,
        I wan' Jesus, de Lamb o' Gawd,
        To walk aroun' my bedside.

        When I'm blue,
        To walk aroun' my bedside, *etc.*

> When I'm sick,
> To walk aroun' my bedside, *etc.*
>
> When I'm doubtin',
> To walk aroun' my bedside, *etc.*
>
> When I'm dyin',
> To walk aroun' my bedside, *etc.*
>
> *Refrain:* I wan' Jesus, I wan' Jesus,
> I wan' Jesus, de Lamb o' Gawd,
> To walk aroun' my bedside.

Elmira[2] likewise bears testimony of heavenly visitation in time of need. The last time I saw her she was feeling very serious and deeply spiritual. She had recently lost her mother. I have known those two long enough to understand a little of their devotion to each other, and I know how Elmira misses "Mama," as she calls her. Reaching out for comfort to her longing heart, she was ready on that day to say something of the visible ministrations of God and of spirits of loved ones. Her explanation of the phenomenon of ghosts is a bit unusual. It is based upon the accepted theory of dual personality. She took pains to explain it to me in this way:

"I don't remembah whetah I read it in de Bible or not, but it seems to me lak I read it som'ers dat all of us is got two spirrits, an' dat when we die, one o' them spirrits don' nevah leave this uth. It may be the good 'un, or it may be the bad 'un that don' cross ovah. But it goes aroun', an', 'cordin' to whichevah one it is, it tries to do good an' he'p us, or it jes' goes aroun' scarin' folks an' actin' thataway.

"Now, youk'n see they's two spirrits, all right, by when you light a candle. Lots o' times I's seed two

---
[2] For a description of Elmira Johnson, see *Publications*, Number X, p. 59 and footnote.

shadows from the same candle, an' it's the same way with folks.

"I 'membah once 'way back, I reck'n hit'uz fifty-fo' yeahs dis comin' summer, I had a cousin that when she'uz a-dyin' she'd tell 'em all, she'd say, 'What makes y'all cry an' go on thisaway 'bout me? I ain't a-worryin' 'bout nothin'. I ain' sufferin'. I'm jes' a-layin' heah waitin' foh de Lawd to come git me an' take me on home. I cain' hahdly wait, an' I'm jes' as happy as I k'n be.'

"Well, I jes' couldn' see how it 'twuz that anybody'ud jes' natchelly wanna die. I tole my mothah 'bout it. I say, 'Mama, I don't see how come Rosie can jes' sho' 'nough wanna die.' An' Mama say, "Well, Baby, she say, 'I reck'n de Lawd takes keer of 'er an' makes de way plain foh 'er.' I nevah say no mo', but I kep' a-worryin' 'bout it.

"Well, finely, one night, I went to baid, an' I'uz a-layin' theah on de baid, an' I couldn' git to sleep. But pres'n'y I drap' off, kinder dozin', an' I had a dream, I reck'n you'd call it, or a vision, or some'n', an' I'uz daid. I could see myse'f jes' as plain as anything, even when they put me in the coffin. But hit seem' like my spirrit was a-watchin' an' a-lookin' on f'om de outside like. An' I seen 'em a-fixin' me away in de box an' all, an' I thought I'uz jes' as happy about it all. Then when we went to the fune'l, I wen' along wid de res' of 'em— Elmira watchin' Elmira. I could heah 'em singin' ovah me, an' a-prayin' an' a-takin' on. I wanted to speak to 'em, an' tell 'em not to cry, but I'uz scared to, foh feah I'd scare 'em. Finely they lowered me down into the grave—I'uz inside too, an' I could heah them ole clods a-fallin' *thump, thump, thump,* right in on me. Mothah she'uz jes' a-takin' it *so* hahd that finely I retch' ovah an' tech' 'er on de shouldah, but I nevah say nothin'.

"Then de Lawd spoke to me, an' He say, 'You'll be awright. I'll be right wid you.' An' I woke up. But evah sence dat day, I've sorto' felt like de Lawd'ud come to me in my dyin' houah.

> "I wan' Jesus, I wan' Jesus,
> I wan' Jesus, de Lamb o' Gawd,
> To walk aroun' my bedside."

To a people whose imagination is so vivid, whose minds are so pictorial, it is an easy step from our conception of spiritual aid and reassurance to the idea of the visible presence of spirits. Somehow for them there is no definition between things ethereal and things of the earth entirely earthy. The tendency to clothe the abstract and the spiritual in the trappings of the flesh is at once grotesque and humorous to us, as in:

> Meet me, Jesus, meet me,
> Meet me in de middle of de aiah,
> So's if my wings should fail me,
> Meet me wid another paiah.[3]

In the same way, the persistent influence of those gone before is embodied and made potent in the Negroes' lives as ghosts, or "sperrits." A good spirit—unless for some reason the person did not die satisfied—returns only on errands of mercy. It comes only to warn, to help, or, as Susan says, to walk around one's bedside—to comfort and sustain.

Often the carnally-minded miss these gentle ministrations, because they are just not equal to meeting the ethereal one on his own ground, and dealing with him after the manner of spirits.

Tennyson raises the question in *In Memoriam:*

> Do we indeed desire the dead
> Should still be near us at our side?
> Is there no baseness we would hide?
> No inner vileness that we dread?
>
> There must be wisdom in great Death.
> The dead shall look me through and through.

---
[3] *Publications,* Number X, p. 61.

Some such hesitation must have been in the mind of Elmira. She said that often her father's spirit used to "come back" to her, but that in spite of her knowing that he was there to help her, yet she shrank from his ghostly presence.

"O, many, many's de time my Papa come back to me. I'd see 'im jes' as plain. Lots o' nights he'd come an' stan' right at de head o' my baid. But hit'ud jes' scare me to death, an' I'd covah up my haid. One night he stood theah, an' looked lak he'uz gonna take me by the han', an' he turn' the covah down. I wanted to talk to 'im, but I jes' couldn'.

"Nex' day I wen' ovah to see Mama—she lived 'bout a mile up de road, an' I say, 'Mama,' I say, 'do Papa evah come back to you at night?'

"Mama she say, 'W'y, yes, Baby,' she say, 'yo' paw's been back lots o' times.'

"I say, 'Well, I wish you'd tell 'im not to come back to me no mo'. Jes' seem lak I cain' stan' it.'

"She say, 'W'y, honey, you know yo' Papa ain' a-gonna hu't you. Maybe he wanna tell you some'n. Why'n't you jes' look at 'im an' say, "What in de name o' de Lawd do you want heah?"'

"I wen' on home, an' that ve'y day, when I'uz out in de road, I look' up, an' theah, stan'in' right befo' me, was Papa. I seen 'im jes' as plain as I evah seen 'im in my life. His face looked jes' as kind, an' he look' lak he jes' sorto shuck 'is haid, an' looked sad. I nevah say nothin', an' I run on home jes' as soon as he lef'.

"An' that ve'y night, Mama say, he come to her, an' fust he kindo' looked at 'er, an' then he stooped down lak he'uz gonna pick up some'n, an' Mama say, 'Youk'n have that.'

"She don' know what he'uz pickin' up. She nevah miss' nothin' nex' day. But f'om dat day to this he ain' nevah been back no mo'. She ain' see 'im an' I ain' neithah."

If, then, the spirit world be so near us, and if ghostly attendants are to be had for the asking, small wonder that the Negro dreams of the day when he will triumphantly cross over "the chilly waters" to be "in that numbah." To me there is pathos, there is tenderness, in the Negroes' songs of sweet release, such as this one:

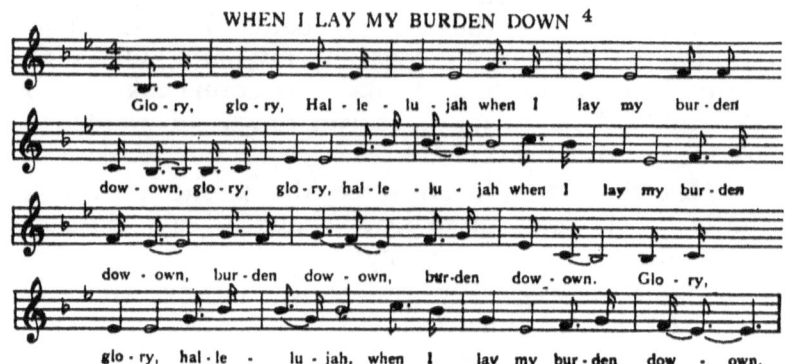

WHEN I LAY MY BURDEN DOWN [4]

O my sistah, O my sistah,
When I lay my burden down,
O my sistah, O my sistah,
When I lay my burden down.

Refrain: Burden down, burden down,
O my sistah, O my sistah,
When I lay my burden down.

O my brothah, O my brothah, *etc.*

O my deacon, O my deacon, *etc.*

Glory, glory, hallelujah, *etc,*

Lawd, I jes' cain' keep from shoutin',
When I lay my burden down.
Lawd, I jes' cain' keep from shoutin',
When I lay my burden down.

---
[4] I first heard this song at Lovers' Leap Baptist Church (colored), Waco. Since then I have had some private coaching by Roberta Walker, a colored employee of the State Home. Roberta assured me, "Ef'n you cain' learn dat song, 'tain' nobody else can."

I'SE SHO' NUFF LUCKY

By AYLETT ROYAL

"Yes'm, Miss Aylett, I'se sho' 'nuff lucky." This from the three hundred-pound black mammy who has been in our family for years. Her thick, shapeless lips parted, showing vacancies and gold work, and she broke out into a broad grin at the attention she had attracted. My questioning came as the result of the vigorous chewing which she had kept up for hours, accompanied by a studied, interested expression, interrupted only when she talked.

"That's John-the-Conqueror-Root," she said earnestly. "Aunt Mandy done sent it to me all the way from New Orleans. I chews it every day to bring me good luck."

After much coaxing and swearing to secrecy, I succeeded in persuading Stella to let me in on the wonderful mysteries of leading a lucky life. I was led apprehensively into the inner recesses of the pantry, and there initiated into the awful miracles so earnestly believed in by my black friend.

The root, taken from the top shelf, proved to be a round, brown mass from which projected tiny threads. This was the part to be chewed. After revealing John-the-Conqueror, Stella cautiously produced an old black purse, bulky in size and bulging everywhere. This was the storehouse for all her charms. She only let me look at it at first, fearing my anxiety was pure curiosity. She never stopped talking, and before I know it I was listening to a remarkably full and free revelation of luck and charms as believed in by a Negro of the old Southern tradition.

Stella practically undressed in an endeavor to show me the various articles worn on her person. A buck-eye around her neck was polished to the nth degree; a pierced dime was tied around her bulky ankle with a pink ribbon, to break the charm of stepping in devil-dust; a needle (she vowed that steel is lucky) was carefully pinned under the collar of her dress; a sack of bluestone and saltpeter (to bring health and happiness) hung from her waist; and the left hind foot of a rabbit was worn on a string and carefully hung around her neck and down her back, resting between her well-covered shoulder-blades. "I jes' *cain't* have no bad luck now," she boasted. "I'se *protected!*"

Then, one by one, Stella produced the treasured objects from her purse, explaining each as she did so. The first was a rusty knife, which she declared she had no use for, but which she had found. "That means I'll git some money, and I wouldn't part with that knife for nuthin'." She was perfectly confident that before the week ran out she would be rich. "That's really true, Miss Aylett."

The second object was a large piece of sandalwood. Her preacher had given that to her, telling her to chew it so that she would go to heaven. "I give a piece to a friend of mine who was goin' to be tried for shootin' a nigger, oncet, and tol' him to chew it durin' the trial and spit it on the prosecutor. He wasn't convicted, neither." Then she enumerated ten of her friends who had had similar experiences with sandalwood. "That's really true, Miss Aylett," she added.

The third object was a highly polished cross-section of a bois d'arc limb. "An ol' man in East Texas done give me this. He say it'll make me happy all day if'n I kiss it every mornin'." With that she raised her eyes to heaven and reverently touched her lips to its surface.

The next article was a Jabric sack from which she poured twenty-five or thirty buttons, each with four holes in it. She had found all of the buttons, she said, and believed that she would get a dollar for each one. "That's really true, Miss Aylett."

The last and weirdest article of all proved to be a long, thin, white, hard, stone-like thing which she swore to be the lower bone of the right leg of a black cat. "How on earth did you get that, Stella?" I asked incredulously. "Well, I fotched me an ol' can," she said, "filled it with the strongest, boilin' lye I could git, set it in the back yard, waited till a ol' black cat that had been a-hangin' roun' my yard appeared, then pushed him in the can and banged on the lid. I walked away from it 'thout lookin' back, and left it there nine days and nights to be shore and kill the nine lives. Then I puts it on the stove, biled it good, and taken out the bone!" This leg bone of a black cat is the luckiest talisman one can possess, I discovered. It will counteract the seven years' bad luck of breaking a mirror. "That's really true, Miss Aylett."

At this point Stella seemed to drift off into a silent orgy of belief, slowly stamping her right foot. I later found that this was one way of calling the good spirits. Suddenly her eyes got wider, and she whispered loudly, "Miss Aylett, is you ever heard of *hoodoo?*"

To my negative answer she replied with a thirty-minute recital of her experiences with it. "I knowed a woman once who was furiated at a girl cause she done tried to steal her husband. She asked the hoodoo doctor what to do and he done told her to kill a horned frog, salt it like salt pork, cook it with cabbage, and feed it to the girl. That's just what she done, Miss Aylett, and the girl went plum crazy, honest she did, and had to go to Louisiana to git a hoodoo doctor to cure her. I sprinkles salt and red pepper on my door sill for to keep off the hoodoo, myself. You better do it too, Miss Aylett.

"My best girl friend done said she come home last week and found a heap of white powdered devil-dust all over her house. She thinks a man what is mad at her got a hoodoo doctor to sprinkle it when she was gone. And you know, the minute that gal stepped on it she got a pain in her laig? But that salt and red pepper done made it go away. That's the truth, Miss Aylett.

"Nother friend, she wanted to git rid of her husband, she did; so she took one of his dirty socks, went in the graveyard at midnight, and buried it standin' up at the foot of the grave. And, you know, that man flew the coop the next day and ain't been heard of since?

" 'Twas nother girl friend, she loved a man what didn't love her; so she wanted to bring him some bad luck. She talked to a hoodoo doctor and found out she had to git his pitture and bury it face down over a corpse's face in a graveyard at sunrise. She cain't look while she's a coverin' it up, and must say over and over what she wants to happen to him. She wished he'd be sent to the jail-house, and sho' 'nuff he stole a diamond ring and is in the pen now for fifteen years!

"I knowed a girl oncet that owned a bootleg joint. She was 'fraid the police would git her; so she went to the voodoo man [*Hoodoo* and *voodoo* seem to be utterly interchangeable.] to find out what to do. He told her to git a flower pot, put a thin dime in the bottom, plant a root that he give her in some red sand on top, and set it by the door. Every mornin' she got to blow on it and the police wouldn't bother her that day. He told her to put a pan of boilin' lye 'neath the front steps so's it would burn the foot of any policeman what would come in. Sho' 'nuff, she done these, and lots a places has been raided all 'round her, and she ain't been bothered yet, after three years!

"Miss Aylett, you know that the wives of hoodoo men is witches, and is they mean! A broom is their favorite weapon; so you'd best be careful how you step over one or they'll sho' kill somebody in your family. The onliest way to break their spell is, if'n you step over one while it's on the floor, take three steps backwards over it, turn around and spit in front of you 'thout ever lookin' backwards or down. With your head still up, make a cross in your spit with your foot, and take three steps forward. Turn round and look, and ifn' the cross is good, the spell is broke!

"Is you ever wanted a man to love you real good, Miss Aylett? I'll tell you how to make him love you so good that he cain't never stop. First you take the ribbon bow from the sweat-band of an old hat of hisn; then you take a little piece of one of your slips that's old and you've perspired on. You puts 'em both in an airtight bottle and burries it nine inches under the ground, where nobody'll step on it. Then, whatever you wants him to do, all you gotta do is wish and he'll do it, cause your sweat and hisn is so mixed that you got a hoodoo spell on him." At my wry face, Stella looked horrified as if I were sacrilegious, and started stamping her right foot again, in order to keep the evil spirits from getting mad.

Soon she came to, and her face, ugly almost to the point of repulsion, relaxed in a proud smile. "Miss Aylett, you know why I'se so popular with the men, and they admires my hair so much? [Her one object in life seems to be popularity with the opposite sex.] Well, it's cause I done charmed 'em like the hoodoo doctor done said! I took some of my hair, I did, snetched some from the heads of some of my boy friends, and put 'em in a hole, hand deep. [This "hand" measurement, I learned, is derived from the fact that one uses his hands to arrange his hair.] They got to be right under a fawcett what drips all the time so's they'll be watered. They growed together, and now folks is always tellin' me how beautiful I is!" Here she seemed to forget her religious devotion and lapsed into a revery of self-admiration and pride.

Fearing this self love would break up the seance, I hastened to change the subject by asking Stella if she believed in ghosts.

"Yau means *hants*, Miss Aylett? Sho', they's really true!" She shivered slightly and came closer to me, registering genuine belief and fear. "I was born wid a veil over my face, and that means that I can see 'em plain as I can see you!"

"Stella," I exclaimed, "do you really mean you've seen some?"

"Yes ma'am, I'se seen plenty! They allus appears first like a dog. Then, when you looks again, they *re*sembles a human bein'. But don't never let one hit you, Miss Aylett, 'cause that means sho' death. Oncet I was a-walkin' down the street when I seen a white dog a-follerin' me. I turned round to hit it and make it go away, and guess what it did! It turned into a man and tried to *hit* me! Did I run? Miss Aylett, you ain't never seen nobody run so fast! I peeked back at it two blocks later, and the devil just plain vanished, right 'fore my eyes! That's the plain truth, Miss Aylett!"

"Did a ghost ever hit anybody?" I asked.

"Sho', they hits people all the time. Did you ever read 'bout those people what died of heart attack? That wa'n't no heart attack; that wa'n't nuthin' but a ghost what hit 'em!"

From this Stella launched into the detailed experiences of her family and neighbors with ghosts. She became so engrossed that she almost forgot I was present. At length, however, she looked at me, terrified, as if just remembered something. "I *dreamed* 'bout one last night, Miss Aylett, and that's the sign of *double bad luck!*" She began rolling her eyes and stroking the buckeye around her neck, mumbling, "I'd forgot 'bout that!"

"Do you dream much, Stella?" I asked, trying to get her mind off her impending fate.

"Every night, Miss Aylett, and every dream got a meanin'."

Thrilled to get her on this fascinating subject, I urged her on, and soon had her dissertating on it with an enthusiasm almost beyond that already expended on lucky charms and man-hitting ghosts.

I'SE SHO' NUFF LUCKY 143

"Dream of your teeth bein' pulled is a sho' sign of death, Miss Aylett. Last week I dreamed that, and the lady next door dropped dead as a door-knob, yes sir! Dream of muddy water, beware of your house a-burnin'. If'n you dream of combin' long hair, that's really a sign of a operation. I know that's a fact, Miss Aylett, cause I seed it happen lots of times!

"Don't never dream of no cats, cause that means you'll be disappointed in somethin' for sho'. But if'n you wants to git some good news, you dream of a baby. The only time I ever gets good news is after I done dreamed 'bout a baby. And does dreamin' bout the moon mean strong affection! Miss Aylett, you don't know what that is till you dream 'bout the moon! That's really the fair truth, Miss Aylett.

"Did you ever dream 'bout gettin' a letter? Maybe you didn't know it, but any bad luck you had after that was caused *di*rectly by that dream. And dreamin' 'bout diamonds shorely means you gonna be deceived. But just dream 'bout a lil' old dog, and sho' as he got a tail, you'll be surrounded by faith. You oughta see how my old man stays home every night for nigh on to a week after I dreams 'bout a dog!

"I dreamed 'bout washin' clothes, oncet, and the preacher done mentioned my name the next Sunday in church for bein' the best nigger in the conflagration that week! Yes sir, dream 'bout washin' *always* means you'll git honor, it sho' do!

"If'n you see somebody kill they selves in your dreams, you'll really lose your health. I had a headache for three days oncet after I dreamed 'bout that; and dreamin' 'bout lightenin' is a sho' sign of a misunderstandin'! I knows that to be a fact, Miss Aylett."

From here on Stella's recital of dream signs and instances of their working was in such a fast-running sequence that I fully believe she had them memorized out of some dream book or collection of her own.

"Dreams of a doctor, that means profit; dream of a dove, you'll git *suc*cess; dream of a angel, you'll have wonderful joy; dream of a burglar, you'll really and truly be safe; dream of aiggs, and you'll be rich, sho' as you're born; dream of a dinner, that means punishment; dream of a nigger, Miss Aylett, and you'll always be happy!"

If she hadn't paused for breath here, I'm sure she would never have stopped, for she seemed to know an indefinite number of results of those baffling things called dreams.

Taking this opportunity to change that subject, I asked, "Stella, aren't you afraid of these spells and ghosts and dreams and things? Don't you ever worry about your future, with all the things that you say could happen?"

"No'm," she said confidently, "I just hopes for the best. Some day I's goin' to git some money and go to *Mon*roe, Lou*isi*ana, to see the Seven Sisters. They'll tell me whether I ought to worry or not. Six of my friends have went there, and they says there ain't nuthin' 'bout your past, present or future that those sisters can't tell you."

"I've never heard of them, Stella," I confessed. "Who are they?"

"They's hoodoo doctors, Miss Aylett, what have made so much money that they's built them a big house just to practice voodoo in. My sister, she say it's a long house with four rooms, one right behind the other. The first one, it's got a mirror floor; the second one, it's full of snakes what hang from the ceilin' and walls and spit at you; the third's got black cats and rabbits and crows. You gotta go through all these, alone, to wash off all your bad luck. Finally you gits to the one with the Seven Sisters, full of herbs and roots and sich. And is those gals awful! People do say that one she got six fingers on each hand; 'nother, she got eyes in her forehead; 'nother, she got one big ear; 'nother, she got only four fingers on each hand; 'nother she ain't got no hair. Only one of 'em looks like anybody else, and she never says much. They really tells you all you wants to know. Yes'm, Miss Aylett, I'se really goin' there some day. That's really true, Miss Aylett."

Suddenly Stella glanced at the pantry clock, gathered up her belongings, and waddled out the back door before I had a chance to ask her why. This priceless old mammy with her peculiarities of habits, beliefs, and expressions, her sincerity and devotion, had aroused in me combined pity and admiration, sympathy and understanding, and had so affected my imagination that I shall never forget her. Her first sentence so utterly exemplifies the spirit of her nature that it keeps revolving in my mind: "Yes'm, Miss Aylett, I's sho' 'nuff lucky!"

I have chosen only the unusual superstitions in which Stella believes. Those recorded are only a small part of her repertoire.

THE HUMAN COMEDY IN FOLK SUPERSTITIONS

By TRESSA TURNER

During several years of teaching prior to 1925, in Southwest Texas State Teachers College at San Marcos, R. C. Harrison canvassed students, representing scores of counties and varying cultures, for folk superstitions. Following his death, in 1927, Mrs. Harrison turned the extensive collection thus made over to the Texas Folk-Lore Society. From it have been taken the majority of superstitions noted in this paper. It has been largely supplemented, however, by two other collections: one that I assembled from my home town, Kildare, Texas, and from Flatonia, Texas, where I taught; the other made by J. Frank Dobie from students in the Agricultural and Mechanical College of Oklahoma, at Stillwater, where he taught during the years 1923-1925, plus a considerable number of superstitions from Texas sources.

In order to prevent duplication, I have checked all this material against articles on superstitions already published by the Texas Folk-Lore Society,[1] though certain overlappings necessarily remain, for many omens are divergently interpreted. Numerous superstitions

---

[1] "Customs and Superstitions among Texas-Mexicans," by Florence Johnson Scott, and "Weather Wisdom of the Texas-Mexican Border," by J. Frank Dobie, both articles in *Publications* No. II of the Texas Folk-Lore Society, 1923; "Superstitions of Bexar County," by E. R. Bogusch, *Publications* No. V (1926); "Ranch Remedios," by Frost Woodhull, *Publications* No. VIII (1930).

are reported over and over from different communities, but those from Oklahoma have no particular characteristic that distinguish them from the ones found in Texas. Superstitions fixed in rhyme vary least in interpretation as well as in phraseology. These frequently, though not always, tend towards the wisdom of proverbs.

Mr. Harrison seems to have asked his students to write after each superstition they set down for him a "Yes" or a "No" to indicate whether or not they believed in the superstition. Some of the students went further and adduced instances in which the superstitions proved themselves valid. Such instances add flavor to the superstitions and help keep them in their right and proper setting, out of which they lose their interpretative value as folk-lore. Literary geniuses have throughout the ages made use of people's belief in and practice of superstitions. Someday perhaps a literary genius will appear in the Southwest—whatever the Southwest may include—to utilize the hopes, the fears, the humor, the tragedy, the humanity inherent in the superstitions of the region. For this genius I leave the superstitions of this paper.

Perhaps I have not composed them as well as Mr. Harrison or Mr. Dobie might have done, but I hold the belief that I have more right to write the paper than either of these gentlemen. It is mine by virtue of a superstitious gesture attending my advent on this earth. Arriving a month ahead of time, I caught my father at work away from home. He rushed thither as quickly as possible, but arrived only in time to see my black mammy, Aunt Mattie Faust, solemnly marching around the house with me—not yet bathed, but closely bundled in an old quilt—in her arms. In spite of having fathered seven children before me, such proceedings were not familiar to him. When he asked Aunt Mattie what she meant, she, scorning his ignorance, replied: "Dis gonna keep de chile from having de measles and wetting de bed, whut works a woman to death." As to the efficacy of Aunt Mattie's gesture, I have no comment. My only point is that, coming as it did, it gives me a peculiar right to deal with superstitions.

I. MARRIAGE, LOVE, AND COURTSHIP

If you sleep with a piece of wedding cake under your pillow, you will dream of the one that you will marry.

Cut a boiled egg in equal parts, remove the yolk from one half, and put salt in its place. Then fit the halves back together and eat the whole egg just before retiring for the night. Whoever brings you water in your dreams will be the one you will marry. A kindred version of this superstition directs you to eat a thimble-full of salt just before going to bed. You will dream that someone brings you water, and that person will be your future husband or wife. If the latter version is carried out by two girls, silent all the while, it is called a "Dumb Supper,"—a very old superstition.

Another form of "Dumb Supper" is for a group of girls to prepare food in unison, eat equal parts of it at the same time, and then all go to the corner of a dark room and stand. No word must be spoken during the supper or period of standing. After a while each of the girls who is to marry will see her husband's image appear on the dark wall in front of her. The girl who does not see an image will never marry.

Put a holly leaf with nine stickers on it under your pillow, and you will then dream of the one you will marry.

Sleep with mistletoe under your pillow and you will dream of your future husband or wife.

Sleep with a mirror under your pillow for three nights, letting the third night fall on Friday. On the third night you will dream of the person that you will marry. Another version has it that one will dream of the same person all three nights.

To dream of a death is a sign of a wedding, of a funeral, an invitation to a wedding.

To dream of a baby is a sign that one will be happily married; but to dream of being married means that one will never get married. Mrs. R. O. Crane of Cuero says that she has known the latter superstition to fail.

If a girl will stick a half of a lemon over one of her bed posts at night, she will dream of her future husband. And if a girl happens to dream of her lover, she will see him the next day.

Write the names of several people in whom you are interested on slips of paper and place them under your pillow. Every time you wake during the night throw one of the slips away. The last one remaining will have on it the name of the person you will marry.

Name two nuts and pitch them into the fire; the nut that pops open first will bear the name of your future husband or wife.

Twist the stem of an apple till it comes out, saying a letter of the alphabet every time you give the stem a twist. The letter that you are saying when the stem comes out will be the first letter of your future husband's name. Also if a pin sticks out perpendicularly to your dress, flip it with the forefinger till it comes loose, saying the letters of the alphabet as you flip the pin. It will come out on the first letter of your future husband's name.

If a girl puts her handkerchief out on the grass the first night of May, the name of her future husband will be found written on it the next morning, provided it "dews" that night. Morris Warwick of San Marcos says that this does not work.

Write each letter of the alphabet on a separate slip of paper, put all of the slips in a pan of water, letters down, and place the pan under your bed. Some of the slips will turn over during the night so that the letters will face upwards, and these can be arranged to spell the name of your future husband or wife.

If you slip a person's hand into a pan of water while he is asleep, he will speak the name of the one he will marry.

Count seven stars before going to bed at night, and then name the four corners of your bedroom after four gentlemen in whom you are interested. The corner that you look into first upon waking will bear the name of the man that you will marry.

If you are sleeping in a room for the first time, it is not necessary to count the seven stars before naming the corners.

Name a fire that you are making. If it burns, the one for whom you named it loves you; if it goes out, he does not love you.

When you go fishing, name your hook after your sweetheart. If a fish swallows it, your sweetheart loves you and will swallow anything you say.

If a girl wants to find out whether she will marry a man, let her get a picture of him and see if she can find a similarity between his features and hers. If she does, she will marry him.

If you can swallow whole the heart of a chicken, you can marry the man or woman of your choice.

A girl may find out the occupation or profession of her future husband by counting the buttons on her dress, saying as she counts them:

    Rich man, poor man, beggar-man, thief,
    Doctor, lawyer, merchant, chief.

If she is saying "poor man" when she comes to the last button, she will marry a poor man, and so on down the list. "Indian chief" sometimes is substituted for "Merchant."

If you take the last piece of bread on the plate and turn it over three times, you will marry a good-looking person; but if you fail to turn it over three times, you will never marry—and in addition will have to kiss the cook. The latter superstition is said to have been made chiefly for the purpose of teaching children "table manners." The cook was supposed to be a darky.

If a boy and a girl see a star fall while they are together, they will marry.

If a girl will hang a horseshoe over her door, she can marry the first unmarried man who walks under it.

Place three bowls of water on a table, one full of water, another full of milk, and the third one empty. Blindfold a girl and have her reach for the bowls. If

COMEDY IN FOLK SUPERSTITIONS   151

she touches the one with water in it, she will be an old maid. If she touches the one with milk in it, she will marry. But if she touches the empty one, she will die soon. Imagine how a trusting girl must have felt upon touching an empty bowl!

On Hallowe'en night a girl should take a comb and a mirror and go to a vacant house to comb her hair. If she will look at her mirror as she combs her hair, she will see the image of her future husband looking over her shoulder into the mirror. This superstition is a good one, as good as the one Keats used in "The Eve of Saint Agnes."[2] Keats, where art thou?

On New Year's Eve go from one room to another and throw a shoe over your shoulder; then look in a mirror, and you'll see the one that you are going to marry.

Count fifty white horses, and the first unmarried man that you shake hands with after counting the fiftieth will be the man you will marry.

To find out how long it will be till you marry, tie a wedding ring to a strand of your own hair and then suspend it over a glass of water. The ring will start swinging, and the number of times that it hits the glass will be the number of years to pass before you marry.

When a quilt is finished at a quilting bee, all hands gather around for the shaking of the cat, which must be black. The cat is tossed upon the quilt and is generously shaken till he jumps off. If he runs off close to an unmarried woman—and of course, he will, being shaken in her direction—she will be the next one of the group to marry. This superstition is practiced at Kildare yet.

By looking at high noon on the first day of May into a well—an old-time dug well—that has no shed over it, a girl can find out whom she will marry, or whether she will marry. If she is to marry, her future husband's image will appear quite distinctly on the surface of the

---

[2] It was believed that on the Eve of Saint Agnes a maiden might see in her dreams the form of her future husband if she went to bed supperless, lay on her back, hands clasped behind her head, looked neither sideways nor behind her, but upward, and thought of the wonders that would come in her dreams.

water. But if she is not to marry, a coffin will appear. I know several women who saw strangers in wells. Later they met and married men whom they recognized by images they had seen in wells. The same knowledge can be obtained by looking into an open well at midnight on Hallowe'en or on May the first.

To find out if your sweetheart loves you, strike a match and let it burn as long as it will. If it burns up without breaking into two pieces, your sweetheart loves you.

To find out if a certain boy or girl is in love with you, pluck a string of love vine, or dodder—that orange tangle of leafless parasitic threads clinging around weeds and low shrubs—swing it around the head three times, at the same time thinking of the boy or girl about whom you are in anxiety, and cast it behind you. Three days later, go to the spot to which the vine was cast. If it is growing, then the person for whom it was named loves you; if not, then not. "I don't believe in the sign," says the contributor, "but when I lived in 'Boyville,' I tried it more than once, always the same name, always hoping that the vine would grow, and when it did grow, as it always did, wondering if it told true."

One has as many sweethearts as he has white spots on his finger nails.

A girl will marry soon if she stumbles near the top of a stairway, but if she stumbles near the bottom, many a day will pass before she marries.

Cut a strand of hair from a girl's head and another from a boy's. Place both strands over a door. If both the boy and girl walk under the hairs, they will marry each other.

One may find out the color of one's future husband or wife's hair by turning around three times, taking nine steps backward, and picking up the first object seen. The color of the object indicates the color of the hair of the husband or wife-to-be.

Upon hearing the first coo of a dove in the spring, take off your left stocking and look in the heel of it.

There you will find a hair the color of that of your future wife or husband.

If the sun shines while it is raining, turn over a rock and look carefully under it for a hair. If you find one, it will be the color of that of your future wife or husband.

Don't sweep under the feet of a girl; if you do, she cannot get married.

If a maiden completes a patchwork quilt alone, she will never marry.

If a girl peels all the bark off an elm or blackgum toothbrush, she will lose her beau. (A hackberry twig makes a good toothbrush, too.)

When your shoestring comes untied, your sweetheart is standing on his head to see you.

When a pin comes out perpendicularly to your dress, your beau is out driving with another girl.

If you stump your toe, kiss your thumb and you'll see your beau.

If it is raining when a couple marry, they will have a dreary life.

If a girl, when washing dishes or clothes, gets her dress wet over her stomach, she will marry a drunkard. If she sings at the table, she will marry a crazy man. If she has a little coffee in her cup and pours more into it, she will marry a widower.

If the left thumb is on top when a man clasps his hands together, he will rule the house; if the right is on top, his wife will rule. If a girl's second toe is longer than her big toe, she will rule the house.

Then after one has found someone to marry, he must listen to admonition and warnings in regard to the wedding itself. A bride should wear something old as well as something new, something borrowed, and something blue. It is unlucky to try on the wedding ring before it is put on the bride's finger at the altar. It is bad luck for a bride to look at herself in the mirror before she is dressed or to glance behind herself while on the way to church. It is lucky to marry at full noon or with the flowing tide, or to see a flight of birds while on the way to the church.

> Monday for health, Tuesday for wealth,
> Wednesday the best day of all;
> Thursday for losses, Friday for crosses,
> Saturday for no luck at all.

The next rhyme for the different months of the year tells that:

> Married when the year is new,
> He'll be loving, kind, and true.
>
> When February birds do mate,
> You wed, nor dread your fate.
>
> If you wed when March winds blow,
> Joy and sorrow both you'll know.
>
> Marry in April when you can,
> Joy for maiden and for man.
>
> Marry in the month of May,
> And you'll surely rue the day.
>
> Marry when June roses grow,
> Over land and sea you'll go.
>
> Those who in July do wed,
> Must labor for their bread.
>
> Whoever wed in August be,
> Many a change is sure to see.
>
> Marry in September's shine,
> Your living will be rich and fine.
>
> If in October you do marry,
> Love will come, but riches tarry.
>
> If you wed in bleak November,
> Only joys will come, remember.
>
> When December's snows fall fast,
> Marry, and true love will last.

COMEDY IN FOLK SUPERSTITIONS

Upon the color in which one marries, it is predicted that:

Married in gray, you'll go far away.
Married in black, you'll wish yourself back.
Married in brown, you'll live out of town.
Married in red, you'll wish yourself dead.
Married in pearl, you'll live in a whirl.
Married in green, ashamed to be seen.
Married in yellow, ashamed of your fellow.
Married in blue, he'll always be true.
Married in pink, your spirits will sink.
Married in white, you have chosen aright.

II. GOOD LUCK SIGNS

It is good luck to carry a buckeye in your pocket; to wear a dime in the bottom of your shoe; to dream of a basket of eggs or of climbing stairs; to find a spider in your room, provided you do not kill it; to spit on a horseshoe and then take ten steps backwards; to touch the hump on a hunchback; to wear around the neck a string with a piece of clover tied to it; for a chaparral cock to run across the road in front of one; and for daddy-long-legs to walk over one.

One will have good luck all day if he puts his left foot to the floor first as he gets out of bed in the morning.

If a buzzard's shadow goes directly over one's head, he will have good luck the next day.

See a pin and pick it up,
All the day you'll have good luck;
See a pin and leave it lie,
To good luck you'll say "Goodbye."

III. BAD LUCK SIGNS

It is bad luck to go into the house with a rake, a hoe, or an axe on the shoulder; to walk over a grave; to trim the fingernails on Friday; to kill a bat, an owl, a blue bird, or a cricket; to dream of fruit out of season; to sweep the floor after dark (If you sweep the floor after dark the witches will ride you.); to sit on a trunk; to walk with one shoe on and one off; to put the right shoe on first; to turn over a chair; to rock an empty chair; to carry a broom while walking; to give away parsley; to walk under a ladder; to walk over an ant bed (If you walk over an ant bed and do not step back over it, the ants will build nests in your grave.); to wear one's wedding dress after the wedding; to kick the left foot against something and pass on without going back over the object.

It is bad luck to raise an umbrella in the house. On this superstition a clerk in a dry goods store said, "I have seen many customers refuse to let the clerk open an umbrella that the customer was inspecting."

If a ball team, while on its way to play a game, passes dogs fighting, it will lose the game.

If you go somewhere on one road and return by another, you will have bad luck before you get home.

Never turn back when you have started somewhere, unless you make a cross in the road and spit on the cross.

If a black cat crosses your trail, turn back or go around him, or you will have bad luck. In Dallas two boys walked half the night trying to go around black cats which appeared at every turn they made. Finally they turned back and started home. Just as they reached home, the superstitious one of the two found a $10.00 bill!

It is bad luck for a family to move a black cat. In fact, it is bad luck to move a cat of any color. If a cat comes to a house and then leaves of its own accord, it is a sign of bad luck. But if a cat comes and stays, it is a sign of good luck. If a cat that comes and stays is black, it will bring prosperity. For every cat that one kills the killer will have seven years of bad luck.

For a rabbit to cross one's trail going to the left is bad luck; to the right, good luck. Too, if a rabbit crosses one's trail, calamity will come to the errand that he is on. By spitting and saying, "Damn that rabbit," one can ward off bad luck.

COMEDY IN FOLK SUPERSTITIONS

If a person doesn't knock on dead wood when he brags on himself, he will have bad luck. (Knocking on one's head won't suffice.)

If one spills salt and doesn't burn some of it, he will have bad luck. It is bad luck to borrow salt—and bad luck to thank anyone who lends one salt.

It is bad luck to pick up scissors that you yourself have dropped. If, however, someone else picks them up, it is good luck.

Kiss your thumb to ward off bad luck when you stump your toe.

If a pupil drops his school books, he will have bad lessons the next day, unless he stamps his feet on the books.

Sleeping in the light of the moon will cause a person to go crazy—as the etymology of the word *lunatic* proves.

A person will have bad luck if he looks at the new moon through trees or brush. If he looks at a new moon through a glass window, he will have bad luck all that moon.

If a person is sitting when he hears the first coo of a dove in a season, he will have bad luck, but if he is standing, he will have good luck.

If two persons walking on opposite sides of a post or some other such object will say simultaneously, "Yellow," they can ward off bad luck or a quarrel. Or, one may say, "Bread and butter," and the other, "Come to supper."

If a person is hit with a broom, he will have bad luck if he does not spit on the broom.

If a card player is having a run of bad luck, let him change his method of picking up the cards. For instance, if he has been picking up the cards as they are dealt, let him wait till the last one has been dealt before he touches his cards. So, too, if a man's betting is lucky, let him increase it by half. A person standing behind a player may "joner" (Jonah) him. It is bad luck at any time to carry a two-dollar bill, but poker players consider such a bill especially unlucky and will hardly receive one in a game.

To hear a screech owl's cry near a house is a sign of bad luck, perhaps loss of money, sickness, or death in the family. Bad luck can be avoided by turning over three times an old shoe or by a complete turning of all pockets present. I have been present at a good many turnings of the pockets.

If one's right eye itches, he is going to cry; the left, be pleased. The one whose right eye itches may "pass the buck" by saying to the person next to him, "My right eye itches." My schoolmates and I used to pass this sentence around till the teacher would ask what we were saying—which was exactly what we wanted her to ask us. Then we would tell her, thus passing the buck to her.

It is bad luck for a person to pull off his hat and toss it on a bed. My imagination can create many scenes wherein this superstition might have had birth. Suppose, for instance, that the members of a large family were in the habit of tossing their hats on the beds. Might the housewife not shrewdly invent a superstition to prevent the development of such an untidy habit, all other methods of prevention having failed her?

Never start anything on Friday that cannot be finished on Friday—or on Saturday, according to an Oklahoma version of the superstition.

A person will go blind if a devil's-horse spits in his eye. Mexicans claim that if a cow swallows a devil's-horse, which she may easily do while grazing, she will die. Like many another harmless creature, the devil's-horse is supposed to be poisonous.

Burn up the hair that comes out when you comb your hair, or birds will build nests with it, which will cause you to go blind.

It is bad luck to step over a person who is lying down. If one steps over an adolescent who is lying down and does not step back over him in exactly the same way, the adolescent person will stop growing. If a child sits in or climbs out of a window, he will stop growing.

COMEDY IN FOLK SUPERSTITIONS 159

If children are allowed to play in the fire, they will develop the habit of wetting the bed.

If one dreams of a snake, it means that he will have an enemy; of muddy water, that he will have trouble. Dreams told before breakfast come true.

It is bad luck to sing at the table. A more detailed version of this superstition has it that one will lose all of his teeth if he sings at the table.

It is bad luck for a dog to howl near the house of a sick person. Once a neighbor of ours was sick with a fever. His bird dog came and howled under his window about twelve o'clock one night. The women who were sitting up with him went home and sent their husbands back so that they would be there to help lay the man out. The next morning the man was dead. The women's faith had been rewarded.

If you kill a frog, your cow will either go dry or give bloody milk. I know of one instance of a frog's reproving a man's conscience for a debt he owed the local grocery-man—mostly for chewing tobacco. This man's farm lay along Frazier Creek. Such heavy rains came in the spring that the creek went on a rampage, overflowed, and washed the farmer's crop away. Late one afternoon he rode his horse down to the fields along the creek. As he sat on his horse looking at where his crop had been, a big bull frog over in the creek kept booming out, "You owe me; you owe me." Finally the man said to the frog, "What do I owe you for?" Thereupon about a thousand little rain frogs answered back in a rattling chorus, "Terbaccer, terbaccer, terbaccer, terbaccer."

To see one buzzard is a sign of sorrow. Sorrow can be avoided by watching the buzzard until he goes out of sight or flaps his wings, which a buzzard only occasionally does. I have seen many people exercising these precautions against sorrow. The turkey buzzard at Kildare forewarns of so many things that his powers defy a strict classification, but the following rhyme fairly well covers them:

One for sorrow, two for joy,
Three for a letter, four for a boy,
Five for silver, six for gold,
Seven for a secret that's never been told.

It is pretty commonly known that for a girl to whistle or a hen to crow is a sign of bad luck, and from the belief have come these rhymes:

A whistling girl and a crowing hen
Would drive the devil out of his den.

and

A whistling gal and a crowing hen
Always come to some bad end.

One of my earliest remembrances is of my grandmother's rhymed warning against the whistling girl. It bothered me until Uncle Jim Huggins told me that:

A whistling gal and a flock of sheep
Are two good things for a farmer to keep.

Thereafter I whistled peacefully, but the poor hen is still under the curse of bringing bad luck when she "outs" with her crowing.

IV. SUPERSTITIONS ON DEATH

If one dreams of muddy water, a nude person, or of being married, someone in his family is going to die soon. If one dreams of losing a front tooth, he will lose a relative in death soon; of a back tooth, a friend.

If one bathes between Christmas and New Year, someone in his family will die soon. This certainly belongs to the days before running hot water and warm bath rooms.

If a man trims his finger nails on Friday, his wife will die before the next Friday.

If a rooster flaps his wings after dark or after he has gone to roost, someone in his owner's family will die soon. A crowing hen is thought by some to presage death.

If three people look in a mirror at the same time, the youngest of the three will die at once.

COMEDY IN FOLK SUPERSTITIONS   161

If two people comb a third person's hair, the older of the two will die soon.

Sweep under a sick person's bed, and he will never get up.

A shooting star is a sign of death.

If a person has a mole on his ear, it is a sign that he will drown.

If you pass a funeral procession, someone in your family will die soon. If you count the cars or wagons in a funeral procession, you will die soon. A rain upon a newly made grave means that someone in the deceased one's family will die soon. Someone in the neighborhood will die soon if a grave is allowed to stand open. If a corpse is brought into a house feet first, someone living in the house will die before the year has passed.

Any kind of owl or bat in the house foretells death. At Kildare the horned owl, usually called the hoot owl, is particularly dreaded because of a belief that if he comes to sit on the foot of a bed and cry, the person to whom the bed belongs will die soon. Though the belief is widely held, my mother tells the only story that I know wherein an owl actually sat on a bed and prophesied death. This is her story: A Mr. Johnson was killed by a log train. At the very hour of his death, as it was later ascertained, an owl flew into the Johnson house, which was unscreened, and lit on Johnson's bed. It began its mournful sounds and refused to be removed. Yet when the report of the accident came, the owl left immediately. It would be hard to convince that family that the owl's visit was merely a coincidence.

Niles Graham, of Austin, woke up one night last summer to find an owl perched on the foot of his bed. No member of his family has died since, but one of his dogs had rabies and had to be shot.

Measure a baby's length, and you measure its coffin.

If a baby is allowed to look in a mirror before it is a year old, it will die before it is three.

If an old clock stops before it is run down or starts before it is wound up, someone will die soon. Glen Van

Noy of the Agricultural and Mechanical College, Stillwater, Oklahoma, tells of two occasions when clocks stopped simultaneously with the death of people. One time he was sitting up with a person who was very ill. Just before the person died, Mr. Van Noy chanced to glance at a clock in the room, and it was running. Presently he looked at it again, and it had stopped, apparently at the exact moment that the sick person had died. Another time he was sitting up with his wife in a hospital in Miami, Florida, when a woman next door died. The nurse waiting on the woman told him that her watch stopped at the moment the patient died. "Grandfather's Clock," a song popular during the latter part of the nineteenth century, depended upon this motif. In January, 1935, the grandmother of a girl in Flatonia High School died, and the clock in her room stopped at the moment of her death. When I was told about this occasion, another girl present said that when her great-grandfather died, the clock in his room struck one hundred forty-seven times without pausing. This strikes me as the prize-winner.

A mirror that falls from the wall presages death. To break a mirror warns of a death. Death may be warded off by burying a piece of the broken mirror.

There will be a death in your family soon if someone sweeps toward you as you are entering the house.

A person who plants a cedar or a willow tree will die when the tree grows to such size that its shade is large enough to cover his grave. This superstition is said to have come from the mountains of East Tennessee. It has probably excused lots of men from the work of planting shade trees.

If a person casts an evil eye upon an animal, the animal will die.

A horse or dog will die if his picture is taken.

V. LETTERS, NEWS, AND COMPANY

To see a red bird or to dream of a dead person is a sign that one will see someone unexpectedly. Also a buzzard's shadow going over foretells seeing someone unexpectedly.

If you pass a Japanese, kiss the back of your hand and you will soon see someone that you have long wanted to see.

If a rooster crows at the dead of night, ghosts are going to appear.

If a person takes two pieces of bread at one time, it is a sign that someone is coming hungry.

To drop a knife is a sign that a man is coming; a fork, a woman. The direction in which the knife or fork points is the direction from which the company will come.

If a straw falls from a broom that is being used, someone is coming.

A rooster's crowing means that company is coming—and from the direction that his tail points. If a rooster crows right in the door, it means hasty news. Sometimes, however, his crowing may have an entirely different meaning. Once an aunt of mine was spending the day with a neighbor. A rooster crowed so persistently that my aunt remarked that someone was coming, to which the other woman replied that it was a sign she was needed at home. As my aunt had not heard that version of the rooster's crowing, it riled her, and she went home in a huff.

If a housewife leaves a kettle uncovered, someone is coming.

If you drop a dishrag, someone nastier than you is coming.

One will hear hasty news if a "news bee" buzzes around him; important news, if a glow is apparent after a candle has been snuffed.

If you find a pin, pick it up and you will get a letter. If a bird flies into the house, someone in the house will get a letter from across the ocean.

The number of grounds that float on one's coffee cup denotes the number of letters that he will receive the next day. Also the number of gray horses that one sees one day indicates the number of letters to be received the next day.

When the bottom of a person's left foot itches, he is going where he is not wanted; the right, he is going to walk on strange land.

When the hem of your dress turns up, spit on it and you will get a new dress. When a measuring worm crawls over a garment that you are wearing, he is measuring a new one for you.

When a butterfly lights on a girl's dress, she will get a new one the color of the butterfly. The following superstition makes a girl earn the dress prophesied: If she will bite off the head of a butterfly that lights on her dress and then throw the head over her right shoulder, she will get a new dress the color of the butterfly. To see a butterfly means that before the day is over one will see a friend wearing a dress the color of the butterfly.

If you spit on yourself—your hands, for instance—you will get a pair of new gloves soon.

You have a disappointment in store for you if you see one Catholic sister or nun; an agreeable surprise if you see two.

If two people bump heads, they are going to sleep together the following night.

If two people hoeing near each other strike their hoes together, it is a sign that they will have something good to eat for dinner and also that they will hoe together the next year.

VI. WISHES

Make a wish and then open the Bible in three different places. If you find "And it came to pass," your wish will come true.

If two people say things simultaneously, they should link their little fingers and make a wish. The one who finishes first should say, "Longfellow"; the other, "Shortfellow." Together they must say, "Hope this wish may never be broke." Or, they may finish by saying each other's names.

If one makes a wish on seeing a falling star before it goes out of sight, his wish will come true.

Spit on a bridge, then go away, and the wish will come true.

If one makes a wish while trying on another person's shoe, his wish will come true.

Place a person's ring on his finger, making a wish as you do so. Tell the person when he may pull off the ring, and if he does not remove the ring before the appointed time, your wish will come true.

Swallow whole a brown bean found among a bowl of white ones, making a wish as you do so. The wish will come true.

Kiss the hem of your dress when it turns up, making a wish as you do so.

At the sight of a white mule, a white horse—particularly two white horses—or a hay wagon—"send" a wish; but you must "stamp" it if you expect it to get to its destination and bring a return. To "stamp" it, place the tip of the right forefinger, or the ball of the thumb, to the end of the tongue as if licking a stamp, then press the finger-tip, or thumb, down on the palm of the left hand, as if adjusting a stamp to an envelope, giving the "stamp" a smart pat or slap so that it will stick. According to one version of the belief, the wish will come true only after one hundred horses have been seen and counted, the stamping act to be enacted for each horse. A white mule counts for twenty. Children, with whom this form of wishing is popular, usually lose count long before they reach the hundredth white horse.

If you drop a pair of scissors and they stick up in the floor, make a wish on them before picking them up.

VII. MONEY

If one says "Money" three times before a shooting star goes out of sight, he will get some money.

If one does not put his tongue in the place from which a tooth is pulled, he will get some money, maybe a gold tooth.

A person who has money in his hand when he sees a new moon will make money the whole month. If one will shake his purse at a new moon and say, "Fill my purse full of money," he will get lots of money.

A person whose eyebrows grow together across his forehead will be rich some day; also the growth is a sign of jealousy.

If one can catch a hummingbird—or put salt on any bird's tail—he will be rich some day.

If a man has a dime in his shoe when he marries, he will always have money enough.

If one dreams of a diamond, he will be rich some day.

If one's left hand itches in the palm, he is going to handle money; if the right palm itches, he should scratch it on wood, making at the same time a wish; he will get some money and his wish both.

Count the "miller" bugs on water. For every bug counted, you will get a dollar.

When you see a lizard, say to him, "Lizard, lizard, show your money." If he shows his money, you will get some money. A lizard shows his money by opening wide his mouth or flaring his jaws so that something red may be seen. The chameleon shows his money best. The sand-sifter will drop his tail if sufficiently excited, but he will not show his money.

In order to have money the year round, bake a poppy-seed cake at Christmas and have some of it left for New Year.

People who burn onion peels will have money.

VIII. REMEDIES AND CURES

Rub a wart vigorously with a gold band ring and say, "Hocus, pocus, presto, warts, go away." Soon the wart will disappear.

Rub spittle on a wart seven times a day for seven days to make it go away, or spit in one hand and rub the wart with the spittle for five minutes, saying as you rub, "Wart, wart, go away." The wart will disappear within five days.

Rub a wart with a bean and throw the bean in a well. When the bean decays, the wart will go away. Or steal a piece of bacon from a neighbor, rub the wart with it, and then bury the bacon. When it decays the wart will go away. A woman in Flatonia has a very learned brother-in-law who removed a wart in this way. If a remedy works for the learned, surely it must be effective for the less learned.

Rub a wart with the jawbone of a horse or mule; hide the bone from the one who has the wart; if he can not find it, his wart will go away.

A raw Irish potato carried in a pocket or a nutmeg tied to a string and worn around the neck will prevent rheumatism.

A tea made from bear grass roots will cure rheumatism.

A sure cure for rheumatism is extract of poison oak. Boil the leaves and stems of poison oak till the juice is well extracted. Then take two drops of the juice in four ounces of water before each meal.

Equal parts of turpentine, sweet-gum, and beef tallow melted and mixed make a good compound for rheumatism. Rub the mixture on the rheumatic parts.

Boil snake root till all the juice is out. Mix the juice with water and whiskey and take every two hours for rheumatism, jaundice, and chills.

Tea made from the white lime of chicken droppings or from sheep balls is a cure for a baby's colic.

A sure cure for four-month colic is asafoetida in whiskey.

To stop the colic in a baby, pull a hair from the mother's head and place it on the baby's head.

To prevent the nose from bleeding, drop a pair of scissors down the back steps, tie a piece of woolen string around the big toe, or wear a coin hung from a string around the neck.

Grease the bottom of a baby's feet with pure hog lard to cure a cold.

For a sore throat tie your old dirty sock around your neck at night.

A stye may be cured by rubbing it with a gold ring. Too, a person having a stye may get rid of it by going to the forks of a road and saying, "Stye, stye, leave my eye; catch the next one that passes by," or by saying to the first person who mentions the stye, "You're a lie."

Either butter and lime, or bear grass roots beaten to a pulp make a good poultice for boils, though nothing will draw a boil to a head so well as raw fat meat.

To cure hives in a baby, find a man who has never seen the child's father and have him blow his breath into the baby's mouth. Likewise have a seventh child to blow his breath into the baby's mouth. Catnip tea is good to break out the hives with.

A string of beads made of elderberries is good for a baby to teeth on. A string of beads made of different spices will cause a baby to teeth rapidly and painlessly.

Tickling a baby's feet will cause him to stammer.

An aged person can blow the fire out of sun-blisters.

Press your thumb hard against the roof of your mouth to stop a headache.

A sure cure for chills is to go to a dogwood tree before sunrise and stand beside it till the sun rises.

A successful cure for the itch is prickly ash salve. To make the salve, "Take prickly ash bark, scrape off the outside surface. Take about as much as you can hold between thumb and trigger finger, pieces to be about eight inches long. Put one cup of lard in a skillet, add the bark, and fry till brown. Now remove the bark and add one pound of sulphur. Stir till cold, then put in a close top can." This recipe was given to me by one whom I know to be proficient in the art of making prickly ash salve. Experience with this compound forces me to observe that the "close top" can is a measure of self-defense against the odors of prickly ash salve.

Tea made from the linings of a chicken gizzard settles the stomach; so does water in which writing paper has been soaked.

COMEDY IN FOLK SUPERSTITIONS 169

Mullein leaves boiled for several hours in a small quantity of water will leave a syrup that is a fine cough medicine.

Cut a green walnut and rub the fresh juicy part of the bark on a ring worm to kill it. Making a cross of soot on a kernel will cause it to disappear.

To cure a "bone-felon," run the affected finger around the neck of a bottle.

Asafoetida worn on a string around the neck will cure almost any kind of disease. In 1869 Uncle Jim Huggins was coming with his father and their families from Butler County, Alabama, to Caddo Parish, Louisiana. When they reached Rodney, Mississippi, they heard that the town was quarantined against smallpox. As Rodney was the most convenient place for them to cross the Mississippi River, they were anxious not to have to hunt another crossing. So Uncle Jim's father went on foot ahead of the wagons to see if he could arrange a rapid passage through Rodney. He consulted the town physician, who told him that if he would tie a bag of asafoetida around the neck of each person in the party, it would keep them from taking smallpox. This he did, and the whole wagon train passed safely through the smallpox-infested town.

A spider in a nutshell worn around the neck will ward off fever. In 1869 Uncle Jim Huggins and his folk arrived in Shreveport, Louisiana, where at that time there was an epidemic of yellow fever. Uncle Jim says that he saw men go out to the Red River docks and hang up eight or ten beef quarters to draw the yellow fever out of the town. He says that it worked, too, that the meat just turned yellow and fell from the bones.

Hot poultices of "dinner" tea leaves applied, one after the other, will cause the swelling to go out of a rattlesnake's bite.

The hoof-like substance from the inside of a horse's foreleg shaved finely and put in the hollow of a tooth will cure or prevent toothache.

To cure asthma go to a tree and measure your height on it, driving a nail into the tree to mark your height.

When the bark grows over the nail, the asthma will go away.

Bluing water is mighty good for horses or dogs that have distemper.

K. Willard Brown, a Negro who lives at Kildare, recommends the following remedy as a cure for fits in a dog: "Resolve a fair size lump of blue-stone in water. Den give it to him often and lots."

Give a foundered cow a lump of alum the size of a walnut and three raw eggs three times a day.

If a watchdog has ceased to do his duty, give him a piece of garlic on Christmas Eve and force him to eat it. He will then resume his duties.

IX. WEATHER SIGNS

"When I want to believe that the weather is going to be good or bad, I make my own sign," says an Oklahoman. His remark probably explains the origin of many weather signs.

It will rain somewhere within sight every day in June if it rains June 1. The number of stars within a circle around the moon indicates the number of days that will pass before it rains.

It is going to rain soon when snakes fall from trees; when doodlebugs and angleworms come to the surface of the ground and crawl around; when ants fill their holes; when crickets congregate; and when the sun sets red for four consecutive days. If there is a red circle around the sun when it sets, it will rain three days later.

A snake hung up with his belly to the sun will bring rain. An old Cherokee Indian was by the Illinois River in the fall of 1923. He saw a stick come floating down the river with a snake on it; he went back the next day and saw another stick, much larger, with another snake on it. He predicted two floods, the second larger than the first. The floods came, all right.

When the wind blows from the east, rain will come; from the west, fair weather will come.

If a fog goes up, rain will come down; but if the fog falls, the weather will be clear. Heavy fogs for several mornings predict big rains forty days later.

> Rain before seven,
> Fair before eleven.

> Evening red and morning gray
> Will set the traveler on his way,
> But evening gray and morning red
> Will bring down rain upon his head.

To ride a horse with feathers in its mane is a sign of rain.

If the sun shines while it is raining, it is a sign that the devil is beating his wife around the stump, or that it will rain at the same time the next day.

If it thunders while it is raining, it is a sign that the Lord is scrubbing the floors of heaven. The thunder is the sound that his water barrels make as he rolls them over the floor of heaven.

If the sun sets clear, the next day will be fair.

A rainbow in the west means that a month of dry weather will follow.

"Dust devils" (whirlwinds) are an infallible sound of dry weather.

If it thunders shortly before or after Easter, there will be a dry summer.

A buzzard sailing high in the sky is a sign of dry weather. I have heard it said, too, that a buzzard's sailing high in the sky means that he was getting above rain clouds.

If birds hover in one place, or an old sow carries sticks and straw with which to build a bed, a cold snap is coming.

If it thunders in December before Christmas, there will be a bad, cold spell of weather at the end of January or the first of February. If it thunders in February, it will frost in May and the following winter will be severe.

Wasps fly into the house when a cold spell approaches. So do flies, for that matter.

If a turtle bites a person, it will not turn loose till it hears thunder.

Stick a double-bitted axe up in the ground to split a norther.

Put feathers on the ground and stamp them to stop a rain.

Butcher hogs in the dark of the moon, and the meat will be firm and the lard will render abundantly; otherwise, the meat will be flabby and the lard skimpy.

Soap made in the light of the moon will be firm; in the dark of the moon, soft. The best time to make soap is between the last quarter and the full moon.

If you plant potatoes in the light of the moon, the new potatoes will grow large and be near the surface; but if you plant them in the dark of the moon, the potatoes will be small and grow deep in the soil. To prevent potatoes from rotting, borrow a potato from a neighbor and put it with your potatoes.

Melons and corn should be planted in the dark of the moon. The moon even affects the breeding of cattle, for a cow bred in the dark of the moon will have a male calf.

Cucumbers planted "on the twins" (during the zodiacal sign of Gemini) will bear a good crop. When cherries bloom, plant cucumbers.

Plant turnips on the twenty-fifth day of September.

The major part of a garden should be planted on Good Friday to insure a good yield.

Plant beans, peas, melons, all crops that yield fruit above the ground, before ten o'clock in the morning to keep the blooms from shedding before the fruit has formed.

X. MISCELLANEOUS SUPERSTITIONS

Cold hands, warm heart; warm hands, cold heart.
Cold hands, warm heart; cold feet, no sweetheart.
A dimple on the chin, the devil within.

For every gray hair pulled out of one's head, two more will appear.

How to find lost articles: Throw a horseshoe over the right shoulder, and you will find the lost article in the direction to which the prongs of the shoe point; or, spit in the palm of one hand and slap the forefinger of the other in the spit. Look for the lost article in the direction that the spit flies.

If a dog steps on a tooth that has been pulled, the child from whom it was pulled will grow a dog tooth.

If a person trims his finger nails on Sunday, he will do a wicked deed every day of the week.

A baby will grow up to be a thief if his finger nails are trimmed before he is a year old.

The following rhyme explains other complications that arise from the trimming of the finger nails:

Cut your nails on Monday, cut them for news;
Cut them on Tuesday, a pair of new shoes;
Cut them on Wednesday, cut them for wealth;
Cut them on Thursday to bring you good health;
Cut them on Friday, cut them for woe;
Cut them on Saturday, a journey to go.

Sneezing likewise has a variety of meanings that are determined by the day upon which one sneezes.

Sneeze on Monday, sneeze for danger;
Sneeze on Tuesday, kiss a stranger;
Sneeze on Wednesday, sneeze for a letter;
Sneeze on Thursday, something better;
Sneeze on Friday, sneeze for sorrow;
Sneeze on Saturday, your sweetheart tomorrow.
Sneeze on Sunday, your safety seek,
For the devil will chase you the rest of the week.

If one burns food while he is cooking, he is feeding the devil.

If a woman burns bread, it means that her husband will come home angry.

A simmering kettle foretells a fuss in the family.

If one pricks her fingers with the needle when sewing, she will get a kiss for every prick.

If one wishes to find the direction in which to look for water, let him find a doodlebug's hole, bend over it, and say, "Doodlebug, doodlebug, come get your bread and coffee." If the bug comes out and knocks up dirt, the person may look for water in the direction that the dirt falls—which will be down.

A light left burning at night will keep danger away.

A person who can swallow whole the floater of a fish will learn to swim easily.

All left-handed people owe the devil a day's work.

Every time a star falls, someone is indulging in sin.

Go to a graveyard and jump over three graves, saying, "What are you doing in there?" The answer will be—nothing at all.

The following belief, said to be of Negro origin, tells how to become a witch: Take a live black cat in a sack and put him in a pot of boiling water. Leave him there until the flesh has all come off the bones. Then with a mirror before you, put the bones in your mouth, one at a time, till it becomes impossible to see yourself in the mirror. The bone that finally makes it impossible for you to see the mirror will be your witch bone. You can take it in your mouth and go anywhere without being seen.

A fisherman will have good luck if a frog jumps into the water and then swims directly to the bank.

A sailor does not want to serve on a ship the name of which ends in the letter *a*.

An ill person reported dead will live a long time.

A person has told as many lies as he has ulcers on his tongue.

A fever blister says, "I've kissed someone that I had no business kissing."

It takes a lazy man to be a singing school teacher.

It takes industrious people to build quick fires and raise pepper. In order to make peppers hot, plant them while you are "mad."

COMEDY IN FOLK SUPERSTITIONS

Red pepper fed to hens will make them lay many eggs.

To keep weevils out of seed, keep the seed in closed cans with wood ashes.

A good way to get rid of chicken mites is to put freshly peeled pine poles in the chicken house for roosts. The mites will crawl off the chickens and onto the poles to eat the sap or resin, which will harden and hold them hard and fast. This is how we get rid of mites on the Turner Farm.

If you will cut off the hair at the end of a dog's tail and bury it under your front steps, the dog will stay with you and be your friend.

If the cows are lost, find a grand-daddy-long-legs and say to him, "Grand-daddy, grand-daddy, where are the cows?" He will lift one of his legs and point in the direction that the cows are.

The witches sweep the cobwebs (whippoorwills) from the sky on Hallowe'en night in preparation of a happy New Year.

WITCHING FOR WATER WITH THE BIBLE

By DAVID HALL

Man's most extended quest has not been for a Golden Fleece, a Gran Quivira, or El Dorado, but for a prosaic thing, a simple human necessity—water. Yet, whereas gold, the quest for which has always stimulated men's imaginations, has produced a myriad of legends, water has given rise to only a scattered few. Nevertheless, the search for water has been sufficient in itself to have influenced folk-living and folk-thinking.

Out of it have come "water-witches" and prognosticators of many home-spun varieties. These men are usually close to the soil, and their ways have been a part of the folkways of the people to which they belong. Of them and their practices with divining-rods and switches a great deal has been told and written. The Bible-and-key rite, however, seems to be little known. Let me reconstruct a scene which took place several years ago on the San Saba River some nine miles below Brady.

An oil lantern spluttered in the face of a south wind. By its light two men squatted on the ground under the walking-beam of a well-drilling outfit. Between them they held a closed Bible from the side edge of which, at the middle, protruded the head of a door key; a string tied around the book caught the key so that it could not pull out. (See illustration.) Allowed to pivot at the key, by which the men supported the book on their forefingers, the Bible would swing uncertainly for a brief second; then, as if impelled by some force, it would turn sharply to the right. Each time it turned, a count was made and the procedure was repeated.

"Two seventy-six, two seventy-seven, two seventy-eight—"

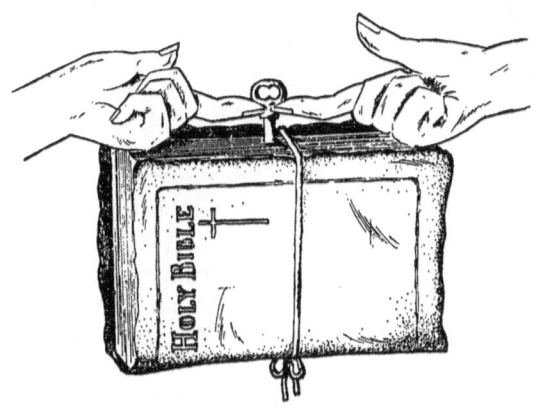

"There's where the bit hangs in the well," interrupted one of the men. It was the well-driller speaking. He anxiously watched the turning book, for his pay depended upon the successful completion of the well. Now long past the depth at which he had expected to find water, he had called in a "witch" to see if there was reason for going deeper.

The counting continued: "Two seventy-nine, two eighty, two eighty-one."

For each such count, representing a foot in depth to water, the Bible had completed a half-turn to the right, always to the right.

"Two eighty-two, two eighty-three, two eighty-four, two eighty-five. . . ." The fitful light waved Gargantuan shadows against the mass of machinery behind the men. The counting continued in a monotone.

"Two ninety-four, two ninety-five." The Bible began another turn, wavered, reversed, and veered sharply to the left. The depth to water, according to divination, was approximately 295 feet—just seventeen feet to the water-sand from where the bit hung in the well. The driller was stirred to sudden activity. He assembled his crew that night and by morning the well flowed water. Today it is still flowing water.

The "water-witch" was Roy H. Wyres, a ranchman about thirty-five years old who lives in the north part of McCulloch County, and who enjoys a local reputation for his success at "witching" for water with the Bible. But Mr. Wyres does not call himself a "water-witch"; he accepts no fee for his services, and he does not guarantee results. He took up the practice, he says, because it was interesting to him and because, in spite of his better judgment, he believes "there is something to it" he can't explain.

"I learned about the Bible-and-key," he relates, "from an old man who used to work on my father's place. His name, I believe, was C. C. Rister, and he came here from Bell County. I heard him talk a lot about 'witching'. Finally I thought I'd test the accuracy of his method. So I took the old man to two wells—wells that he'd never been around enough to know their depth. He divined, and in both cases the Bible and key 'witched' the exact depth. So then and there I decided there must be something to it, and right away I started trying my hand at it."

Since he began "witching" Mr. Wyres has also used a mesquite switch, but he believes the Bible and key gives better results. "Both methods," he says, "are worth trying before you dig a well."

According to Mr. Frank E. Simmons, of Oglesby, Texas, a forked switch is useful to find where water is

WITCHING FOR WATER

and the Bible-and-key method to determine how deep the well must go. He says[1]: "In the summer of 1932 a creek running through my pasture dried up. I needed stock water, and so secured the service of 'Crouch the Water Witch.' Crouch cut a forked switch from a plum tree. To demonstrate his power, he bound a nickel into the split end of the switch and told a boy to hide another nickel on the ground. He then circled the terrain, holding the prongs of the switch in his hands, apex up. Within three minutes the point of the switch dropped directly over the coin. Proceeding to the farm, he did considerable witching. Finally the switch dropped. Then with a Testament and a door key he made a depth test. The key was bound at the middle of the Testament. Crouch, kneeling on the ground, held the ring of the key on his index fingers. The Testament turned and fell to the ground. The procedure was repeated eleven times with the same result, but the twelfth time the Testament and key failed to turn. Crouch looked up and said, "Twelve feet won't miss it six inches.' We struck a small stream of water at twelve feet."

Bible-and-key divination for various objects bears evidence of antiquity. To this day it is not uncommon in rural England.[2] The following passage, quoted from Thomas Hardy's novel, *Far From the Madding Crowd*, indicates that the rite in England is substantially the same as that used by Mr. Wyres in Texas:

"The Bible was opened—the leaves drab with age. . . . The special verse in the Book of Ruth was sought out. . . . A rusty patch, immediately upon the verse, caused by previous pressure of an iron substance thereon, told that this was not the first time the old volume had been used for the purpose. . . . The verse was repeated, the book turned around."

The sixth and eighth verses of the eighth chapter of *The Song of Solomon* are usually chosen for love divining. The Yorkshire belief is that a maiden must bind

---
[1] Taken from the McGregor *Mirror*, 1933.
[2] Firor, Ruth A., *Folkways in Thomas Hardy*, University of Pennsylvania, Philadelphia, 1931, p. 44.

the key in the Bible with one of her garters. The practice was also followed to determine the name of a thief, the sixteenth verse of the first chapter of Ruth ("Entreat me not to leave thee," etc.)[3] being preferred for this act of prognostication. Scottish witch trial records show that Bible-and-key divination afforded grounds for conviction.[4]

One instance of love divining in Texas has come to my notice. Mrs. J. M. Coleman, of Menard, says that during her girlhood she divined for the name of her lover by this method. She used a verse in *The Song of Solomon*, but doesn't remember which verse. The key, she recalls, was placed on the verse, and the book was closed and tied with a string. Then she and some other person, usually a girl friend, would support the key on their fingertips and repeat the alphabet slowly. The Bible would stop turning when they called the first letter of "his" name. Mrs. Coleman says, "It always worked, too." She spent her girlhood in Belton, Texas, and believes that the rite was brought into her family by a relative who lived in Comanche County.

In divining for water, the rite as practiced by Roy Wyres does not require that the key be placed upon any certain verse. The center of the Bible, where the key must be tied to assure perfect balance, is in the *Psalms* in most editions. It is not unlikely that the seventy-eighth Psalm (which is in the exact center of at least one edition of the Bible), fifteenth and sixteenth verses, may once have been connected with the rite. The verses read:

> 15. He [Moses] clave the rocks in the wilderness, and gave them drink as out of great depths.
> 16. He brought streams also out of the rock, and caused waters to run down like rivers.

On one occasion when Roy Wyres was a visitor on a neighboring ranch I asked him to perform the rite that

---
[3] Firor, Ruth A., *Folkways in Thomas Hardy*, University of Pennsylvania, Philadelphia, 1931, p. 44.
[4] *Ibid.*

I might see it. With some care he placed a door-key in the Bible and secured it there by several wrappings of string tied around the book. The handle of the key was allowed to extend beyond the edge of the book. The spot selected for divining was on the floor of the ranch-house kitchen immediately above an underground cistern. We balanced the key on the tips of the forefingers of our right hands and suspended the Bible between us. It wavered a little and then moved to the right. Nine times it turned, but the tenth time it was placed in position it refused to move either way. We sat on our haunches and waited. The "witch" refused to coax it. My finger began to grow tired from the weight of the book. But then came the turn, this time to the left.

"Mighty close to nine feet," was the verdict.

Later I measured the depth from the kitchen floor to the surface of the water. It was exactly nine feet and four inches. Roy Wyres was right: there was indeed "something to it" that I could not explain.

THE BLACK CAT OF COLE'S PLANTATION

By JULIA BEAZLEY

In the lean, unlovely years that followed the Civil War, the Smalls loaded their household goods into a covered wagon and traveled from Mississippi to Texas, in search of happier times. At the Cole plantation, located in the region of piney woods and post oaks, they stopped, persuaded by the somewhat liberal offer of wages for farm labor.

A rumor that seemed in the air rather than on the tongues of their new neighbors breathed of dreadful things. It hinted that transient workers on the plantation had been known to disappear just before pay day, and pointed to a certain cornfield which nobody except the eccentric Captain Cole himself dared enter.

It was almost pay day now, and Mrs. Small sat among her sandy-haired brood before the open fire, awaiting her husband's return from work. Night had come early and black. A chilly rain was falling outside, and generous hands had fed the flames with oak chunks and pine knots. Their unsteady light made high relief of the humps and swales of the floor.

"Ma, what makes Captain Cole stare at folks like he had gone to sleep with his eyes open?" It was fifteen-year-old Angelina, eldest of the children, who had broken the silence.

The question was so akin to her own thoughts that Mrs. Small was almost startled out of her usual flat calm. "Worry, I reckon," she replied. "It's enough to run anybody crazy to manage a place as big as his." As she spoke there came from without the penetrating yowl of a cat.

"That's Pa, trying to scare us," volunteered Missy, second in age.

The sound was repeated. Then the door blew open. Everyone was sure it had been securely shut. After a moment Mrs. Small went to close it, and Angelina followed her, a little ashamed of the reluctance she felt.

They were scarcely seated when the dismal cry rose again, and again the door flew open.

"Let's jump out on Pa and catch him," challenged Missy.

The two girls tiptoed around the wall and reached the door. Together they sprang out on the porch. They were back in an instant, and even Missy's eyes were wide. There was nothing out there except thick darkness.

Mrs. Small laid hold of a formidable pine knot. The children crowded closer. Louder and nearer came the melancholy wail. Once more the door flew open, and this time in walked a large black cat, miauling like a lost soul.

"Scat!" shrieked Angelina, with a frantic stamp of her foot. The creature appeared not to hear. Noiselessly it walked about the room, fixing its burning eyes on each face in turn, filling the air with its nerve-shattering cries. The rain had left it untouched. It was quite dry, and left no track. When at length it had satisfied its purpose, whatever that might be, it turned and walked deliberately through the door. Mrs. Small sprang after it and shut the door and placed the heavy bar in place across it. Whereupon there was a great rattling of the knob from outside.

"Who's there?" quavered Mrs. Small.

"Open this door," came the gruff voice of her husband. He was tired and hungry and wet, and did not propose to have his own door barred against him.

The family flew to let him in, and poured out the story of their adventure. He refused to take it seriously at first, but when the uncanny yowls rose again and yet again, he took a pine torch and went out to investigate. Outside was nothing save silence and darkness and rain. Returning, Mr. Small loaded his double-barreled shotgun with buckshot. There were no more disturbing noises, and before long the man spread a pallet against the closed door, and lay down to sleep.

The next morning he was up at break of day. In a remarkably short time he had his family and all his worldly goods in the old covered wagon and was driving westward. The road led past Captain Cole's house, but Mr. Small did not stop to ask for the wages due him.

As to what happened when the rain stopped and the moon came out on that eventful night, absolute certainty is wanting. According to one account Tom Small chased the bodeful cat when it came again, and it led him to the forbidden cornfield. There amid significant mounds of earth he came upon a freshly dug grave yawning for its occupant.

IRISH FAIRIES IN TEXAS

By LOUISE VON BLITTERSDORF MOSES

Mr. Mike Welch, of Thorndale, Texas, was nearly as good as Peter Pan at making people believe in fairies. Of course he was Irish, and he was as loyal to the "wee folk" as he was to his religion. Every Sunday he would dress in his best clothes and ride sixty miles to mass over roads that only a T-model Ford could negotiate. But he has taken that ride for the last time. I hope that he has gone "over the fernie brae" into that "garden green" where the Queen of Elfland took Thomas Rymer so long ago. Mike Welch knew that wonderful country well and loved it. One of the stories he used to tell was of Irish fairies that had come to Texas.

I had heard that Mr. Welch's house was haunted. None of the family cared to stay there alone. I was anxious to know why it was haunted, but no one seemed to know. One summer night we were all sitting on the gallery of the house talking. The full moon brought the landscape into brilliant relief.

"It was a night like this," remarked Mr. Welch, "when I saw the lovers walking in the moonlight."

"What lovers?" I asked.

"Why, those that belong to the house here."

I pleaded ignorance, and he was soon launched into their story.

"When I first came to Texas," began Mr. Welch, "I was only a young fellow, though I had wandered about quite a bit. When I looked on this river-bottom farm, I decided it was the place for me. Right then I made up my mind to settle down here, and, if I could find the right sort of girl, get married. When I located the spot on which to build my house I was surer than ever I had found my lodging place. If you look carefully, you can see that this house is in a flat completely surrounded by a sort of wide ditch. The ditch isn't very plain any more. The rains and washouts of all these years have almost filled it up, but when I first saw it, it could be traced quite plainly. That wouldn't have meant much to you, not having lived in Ireland, but when I saw it, I knew at once I had found a ruined moat.

"Now, in the old days in Ireland when every landowner was a law to himself and lived by strength of arms, he dug a moat around his castle and filled it with water. This was a sure protection against invasion. By my time, of course, most of those old castles had fallen into ruins and disappeared, and only the outlines of the moats were left. I've seen many a one. I remember one in particular only a short distance from my home. We boys often used to go there.

"One Sunday morning another boy and I hid in the moat to play cards instead of going to mass. We were having a fine time and I was winning, when we both looked up and saw a lady all dressed in black coming toward us. My friend flung down his cards and ran, but I stayed there. The woman came up to me, took the cards from my hand and began to turn them up one by one, at the same time telling all about my past and my future. I know it's wrong to believe in fortune-tellers, but every single thing she told me came true.

"When she had finished, she told me I might have three wishes. I was getting kind of uneasy by then; so I up and wished for a happy death and for the safety of my immortal soul. She said she couldn't grant that and begged me to wish for something else. I was pretty scared by then, and remembered that I was missing mass on a Sunday; so I stuck to my wish. Then she started in and talked to me a long time. She gave me a lot of good advice and reproved me for playing cards on Sunday and missing mass. About that time I made the sign of the cross, and, lo and behold, she completely vanished into air! I ran every step of the way to the church and got there just as mass was over. I went to confession right then and told the priest all about my experience. I begged him never to let me see the woman in black again, and he promised me that I never would.

"But that didn't cure me from moats, and when I saw this one here in a foreign land, I just felt like I was home again. I built my house right here in the center where the old castle had stood. I guess you are wondering how such an Old World thing as a moat came to be in Texas.

"Well, that was the doings of the fairies.

"A long time ago there lived in Ireland a good and wealthy man. He owned a large estate, and his lands prospered. He was kind and just to his vassals. Above all, he was a good Catholic, attending mass and holy communion every morning in his private chapel. He was a good friend to the fairy folk, too, and took care never to displease them. Now, this man had a daughter who was very good and very beautiful. When she became old enough to marry, it was soon arranged that she should be the bride of a handsome young gentleman, the son of another Irish lord who lived near. Those old Irish houses kept themselves strong by keeping up such alliances. May Eve, which is a special feast of the fairies, was set as the night for the betrothal of the young couple. A great banquet was prepared in the hall of the castle with friends and relatives coming from half of Ireland to celebrate the event.

"All might have been well but for the English baron who lived to the east. This baron had large Irish estates that he had acquired by very questionable means, and he was anxious to add to them still further. The daughter of the Irish lord had become of interest to him. Maybe he was in love with her beauty as well as with her possessions. I don't know. When he asked for her hand, he was at once rejected, for what Irishman would give his daughter to an Englishman, however powerful he might be, when there was a good Irish lad to the other side of him who was only waiting for a chance? Rejection did not make the baron any friendlier. He determined to have the girl by force. He didn't dare attack the Irish lord openly, for the castle was too well fortified, but he bided his time and waited.

"His opportunity came on May Eve. While the banquet progressed in the great hall above, the servants' quarters were not forgotten, and the retainers of this Irish lord feasted and drank in the hall below. The wine and ale flowed freely. The soldiers who guarded the walls perhaps drank more of it than they should, but who was to reprove them on such a night as this? What if they did become a little drowsy as the night progressed and fail to see the forces of the English baron until they were fairly upon them? The enemy had entered the castle before they had time to issue a warning. The happy revellers were slaughtered mercilessly. The young couple, who were walking in the garden in the moonlight at the time of the attack, did not escape. The lad was cut down as he defended his bride, and she, seeing him fall, plunged his sword into her own body that she might die with him. When morning came, the castle was in ruins, and the moat flowed red with blood.

"When the fairies saw what had happened, their May Day celebrations were ruined for them. They had lost one of their best friends in the very act of celebrating their own feast. They decided to call a council. They begged God to restore the castle just as it had been before the slaughter. God did not approve of that, but He did compromise with the fairies. He offered to restore the castle and its inhabitants just as they had been on condition that the fairies would carry it away to where no Irish would ever see it. The fairies agreed. They picked up the castle, moat and all, and carried it across the ocean to this unknown world and set it down in Texas.

"Then the New World was discovered, and it wasn't a great while until people began to come to Texas. The

Irish among others. The fairies had promised God that the castle should not be seen by Irish eyes; so there was nothing for them to do but put it out of sight. Slowly it began to sink into the earth until it completely disappeared, leaving only the outlines of the moat visible. That is the way I found it when I came here.

"Some people try to say this house is haunted, but it isn't. I know you can hear people laughing and talking, babies crying, and the music of violins, but that is only those people down there in the earth still celebrating May Eve. Once in a while they come up on top, and one can see them. I've seen them warming themselves at my fire on a cold night, and once when I was real sick a woman came across the room and bent over my bed, and I began to get well right away. They aren't dressed in the kind of clothes we wear either. They wear clothes like those of long ago."

"And did you say that you saw the lovers?" I asked.

"Yes," he answered. "On the night before my wedding I was sitting here on this very gallery, thinking about my bride, when right across this space of yard in front of me I saw a young couple walking in the moonlight. I watched them walk clear across and vanish under that mesquite tree there."

PIONEER FOLK WAYS

By AFTON WYNN

Editor's Note: The ways of life among the pioneers, their folk ways, is one of various subjects common to both folk-lore and social history. Prime sources for such material, pertaining to early-day Texas, are Noah Smithwick's *Evolution of a State,* Austin, 1900, reprinted by the Steck Company, Austin, 1936—bully reading as well as informative; the "Reminiscences" of Mrs. Dilue Harris in Volumes IV and VII of the *Southwestern Historical Quarterly,* and of C. C. Cox in Volume VI of the same publication; the *Memoirs* of Mary A. Maverick, San Antonio, 1921; *A Texas Scrap Book,* by D. W. C. Baker, New York, 1875, reprinted by the Steck Company, Austin, 1936; Frederick Law Olmsted's *A Journey through Texas,* New York, 1857; *Texas . . . in a Series of Letters,* by Mary Austin Holley, Baltimore, 1835——reprinted under the title of *Letters of An American Traveler,* edited by Mattie Austin Hatcher, Dallas, 1933; *Texas,* by Ferdinand Roemer—translation by Oswald Mueller, published by the Standard Printing Company, San Antonio, 1935; various county histories, distinguished among them *History and Reminiscences of Denton County,* by Ed F. Bates, Denton, Texas, 1918; John A. Hart, *History of Pioneer Days in Texas and Oklahoma*—an undated work now very scarce, in a much extended form published under the title of *Pioneer Days in the Southwest,* Guthrie, Oklahoma, 1909. *Thus They Lived,* by Joseph

PIONEER FOLK WAYS 191

W. Schmitz, the Naylor Company, San Antonio, 1935, treats of social life in the Republic of Texas, but it is at best a very fragmentary treatise.——J. F. D.

Parker County, Texas, was organized in 1855. Pioneer life here was perhaps typical of pioneer life in Texas, but it lingered here longer than in many other sections and in many of its phases seems to have been more intensive. At the time of organization the county was on the extreme western frontier, and for many years it continued so to be. Rough, broken country amid its fertile stretches kept it from changing too quickly. Much of the land within its confines can never be changed by man. Thus, homespun, gourds, and one-legged beds continued in use up some of the hollows of Parker County until comparatively recent times.

Amid the communities within the area that the very nature of the terrain distinctly separated from each other was The Pool, now better known as Poolville, sixteen miles north of Weatherford, the county seat. It is a decaying little village, but natives still go to The Pool to do their trading, whittling, and open-air domino playing. It took its name from a small lake of water on the Clear Fork of the Trinity River beside which Jim Taylor, some time before 1870, opened a store and another man a saloon. More than fifty years ago the lake gave way to a stretch of sand, and now old-timers can scarcely agree on the exact location of the fine waterhole at which herds once stopped to drink while being driven up the trail.

The settlers knew about the Indians, but they kept believing the government would soon have them safe in hand. The rich bottoms of the Clear Fork, the good water, the pleasant willows and cottonwoods along the course of the stream, and the vast stretches of sage grass and prairie hay made the land a golden promise.

At first the people built dugouts, cellars they called them. But as soon as possible they fell to the task of cutting, barking, lining, and hewing the postoak trees for their log cabins. Some of these were built hurriedly of round logs, the dirt serving for the floor; but hewn logs were used in the structure of the more permanent houses, and one side of split logs was smoothed down to form the puncheon floors.

The people immediately began to cultivate the soil, planting seeds they had brought from their native states; and to build log churches and schools. They strove to establish such community life as they had left behind in Arkansas, Tennessee, or Mississippi.

"The pioneers did not come as hunters of hidden treasures nor buried fortunes, but to build homes and establish citizenship," says one of the oldest citizens.[1] "I have no doubt," another chronicler records,[2] "that a great many imagine that the people of pioneer days were toughs and outlaws, but such is not the case. While I was a small boy when Parker County was first settled, only about thirty families in the county, I remember that all heads of families were Christians at that time, and I am of the opinion that Parker County is only a sample of pioneer days in Texas."

In the new county the commissioners, in order to encourage settlement, sold land in the uplands for as little as fifty cents an acre. But the settlers were not always well-to-do, and by the time they had paid the expenses of the trip to the new county, few had little left for buying land. The early comers with the most money got the best farm in the bottoms, and the poorer families had to be content with the prairie land. Indeed, the latter were about as fortunate as the lowlanders in the long run, for their crops were good when the bottom lands were flooded and the fields ruined by rains.

A tale is told of an old-timer in Parker County who said to a newcomer in later years: "I came here when I could have bought a league and a labor for a pair of boots and a Spanish pony." A league is 4,428 acres, and a labor is 177.

"Well, why didn't you buy it?" the newcomer asked.

"Because I had nary pair of boots nor nary pony," the old-timer answered.

---
[1] Holland, G. A., *The Double Log Cabin*, Weatherford, Texas, 1931, p. 69.
[2] Hart, John A., *History of Pioneer Days in Texas and Oklahoma*, pp. 1-2.

PIONEER FOLK WAYS

The new county officers were elected on March 2, 1856, exactly twenty years after the signing of the Texas Declaration of Independence and eleven years after Texas had been admitted to the Union. On June 24 the commissioners held their first sale of lots in Weatherford. Records show that one hundred and seventy persons attended the sale and bought $9,700 worth of lots. Ten of the front lots on the square, says Smythe,[3] went for $150 each. Deputy Sheriff D. H. Sisk, who had moved from Hopkins County, Kentucky, bought a 50x100-foot lot on the south side of the square for $217. Farming land as late as 1877 could be bought for from $1 to $10 an acre. Unimproved land for from $2.50 to $5 and improved for from $5 to $10, was a general estimate.

Parker County got off to a good religious start, and well it did, for the early home builders needed their religion to sustain them in the perils they were soon to face. Many threw up their claims and went back to their old homes, but most of them stuck it out, and prayed, and fought the Indians—and fought the Indians and prayed.

When the Rev. Pleasant Tackett arrived at the Clear Fork in May, 1854, with his fifteen families, they found the stream raging as only Parker County people know it can rage. The travelers made camp on the banks of the creek, prayed, and sang their hymns. As they awaited the subsiding of the water, the preacher inspected the territory, riding forth on a mule. Suddenly something struck him on the foot; and, looking down, he saw that it was an arrow. He pulled it out and rode on into camp. Thus came the Indian trouble from the very beginnings of the new county.

Later the families crossed the creek and began to choose fertile spots which struck their fancy. One group settled on Walnut Creek at a point about five miles southeast of the big water pool on the Clear Fork, and religiously named the place Goshen. Tackett himself was

---

[3] Smythe, H., *A Historical Sketch of Parker County and Weatherford, Texas,* St. Louis, 1877.

with this group. It was summer and, dugouts being unnecessary, they set immediately about the building of log cabins. Three days of log cutting and house raising had passed when Maggie Lee, a little orphan girl in the care of one of the families, was bitten by a large rattlesnake when she moved some bedding on the ground. The next day she died. In the Goshen cemetery where they buried her, there were soon to follow victims of the ruthless savages, and many slabs in that old cemetery today bear the inscription, "Killed by Indians."

Hugh R. Frazier and his older sons, John and Joe, and the Culwells not only carried Methodism through the years, but they kept alive the spirit of sacred song in the face of Indian raids and atrocities. They liked to sing, and they could sing. Until a very few years ago church was held regularly at Goshen, as well as all-day singings. The four-note *Sacred Harp* was the principal hymnal, but later the *Christian Harmony* came to be used along with it. The *mi-fa-so-la* type of singing was perhaps never better exemplified than by the Goshen singers on a hot Sunday afternoon under a brush arbor. The babies lay on pallets in the aisles between the homemade puncheon benches. The children played about the spring or in the shade of the liveoaks. Older boys and girls courted, perhaps. But most of the men and women sang.

From Goshen emanated the Taylor Singing Convention, named after a master of hymns who covered the county on a song-teaching itinerary. This convention continued many years, being held annually in first one community and then another. Many Sundays were given over to all-day singings, but the convention was an event of events, and usually lasted from Friday through Sunday. The Culwells and Fraziers predominated among the song leaders; the citizens-at-large attended, all wearing their very finest clothes.

John Frazier, who died in 1933 at the age of eighty-six years, was for decades the spirit of Goshen. Relatives and other members of the church gradually drifted into the congregations at Poolville or Springtown, but Frazier and his old friend, Jake Shadle, when they found that they were the only members left, refused to disband. Today the Frazier family holds the old Goshen church book, a volume of considerable interest to the searcher of facts in the development of an humble community.

An instance of the godliness which prevailed long in the Goshen community is found in *Alfalfa Bill*, a biography of William Henry Murray, recent governor of Oklahoma: "Henry learned that the little community at Goshen church-house wanted a short term of subscription school and he went to attempt to enroll enough students to make the venture profitable. He stayed with a family named Kirley, a devotedly religious folk who had little patience with schoolin', believing it too worldly. After a short period, the community's religious folk gathered beneath a rude shelter they had built in the church yard for outdoor services and a shouting evangelist was brought in for a protracted meeting. Often beginning at sunrise and lasting far into the night, the shouting distracted the young pupils and Henry soon became convinced that community interest had drifted from l'arnin' to holiness. He packed his belongings and went back to Springtown."[4]

This episode took place in the summer of 1888.

Before the Civil War, four religious faiths had been established in the county. The log schoolhouses usually served for church in the winter and brush arbors in the summer. Two large arbors were constructed, one for the worship and the other for dining. Small arbors were thrown up for the families during camp meeting, and with a little effort these were converted into private rooms with leafy boughs serving as walls and roofs. By the time the different denominations took time about with camp meetings lasting from two to six weeks each, the summer was fairly well filled. Crowds came to these meetings for miles about, on foot, on horseback, in covered wagons, and in ox-carts. A beef was killed every day, and the women prepared the meals between services

---

[4] Hines, Gordon, *Alfalfa Bill*, Oklahoma City, Oklahoma, 1932, p. 63.

while the men sat or squatted around in their Sunday jeans and discussed the doctrine.

Professions of the faith were many, for those who were turned out of the church in the winter time for dancing or drinking would come under conviction again during the summer and would be readmitted. The women were the best shouters. It mattered little whether a woman was a Methodist or a Baptist, she was equally inspired at all camp meetings if she happened to be the shouting type. She would clap her hands, run up and down the aisles, and shout and scream hysterically at the top of her voice. She would embrace her friends and loved ones, and weep and laugh. Usually her tucking comb fell out and her hair streamed down over her shoulders. Some friend would pick up her comb, fan, hymnbook, and handkerchief and hold them devotedly until her ecstasy subsided. The men would get happy too, but the women always made a more graceful and impressive demonstration.

At the height of religious revelry, a band of Indians was likely to rush into the midst of the worshipers, and kill and scalp or capture some of them. Against such a contingency, every man carried his flint-lock, his shot pouch, and powder horn to church. The guns were always stacked near the entrance to the church or the brush arbor.

Singing at church, especially at the summer camp meetings, was done with a different sort of fervor from that of the singing convention, for the faith of the fathers entered into the strictly religious song service. At the singings there might even be a little fun. At any point in the preacher's oratorical effort, an off-key tribble was likely to break in with "How Firm a Foundation," "There Is a Fountain Filled with Blood," or "The Old-Time Religion." A tuning fork was ordinarily used by the song leader, but it was not always his lot to start the singing. When some gentle soul jumped from the puncheon bench on which she sat, with music in her system, she set the key, and the others followed as well as they could.

Even today the protracted meeting is one of the leading social attractions at the little towns in the northeastern section of the county. Fairs, bazaars, box-suppers, barbecues, picnics, candy-breakings, public Christmas trees, and melon cuttings have had their day along the Clear Fork, but no other social occasion has had the pulling power of the camp meeting.

The women in Parker County suffered considerably through the various interpretations of Paul's doctrine concerning their place in the church. The subject was widely discussed and argued. In the Baptist church in the Erwin community, two miles southeast of The Pool, there was a great stir over this question. Lee Stratton, one of the members, held that a woman should not take part in the business of the church, maintaining that she did not possess a soul. Bud Taylor, a young man with free-thinking ideas, dared to advance the theory that if a man had a soul, it was reasonable to presume that a woman had one too. The thoughts of the people, religious as they appeared in general, ran all the way from fanaticism to professed infidelity.

While the country churches were threshing out the subject of woman's place, the churches in the little town of Weatherford were going right ahead and letting the women help pay for their new brick or frame buildings. The county was only twenty-one years old when its historian, H. Smythe, wrote: "For nearly ten years an effort has been made to rear a house of worship for the Christian denomination. Attempts by man signally failed; the women magnificently accomplished their purpose." This they did "through laborious working with the needle and various knitting appliances, combined with two public festival entertainments."

Circuit riders looked after the Methodist churches, while missionaries, armed with gun and Bible, made the rounds to the small Baptist flocks. Some very small congregations would have a preacher only on Fifth Sunday, an off-day from his regular itinerary. Bible study and family prayer were diligently adhered to by many of the early families. In their log cabins the pioneers always provided a reading shelf if they made any pretense whatsoever toward religious or secular study. These shelves were made of rough boards, but were often covered by the best-knit tidy in the household, on which reposed the Bible, along with a grease lamp or home-made candle.

Few negro slaves were brought to the new county, but those that came were cared for spiritually by being permitted to join the same churches with their white people. They sat apart from them, however.

Weatherford had city ways, but historian Smythe mentions the passing of an ordinance in 1877 which prohibited the firing of any gun in the city on the Sabbath for sport or amusement or for the killing of small game. In the country sections guns were sometimes fired for the purpose of obtaining food, and shooting matches were sometimes held on Sunday afternoons, but in general there was little work done that day. The very religious engaged in no amusements gayer than visiting at each other's houses for dinner after preaching, than talking, singing, praying, inspecting the neighbor's garden or spring house, or walking in the woods or on the prairies to gather wild flowers. There was as little work done as possible. The women did only that cooking and housekeeping which was deemed necessary. If a man looked over his crop on Sunday afternoon, that was not considered work. All religious services were usually attended by all members of the family. It was safer to take all the family to church than to leave a few at home.

All devout families held thorough housecleanings on Saturday, on which day most of the cooking for Sunday was done, and the house put in readiness for a day of rest. Puncheon floors were scoured with ashes and lye soap, and chairs and benches were scrubbed until they were white and slick. Hugh Frazier, at Goshen, permitted absolutely no cooking in his home on Sunday. He and his wife were so religious that they observed occasional fast days, but they did allow the children to eat. In the family of W. T. Taylor in the Erwin community was less religious observance. But prayer was held often in this home, as Taylor had a large domicile—plenty to eat and several marriageable daughters—conditions calculated to help the preachers come often a-praying.[5]

Alongside of the church was the saloon. There seems to be little evidence that the earliest saloons were great dens of iniquity, as they no doubt were later when the Sons of Temperance was organized in 1874 for "the moral elevation of mankind." Its members succeeded in 1877 in voting whisky out, but when it was voted out, it was bootlegged in. It would never stay out long until the tide would turn, and back it would come. When whisky was out in Parker County, there was more going to Fort Worth, that wild outpost where the West began and where the good sons of the Clear Fork could cut up without interference. It was a good day's ride by horseback over the forty miles to Fort Worth.

The use of whisky by the pioneer served a double purpose. It not only helped him overlook his hardships, but it also provided much needed barrels for his home. When the creeks and shallow wells went dry, the whisky barrel set on a "lizard," a sled made of a forked sapling, was used to haul water. Cut in two, with holes at the right places for handles, barrels made good washtubs. Soap, potatoes, beans, syrup, honey and other things could be stored in the barrels.

Parker County has long basked in the limelight of Cynthia Ann Parker, but as far as historians know, Cynthia Ann was in the county but twice. As her captors fled with her, they camped at a site believed to be a few miles southeast of the present city of Weatherford. There, in 1836, they held their customary war dance to celebrate the taking of Fort Parker. Cynthia Ann twenty-five years later passed through Parker County on the way to her uncle's place in Birdville, Tarrant County.

Her uncle, Isaac D. Parker, for whom the county was named, moved from Birdville to the Clear Fork, eight miles east of Weatherford, in 1872, nine years after Cynthia Ann had died at the home of her brother, Silas

---

[5] Frazier and Taylor were great-grandfathers of the writer; hence these liberties are taken in mentioning their religious practices.

Parker, in Van Zandt County. No doubt, every person in Parker County, from ten years up, can relate parts of the dramatic story of Cynthia Ann, but the number of natives who ever heard of Isaac D. Parker are now few and far between.

The Parker capture, which has been related many times in print, was typical of the hundreds of raids and massacres which took place during the first twenty years of the settling of Parker County. These atrocities were a part of the lives of people who dared to settle the country. Worse than a cyclone, worse than a rattlesnake, the Indians struck more often and with less warning. The families and the parts of families that survived had to be cautious, wary and quick on the trigger.

The last Indian raids were made in 1874. During twenty perilous years, it is estimated that the Indians captured and destroyed property within a radius of one hundred miles of Parker County to the value of six million dollars and killed or took into captivity nearly four hundred persons.[6]

"Those who saw it say that the most deplorable and heartrending sensation known was experienced by a visit to a home after a raid where some member of the family had been killed and scalped, and others carried away into captivity——all the stock gone; furniture and dishes broken up and scattered over the yard; the emptied feathers from the beds blown by the winds and hanging on the fences, shrubbery and trees like snowflakes. Even the remaining chickens and house cat knew that something terrible had happened."[7]

The Indians never stole cattle but always went for the horses. They would scalp a family, then rob the house of all food, clothing, and bedding. Beds were split and the feathers emptied, only the ticks being wanted. These the housewives had made by weaving their strong homespun as closely as they could, and later boiling the web of cloth in meal, which was the best sizing they knew.

---

[6] Smythe, H., *Historical Sketch of Parker County and Weatherford, Texas*, St. Louis, 1877, p. 140.
[7] Holland, *op. cit.*, p. 10.

At the time of the raids a story was current that a woman saved herself by running into the woods. When the Indians were gone, she returned. Her loved ones all lay killed and scalped about the place, but her neighbors found her going distractedly about the yard trying to pick up her scattered feathers.

At all times the people were in mortal terror of the Indians. Only the uninitiated went without guns. Even the women kept a gun at hand when there were enough arms in the family to go around. The houses were barred at night, and every family listened to the warnings of its dogs. When the Indians were afar off, the dogs barked loudly; but when they barked softly and came into the house and were restless, it was almost a sure sign that the Indians were near. If the family was fortunate enough to have dug a cellar under the puncheon floor, the women and children were afforded better protection while the men folk took a chance at fighting it out by shooting through the chinks of the walls. The Indians chose the bright moonlight nights for their raids, and the pioneers dreaded the coming of the next full moon.

"A good night for Indians," was a remark that still lives with those whose boyhood and girlhood days were spent on the frontier. Even some of the great-grandchildren to this day have an instinctive fear of the moonlight.

While the depredations were at their height, a family scarcely dared to sit outside on the hot summer evenings. They were ever on the lookout for savages. Barred in their one or two-room cabins they often sat up far into the night with a grease lamp or a candle, or the flickering light from the fireplace to help as they performed the homely duties of picking cotton from the seed by hand, knitting, spinning, weaving, mending shoes or harness, while one, perhaps, read the Bible.

Added to the ever-present dread that the Indians would strike at any time, the families, as the years rolled by, kept alive memories of the atrocities to their relatives and neighbors. The terrifying tales were continually relived. When a household opened its doors for a new relative and his family lately arrived from a civilized state or county, the tragedies of the settlers were promptly recounted.

Sometimes the whites took the offensive; hence, there were tales of bravery and exploit to relate. Sometimes they trailed the marauders and killed them, finding the scalps of white victims on their belts. If the scalped person was still unburied, his detached head covering was brought back and replaced with care to hide the gruesome sight. And sometimes the bloody, lousy scalp of the Indian was brought in as a sort of token of revenge.

It was in 1860, after the murder of Frank Browning, that General John R. Baylor and a group of settlers made perhaps the greatest showing at returning the savagery of the Indians. They overtook the Indians on Paint Creek and killed fifteen. A barbecue was given in Weatherford in their honor, and the people danced all night at the courthouse. A rope was stretched diagonally across the room and on it were strung nine scalps and the bows, arrows, quivers, shields, and tomahawks taken on the expedition. General Baylor took these trophies around to the larger cities of the state, and soon money was pouring into the county for the support and protection of its settlers.

General Baylor started a newspaper in Weatherford which he called *White Man*. The paper, begun in 1860, did much toward inciting the people of Texas and the whole United States against the government's policy of permitting the Indians the use of arms while it made no effort to punish them in a court at law. During the Civil War General Baylor's newspaper, as well as the *Frontier News*, which also was being published in Weatherford, were silenced when Northern sympathizers destroyed their offices.

Just how the frontiersman and his family felt about the Indians may be surmised from the fact that after the report of an Indian killing the people would flock for miles to take a look at the dead warrior or warriors, and often enough the bodies would be hitched to horses, after they had been scalped, and dragged for miles. The Indians were not only feared but they were despised and hated. Those who witnessed displays of barbarity on the part of the settlers have recounted in later years that the dragging of an Indian's body over the roughest of ground seldom resulted in as much as the breaking of his tough skin.

A noticeable effort is now being made by Parker County citizens to keep alive the memories of the hardships endured by the pioneers. Mayor G. A. Holland, Weatherford banker and former school teacher at Poolville, bought an old log cabin several years ago and moved it to his lake resort near Weatherford to be used as a museum. In this cabin in 1873 George McCleskey died while shooting at Indians through the chinks of the wall after he had fallen to the floor from a bullet wound, paralyzed from the waist down. It was the home of his father-in-law, John Bumgarner, who also was engaged in the skirmish. To this McCleskey-Bumgarner cabin has been added another log house, from the Muleshoe Ranch, and the two have been joined by an open hall to make a double log cabin, a typical home of the prosperous pioneer. Holland has named the museum the Double Log Cabin and has spent considerable time in collecting the relics housed by it. The most interesting relic, perhaps, is the buffalo robe worn by Cynthia Ann Parker when she was captured by Captain Ross's men. Also there are guns the pioneers used in killing Kiowas and Comanches, a loom on which Holland entertains his visitors by weaving handspun cotton, examples of the first furniture in the county—a cord bed, stools, rawhide-seated chairs—gourds, arrowheads, handicraft specimens, pots and pothooks, dutch ovens and crude tools of many kinds. The chimneys include stones from Isaac D. Parker's home on the Clear Fork, and the porch is supported by cedar posts from Sam Bass's old camp in Palo Pinto County.

While the double log cabin, connected by a roofed, open hall, was common among the pioneers, the two cabins were more often not connected. They were separated primarily as a safeguard against fire. One was used as a living room and the other as the kitchen, and the two were designated as the big house and the kitchen.

Both had chimneys built of clay and straw. The children watched the chimneys constantly, and often had to scurry up on the low roof with a gourd full of water to cope with a small blaze. Poor families had only one small room, often floorless and windowless at that, in which they did their living, eating, sleeping, spinning, weaving.

Logs for the better homes and for the puncheon floors were hewn with a broad-ax along a line made by a string dipped in poke-berry juice. Puncheons were smoothed with a drawing knife, and the floors were smooth enough for dancing. Boards, rived with a froe, were used to cover the roofs, which were supported on pole rafters. Joists were peeled saplings, and the lathes were split saplings with the flat side up. The rived boards also were used for the doors and for the window jambs—if the house had windows. There was no glass to be had, but when a man decided his family must have a window he made a shutter door for the opening by pegging together some rough boards and attaching them by rawhide hinges.

Chinking the walls was a task never finished. The houses which were hurriedly built of round logs had such large chinks that good-sized chips had to be used in daubing them. It took quantities of clay, straw, and hogs' hair to provide the necessary filler. Poorer families would awaken in rainstorms to find the daubing on a whole side of their cabin completely washed out. If they could find enough old rags and shucks to stuff up the chinks temporarily, they could turn over and go back to sleep, but too often the floor was muddy and the whole household was thrown into an uproar until the rain subsided.

There was seldom more than one door in these first houses, and a tree block served as a step, if a step was needed. The tree blocks served many purposes. They were used for upping blocks by the women and children, being cut often in stair-step fashion. They made substantial tables for the whisky-barrel tubs, and they often were used to hold the gourd wash basin, the water bucket, and such flower plants as the housewife might be trying to grow in any discarded utensil she could find. They made excellent chopping blocks for the cutting up of deer, beeves or hogs. Every home could use a tree block on which to scrape hides if for nothing else.

Each house was enclosed by a strong rail or picket fence with a gate of poles. Gates, doors, and windows were all barred at night.

In the big house were the beds, usually two one-legged beds with a trundle under each. The stationary bed of one leg was made by boring or reaming a hole in a puncheon at the proper place and inserting an upright post. At right angles from this post, horizontal poles would lead to the chinks in the walls, forming a substantial rectangle on which to place board slats. More comfortable, however, were the cord beds, which were of four-legged construction with rawhide strips, ropes or cords laced through bored holes along the lengthwise supporting poles. The trundle beds were about eight inches high and were constructed in the same manner as the large four-legged beds. These saved many a hard bump for the pioneer children.

Going to bed was a delicately handled ceremony in the large families. The children washed their feet in the summer time, and were properly dressed in their night garments and tucked away in the trundles. When it came time for the grown-ups to retire, the men all went outside to give a last look to the stock while the women undressed. The men returned to find the women all in bed. Candles were then extinguished and the men undressed in the dark. The coals were banked in ashes for the night, and on cold mornings the head of the household arose, slipped on his jeans and built the fire. Usually the men arose first and went to see about the stock while the women dressed.

Feather beds were used by all the thrifty housewives. They kept geese and picked them regularly to keep up a supply of feathers for their own use and for their children as they married and started homes of their own. Shucks and straw were used in under beds to give a certain resiliency to the feather beds on top. The feathers were given a good shaking up each morning and the bed turned over. Making a bed was considered an art, and the housewife strove to keep her beds clean and in perfect order. They were not used for lounging on during the day. Some of the earlier settlers used buffalo skins for beds, but the buffaloes did not last long after the settlers came. Home-woven ticks, sized with corn meal, blankets, sheets, pillow cases, shams, fancy coverlids, and hand-pieced and quilted coverings made up the bedding supplies of the average family. A well-ordered family arrived with a supply of bedding, but, as it gave way, the Parker County housewife went ahead weaving, piecing and quilting what she needed.

Those homeseekers who moved in grand style brought their furniture, usually home-made. Most of them, however, made their furniture after they arrived in the new county. Spinning wheels were perhaps the most intricate of the home-made pieces, the wheels often being the handiwork of some specialist. Sleys for the looms were constructed of reeds from the canes found along the creek banks. The canes were made stationary in rawhide frames by deft wrapping with strong, home-spun twine. The cotton was often hand-fluffed for the spindle, but many homes possessed cards made of sharpened reeds mortised vertically into small boards.

Furniture depended for grace of line upon the cabinet-making ability of the men of the family. Artless householders turned out some crude pieces, of course. The paraphernalia for making cloth also included warping bars on which the warp was prepared for lacing into the sley. And there were also reels for measuring the thread. The raw cotton was first picked free of seeds, after which it was washed in lye soap, to give it strength, and dried. With the soap still in it, the cotton was then carded free of motes and shaped into a roll. A broach of shucks was adjusted to the spindle and the wheel set to turning. Held to the end of the spindle, the roll was twisted out into a thread, which was wound on the broach. All operations that followed necessitated running of the thread on to a cane quill, which served as a spool in the shuttle, or for the measuring of thread on the reel, or for the warping process. The reel was made of cross bars set up in horizontal windmill fashion. On each of the fans was a vertical peg on which the thread was strung to form hanks of so many yards each. The warp had to be twisted for strength and was then measured. Often a knot had to be tied to insure the proper length for the new piece of cloth.

These twisted threads were wound off on a smooth corncob or a cane spool and were then ready for the warping bar. If dyed, the process called for hanking on the reel, after which the thread was colored and dried before going to the warping bar. The spools were strung on pegs along a horizontal bar set up outside the house, parallel to it, and about ten feet away. All the loose threads were picked up by hand and the mass was strung out together over pegs on the outer wall. A rough twist here and there, and the lapping over peg after peg as the threads were drawn off the spools, enabled the weaver to get her warp into condition for the loom. Each thread end was fastened to a revolving cylinder of wood at the lower back of the loom, and the whole was wound on. Each thread then was slipped by hand through the harness of threads and thence through the sley. All the threads were ultimately stretched into place for the weaving and were attached to a front revolving cylinder on which the woven cloth would be wound. Treadles had to be adjusted to fit the length of the weaver's legs. The batten for holding the sley and for beating up the woof tightly into place, the temple for holding the woven product at uniform width, the shuttles for carrying the woof threads—even the bench for the weaver—had to be made by hand.

The woof usually was of single threads. These were not as carefully measured as the warp, and in plain weaving they were run directly from the broaches of shucks on to the cane quills and were inserted into the shuttles for immediate weaving. If a woof thread broke, it was little trouble to tie, but the breaking of a warp thread caused a tangle, and meant the splicing with a new piece of thread and the making of two unsightly knots.

Women who possessed wheels and looms of their own often wove for their neighbors on the shares. Most looms stayed busy from dawn until bedtime. In ordinary weaving a housewife could drop her work for a time while a neighbor ran off a few yards of needed material; however, she might have to wait a while before the warp was woven up and she could have her piece of cloth cut out.

Beds, chairs, tables, shelves, stools, and sometimes a chest of rough drawers or a safe were among the articles the man of the house usually had to make for his family. Native oak and elm were most often used, but pine could be bought in Weatherford—if one had the money. Chairs were often made of a wheel off a log, perched upon crude legs, basined out a little in the seat, and supported in the back by a board. The more talented chair-maker could turn out a fair product with a solid, laced, or hair-side-out rawhide bottom. There were always benches and three-legged stools for the children, but seldom was there more than a seat around for the members of the large families. "Bring your chairs and come to dinner," was the welcome call from the kitchen to the big house three times a day.

Families usually included such a host of relatives that it was necessary to have a bed and a trundle in the kitchen as well as two of each in the big house. That made six beds, and with only three on a bed, eighteen persons could be comfortably accommodated. A child could be placed at the foot of each bed, providing for twenty-four. And pallets could always be made down on the puncheons in case of an emergency. Babies had cradles for day use, but at night they slept with their mothers. With a very little effort on the part of the family carpenter, an ordinary chair could be glorified with

PIONEER FOLK WAYS

rockers for spoiling the babies. Cradles varied from a hollow log contrivance, which could be rocked on its own base, to boxes on rockers of half-barrel heads, or to a fancifully carved or latticed fabrication bespeaking the talent of some man in the family.

Basketry was possible, since willows grew on the creek banks, but a gourd served more purposes than a basket and came easier. Crude baskets of thin splints were not uncommon, however.

Hospitality existed in every home and the latchstring hung outside—but that was because it was made that way. The visitor was always welcome, but at night it took more than a pulling of the latchstring for him to gain entrance. When darkness fell, a stout pole was laid across two tree-fork brackets on the door jambs, and the latchstring worked only when this bar was removed and the household considered itself at home to the night caller. Forked limbs made gun and shelf racks. Shelves also were made by laying boards across pegs stuck in the chinks of the wall.

Shelves were covered with tidies of knitted, crocheted, or hand-tied lace. Large tidies, called lambrequins, were draped over the fireboard, or mantlepiece, on which often stood a square, wooden clock, china and glass ornaments, medicines, shells, pretty rocks, and a large conch or a cow horn used to call the men in from the woods or the field for dinner. After enlarged pictures came into vogue, it was considered tasteful to drape the crude likeness of some departed loved one with hand-embroidered or crocheted throw. The picture album of tintypes made an early appearance in the homes of the pioneers. Among the first photographs were the gilt and red-plush case daguerreotypes sent or brought home by the men who fought in the Civil War. Many an old-timer remembers how as a child he inspected the prized likeness of a dead father or uncle so closely with clumsy little fingers that the features went into a dark smudge and were forever obliterated.

Mirrors, sometimes mere broken pieces, with rather billowy surfaces, occupied a prominent wall space, and under them were comb cases made of curled or folded shucks or papers. The pincushion, fancy or plain, was an important accessory, and the pins and needles it held were so valued that each had individuality. Whenever a scrap of paper, white or colored, came into the household, it was promptly put to some decorative use. Frequently it was made into a flower to pin on the lambrequin. Sometimes a tree branch would be wrapped with colored thread or yarn and studded with flowers made of colored paper, or with birds made of bright yarns or cloth. This contrivance, when stuck firmly between the chinks, was about the most decorative item in the house. Ornaments also were made by stringing vari-colored straws on yarn and hanging them about the walls. Every scrap of paper was prized. Descendants of Mrs. Lucy Taylor of the Erwin community recount that she was heartsick when she discovered that her children had made flowers of a letter she had from her brother, Dr. Tom Taylor, of Dallas.

Box-like shelves with home-woven domestic for curtains were used in the kitchen to hold the dishes. The tables of those with a little nicety were covered with a strip of domestic. A backless bench at the table always served for the children, while the grown-ups sat in chairs. There were no stoves in the first homes. Cooking went on in front of the fireplace. After stove agents began to enter the country, a tale was told of one family that couldn't start a fire—because, as it was found by a neighbor who was called in, they thought the little door for the removal of soot was the opening to the firebox. In one-room homes the fireplace was used for the cooking and for heating.

Sanitation was a little-known term, but nice homemakers knew that scalding water, soap or ashes, and long hours of sunning on the high, outside shelf at the back of the kitchen brought a certain purity and sweetness to the milk crocks or gourds.

PIONEER FOLK WAYS

Short-handled gourds were used for milking; and one with two holes in it, plus a square of cloth, served as a milk strainer. Nice people also hung their drinking gourds out of the cedar water-bucket. Trifling folks left the dipper in the bucket to become soggy and greenish-black with mold. Gourds also were useful for storing soft soap, coffee, brown sugar, shelled peas, beans, corn, dried peppers, popcorn, dried fruit, dried pumpkin, etc. The top of the squatty, fatty gourd was cut carefully so as to make a lid. The newcomers took pride in the gourds they raised, but they were never able to grow as large fatty gourds as back in Georgia or the Carolinas. Molasses and honey did not do so well in gourds but kept better in whisky barrels. Lard kept very well in a well-cleaned gourd; and often a small one was used for the drippings, though likely to be soggy. The soft, home-made lye soap was often stored in a tree trough.

Dishes brought from the older states were guarded with the greatest care, for, until the merchants began to carry queensware, a broken dish meant a catastrophe in the business of keeping house. Very early came the peddlers from Fort Worth with tinware, knives and two-tined forks. They also brought shining tin pails, dishpans, washpans, sifters and candlesticks. Each household had its covered dutch oven for all baking purposes, but in Parker County this was called the skillet and lid. In each well-ordered home were to be found heavy pieces of ironware, including teakettles, shovels, pots with lids, washpots, and lidless skillets for frying. Pothooks for the boiling pots were built firmly into the chimneys. Some homes even had wrought iron andirons, but rocks were often used to support the burning logs in the fireplace.

Tumblers were made by burning a string—greased or saturated with coal oil—tied around a bottle, and immersing it in water to break it at the right place. They were also made by see-sawing a strip of rawhide around a bottle until it was hot and immersing it quickly. The rim was then filed smooth to prevent cutting the mouth or hands. Such a tumbler also served as a spoon-holder. Spoons were frequently of pewter and had to be guarded against overheating. It was not uncommon to melt a pewter spoon by snuffing a candle with it. While the housewife had to watch her pewter, the small girls had to watch their wax-faced dolls to keep them from melting —if they were lucky enough to possess a wax-faced doll. In more prosperous homes there might be imported knives and forks with white bone handles. Butcher knives were often made by a local blacksmith.

Artificial light was produced usually by candles, either dipped or molded. The former were made by dipping the wicks, strung on a stick, into melted tallow and beeswax, and then into cold water, until enough tallow and wax was accumulated by the wick to form the candle. Candle molds were a great convenience to the family. The grease lamp, made by placing a wick or a wadded rag in a utensil filled with tallow or lard, was also used. It smoked up a place quickly, and a very particular housewife soon learned to get as much work done by daylight as possible in order to keep from burning the grease lamp at night. Little brass lamps were brought in by the peddlers. They held as little as a half-pint of kerosene ("coal oil") and were burned without a chimney. Many people were afraid to use them, however.

The fireplace was the home center, and the fire had to burn regardless of the heat of a July or August day. If the fire went out, some member of the family had to take a skillet and go to a neighbor's to borrow a fresh coal. Industrious families prided themselves on never having to borrow fire, but it was simpler to run to a neighbor's for a coal than to strike fire with flint and steel. Matches sold at ten cents for twenty-five. Reckless and improvident cowboys carried them before they became common in thrifty homes. If weather conditions and remote location of a house were not favorable for borrowing fire, it could be started in various ways. The usual method was to spread dry cotton, sprinkled with powder, on a skillet lid, which would then be struck by a hammer or a flint rock. If a spark flew, it stood a good chance of igniting the powder and cotton. Flint and spunk were also used. Whenever a hollow tree was felled, it was examined closely for the precious spunk, to be brought home and kept in a dry place.

The fireplace had to be supplied constantly with dry wood to make the necessary coals for baking, boiling, and frying. The storage of sufficient wood in a one-room cabin to last through a long wet spell was indeed a problem.

Cooking was an art, if it were done properly, and the good cook had to know just how to get her coals in shape, and just how hot they must be for the various foods she prepared. Before putting in the dough she would sprinkle a pinch of corn meal into the skillet and on the lid to test how hot they were. If she knew her business, she could pop an iron pot full to the brim of popcorn without scorching a single grain. She could cook a cake as light as a feather and bake biscuits a golden brown that melted in the mouth.

The diet was entirely free of mayonnaise, but there was a salad made by wilting lettuce, tender mustard and spring onions by pouring hot bacon grease and vinegar over them. The keeping on hand of mother-of-vinegar was almost as important as the keeping of fire. After cucumbers had been soaked in earthen pots or barrels of brine, they were made into pickles by washing them well and covering them with vinegar. Pies were often made of vinegar, and the sheep sorrel was used in the spring to make a pie very much like that of rhubarb. There were many forms of wild greens which the people craved after going through the long winter without a vestige of fresh vegetables. Among these were poke, sour dock, careless weed, purslane ("pursley"), lambs' quarter and many others the trained greens-picker knew about. The story is told in the Beaird family of Jim, who went to the woods with his sister Nancy. She eagerly sought the tender shoots of poke, but he was not interested in the labor involved. Growing tired of following her and carrying the greens, he said, "Nance, the Indians'll get you if you don't quit gathering their veggables." People would search for miles for the first wild onions that stuck up their heads in the spring.

Vegetable gardening was all important. The settlers brought seeds with them, and what they lacked they usually obtained by swapping around with their neighbors. They grew tomatoes, pumpkins, corn, squash, cucumbers, onions, lettuce, mustard, beans, peas, radishes, sage, okra, turnips. They put up kraut for winter use. They roasted corn in the shuck, or fried the green corn. They made hominy with ash lye. They could not wait for the corn to mature to make cornbread, but would take the ears as soon as the milk was set and grate off the grains to make a sticky bread they relished. This they called grated bread.

Wild blackberries, wild plums, hog plums, winter and mustang grapes, black haws and red haws abounded in the new country, and while the first settlers knew nothing about canning, they dried what they could of the wild fruit, and made winter pies of it. A fruit cobbler in season or a green grape pie in the early summer was something to look forward to.

Peaches were among the first of the cultured fruits to be introduced. The crop was first saved by drying, but along in the eighties the housewives began to learn to can their peaches in glass jars—an innovation which met the disapproval of many who could not believe the fruit would be fit to eat. Bunch raisins, which the people called "reesons," and dried apples could be purchased at the stores around Christmas time, but all tropical fruits were oddities for years. Apple wagons from Arkansas came through the country now and then—with a fruit-laden limb sticking out for a sign. Teachers in the log schools would patronize the apple peddlers and give their pupils a treat. Mrs. W. P. Wynn, a Parker county pioneer, recalls that Mr. Griffith, teacher at the Erwin School about 1873, treated the children one day with brown sugar, serving it on little squares of paper. Apples were such a rarity and were held in such wholesome esteem by the pioneers that they often had their tintype pictures struck while holding an apple fondly in the hand. Sometimes they held a rose, but roses were as rare as apples.

Poor doo—a very different viand from "poor doe," frontier slang for venison—was a dish often served in the pioneer home. It was made by crumbling cold cornbread into a skillet of grease and pouring in enough hot water to make a soup-like consistency. With less water, and cooked down with a few sliced onions, this made another dish which bore the appropriately homely name of cush—pronounced as in *cushion*. Crumble-in, cornbread crumbled into a glass of sweet milk, was a favorite with the children, as was sweetened clabber. Mush was a staple of the diet, and cornbread was the staff of life. It was usually made into pones without leavening. Corn was the principal grain food in the early days because it was easier to get milled than wheat. Many homes had their own grist mills, which were operated by a primitive contrivance called a show tom. At first, wheat had to be ground at Witt's mill, which was sixty-three miles east of Weatherford. Many took their wheat to McKinney. In 1857 Judge W. F. Carter installed a steam flour mill for corn grinding at Weatherford. Those who did not grind their corn at home could take it to Vardy's mill at Veal Station and have it turned into meal on the shares. During the seventies, a concerted effort was made through the granges of the Patrons of Husbandry to boycott the flour mills when they ceased handling the farmers' wheat direct. At first, the mill returned to the customer his flour, bran, shorts and middlings, taking a portion of each for pay. But when the mills began merely buying the wheat and forcing the farmer to buy his flour from the stores and to do without his bran, shorts and middlings, unless these too were purchased back, there was much protest. The people quit raising wheat, although they had prided themselves on the fine quality of this grain which their county could grow. They waged a futile war against the middle-man; however, they never did go back to wheat raising with their old-time enthusiasm.

Coffee, boiled of course, was considered almost a necessity, but during the Civil War the settlers learned to like a hot drink made of parched grain—corn, acorns, okra, and other substitutes. Coffee was purchased in the green kernel and was roasted at home. If the family had no coffee mill and lived near no fortunate neighbor, the parched kernels had to be cracked by hand. Often the family had a mortar and pestle which could be used for this purpose. Otherwise, a wooden mallet on a block of wood sufficed. It was nothing uncommon to see babies fed on sweetened coffee—and the mothers would have been considered neglectful of their duty had they not chewed for their babies.

The home-building settlers of Parker County had milk, unlike the first colonists in the State, and many who came later. They always tried to find a good spring near which to erect their cabins, and a spring house was usually constructed for the keeping of milk. If there was no spring house, the smokehouse could be utilized by scooping out a place on the ground for the milk and butter crocks, the place being kept damp. Sometimes the family cats gained access to the smokehouse and made inroads on the cream, much to the discomfort of the entire household. If there was no smokehouse, the hams and sides of meat could be cured by outdoor smoking, the meat being hung later from the rafters of the cabin along with onions and strings of peppers. There was always a way to keep the grub.

Frying, of course, was the easiest method of cooking, and into the stomachs of the pioneers went unlimited quantities of fritters (which they called "flitters"), fried pies, fried eggs, sausage, chicken, buffalo and beef steak, bacon, some fish, squirrel, and rabbit—if there was no other kind of meat available—all fried. They had venison, fresh or jerked, quail, prairie hens, wild turkeys, which they called up with the hollow shank of a turkey's leg bone, and now and then a fat opossum. Dumplings were made often, as there were nearly always quantities of beef or chicken stock on hand. At branding time there was that delicacy known as the mountain oyster, unless the women folks were too finicky about cooking it, and tripe and chitterlings were properly prepared at hog-killing time, which also brought in its quota of spare-ribs, crackling bread, souse, and backbones. Hunting went on constantly.

Pumpkin bread was made from the dried pumpkins. Honey from bee trees was plentiful, but care had to be taken not to eat too much of the green honey. Most of the sweet liquid from a tree-cutting was brought home in the comb and left to cure. The wildflowers on the "pararas" afforded the bees with a fine field stretching for miles with honey-laden blossoms. Here and there a family succeeded in luring a hive of swarming bees to some rudely built gum, which was easy to rob. Eggs and sweet potatoes were baked in the ashes, not because the family possessed no cooking vessel but because the pioneer liked a little of the ash flavor in his cooking. Custards, pies, and cakes did not stump the good housewife. She could cook anything with her skillet and lid.

All the buffalo had been driven out of the county by 1876, but adventuresome men, John Stratton among them, would follow the herds westward and kill them by the scores for their hides and tallow. These hunters would run in home with a few choice cuts to be cured by scalding in hot brine. Smokehouses proved their worth during the Civil War. When the people found themselves without salt, it was a lucky day when someone remembered the brine encrusted on the smokehouse floors. The dirt surface was carefully scooped up and dissolved in barrels of water. The water was then boiled down to a strong brine that brought back the zest to meat and vegetables. Jerking of beef or venison was common, the blow-fly seeming not to exist. Some sheep were raised, but more for the fleece than for mutton. Goats were difficult to keep and were rarely included in the stock of domestic animals. After a heavy rain there were always perch and catfish in the Clear Fork. The settlers said they swam up from the Trinity River when the water was high.

The pioneers soon found that sorghum grew well. They usually planted it on a cow lot that had not been used too long, moving the cows into a fresh enclosure of rails or piled brush. In the crudest manner they made their first molasses, squeezing the juice by hand and cooking it in open pots. Soon syrup mills sprang up in various communities. The presses had wooden rollers and wooden cogs, a horse supplying the power. Flat evaporating tanks were introduced in time, and the places where molasses was being made were focal points in the communities. After the sorghum-making was over, a great molasses candy-pulling usually followed.

The people liked their sweets. Molasses, honey, brown sugar, crystalline pink or white rock candy, and red-striped sticks of white sugar candy helped fill their "sweet teeth." From the earliest time the stores handled the little white heart-shaped peppermint lozenges with verses printed on them, an adjunct to the art of courting. Many a proposal and acceptance was handled by the interchanged lozenge, it is said. Large candy hearts with elaborate decorations on them were purchased by the swains for their best girls. Mrs. Wynn recalls a grange dinner at Central at which a cake decorated with these large hearts was placed on the table. It won the admiration of everyone; but, on its being cut, the interest died out as each person served discovered that something had gone wrong in the baking and the cake itself was not fit to eat. The candy hearts themselves, she said, looked the part, but there was not much eating to them, as they consisted of sugared curlicues, verses, lithographed cupids, and pasteboard forget-me-nots.

The only supplies which had to be purchased by the pioneer were salt, soda, coffee, sugar, dyes and matches; but he could often make-shift for most of these. In the first years he even grew his own tobacco. Molasses and honey could be substituted for brown sugar and often were. He could parch grain and call it coffee. He could kindle his fire with flint and spunk. The housewife could use barks, plants, or clay for dye. Bread could be leavened by the salt-rising process, but there was no substitute for salt. From some source it had to be purchased.

Home industries, of necessity, flourished in the new country prior to, during, and long after the Civil War. Outside the importation of dishes, ironware, some cutlery, cedar buckets and clocks, the average family could get along somehow. From the first there was a division of labor. One farmer who could do blacksmithing would open up a little shop in which he would repair articles, make plowshares and horseshoes, recondition the tarpole wagons, or what not. He might even be a wheelwright. Someone would put up a syrup mill or a cotton gin, while another would specialize in harness-making or the cobbling of shoes. Some knew more than others about branding or house-raising or well digging. Labor was swapped for labor or for useful products.

Spinning, weaving, and dying all the textiles needed in the home was the woman's province. The cutting and making of garments was negligible when compared to the task of getting a piece of cloth ready to cut. In the face of the worst odds the Parker County women did all they could to keep up a high standard of style. They came to the new county wearing hoopskirts and spitcurls, and whether it was the Grecian bend or leg-of-mutton sleeves in New York was a matter of concern all the way down to Parker County. There was never a time except during the Civil War when the women had to depend entirely upon the products of their looms. They could buy pure silk, which lasted a lifetime, with good care, in the Weatherford stores for a dollar a yard, and they could buy pretty calico prints for a bit. Nun's veiling was a popular woolen for Sunday wear. But they knew how to weave and they had little money. There was a certain virtue in doing one's own weaving. It bespoke one's talent, industry, and duty to a time-old tradition. The family would journey to Weatherford on an all-day wagon trip to buy a few needed articles, perhaps a silk dress pattern for one of the women, a fancy reticule for a grandmother who had stayed at home with a neighbor, or a portmanteau for the horseback trip one of the men might be planning back to Arkansas.

During the seventies *Harper's Magazine* was among the periodicals that came to the W. T. Taylor home, and the daughters were overjoyed when a paper dress pattern accompanied it. With a new idea of something to wear they had news for every woman in the countryside. The dressing had to go on. The women and girls were always exchanging patterns as the style changed in sleeves, bonnets, or basques. Knitting, crochet, and tatting patterns and quilt designs also were exchanged. Hats of the finest sort with shirred silk underlinings, velvet bows, plumes, or artificials could always be bought in Weatherford. Women affected all the little fads that came and went, and whenever a new woman came in from one of the older states, some new style idea she brought was sure to sweep the settlement.

Men could buy hats in Weatherford and have their best suits made by tailors. Carroll Sullivan, who lived in the Erwin community, was a farmer, but he took time out to make men's hats of sheep's wool. Store-bought pants with a crease down the front of the leg were frowned upon by the best dressers. Many women were forced to make all the clothes their men folks wore. They even plaited hats of straw for them to wear in the fields. Brogans were made at home or by a neighbor cobbler, but dress shoes had to be selected in the stores.

Long after the Civil War some settlers continued to pick their cotton off the seed, though gins were rapidly being installed. Smythe records twenty-seven gins in the county in 1877 and a cotton production of six thousand bales a year. As the members of the family plied their various industries at night, each child was given a task to do. It might be a certain amount of lint to pick from the seed, or a basket of beans or corn to shell. The children helped with all the work at home or in the fields. It was their duty to bring in the wood and the chips, to watch for fires, to help patch the chinks in the walls, to "pull off" the calves while a grown-up did the milking.

The knitting never stopped except for Sunday. A woman would knit as she walked to and from her visits with the neighbors or as she rode in a wagon or ox-cart. When a hole wore in a sock she didn't darn it but raveled it and knit in a new heel or toe. The spinning wheel had a fascination for a woman. She liked to hear it hum. And she liked to weave, for weaving gave her a chance to display her talent in art. In fancy coverlids she could run the gamut in color and design. She liked to see a web of cloth grow under her fingers—linsey-woolsey for herself and daughters, jeans for the men, domestic for a hundred and one purposes. She didn't have to wait around for the plumber, or radio, telephone, or sweeper repair man if anything went wrong in the household. She usually knew how to do her own repairing, and went ahead with the business in hand.

Some buckskin was worn for hunting and heavy work, and caps were sometimes made of dressed deerskin with the hair side out. The dressing of hides was one of the principal home industries, the buffalo hide being used for shoe leather and cowhide for innumerable purposes. Cat and squirrel skins were used for shoestrings. Halters, harness, hinges, chair bottoms—made more commonly of rawhide—and even thimbles were made of leather. Rawhide was used for the first clotheslines, was handy for repairing saddles, and served for bed cords that would last a lifetime. In some instances halters and ropes were made of horse or cow tail hairs. Each home had its graining block and tanning trough. Home-made lye was used to loosen the hair on the hides, and sumac or blackjack bark was used in tanning them.

For many years the weaving of carpets was unimportant. The idea of a carpet on a puncheon floor was a little ridiculous. In the eighties, when frame homes were springing up like mushrooms and the log cabins were becoming eyesores to the progressive citizens, the need for carpets arose. The very prosperous families laid their new pine floors with ingrain carpets from the eastern mills, but the average housewife was glad enough when she had accumulated enough bright-colored rags to have them woven up either at home or by one of the few women who went into the carpet-weaving business as a means of making a living. Mrs. Nancy Beaird Taylor, one of the best-known carpet weavers, plied her trade near Poolville until 1910, when she moved with her daughter, Mrs. W. P. Wynn, to Uvalde County. The rag carpet craze had about run its course at the time, and people were already beginning to buy art squares.

There were many things the pioneer woman could weave if the necessity arose—galluses, girths, saddle blankets, bed cords. She could do anything with her needle that could be done with any needle. All she had to see was the need. Odd pieces from garment making were always worked up into quilt tops. Bright prints were so scarce that quilt-making did not flourish as a fine art in the early days. Every woman knew how to card her bats for a quilt and knew how to lace it into the frame for quilting. There was nearly always a quilt in the frame, rolled up on its hangings to the pole joists at night or when she was too busy in the daytime with other duties to quilt. The home industries never left her a moment to sit and hold her hands.

Dyeing was a problem all to itself. Finding a color was one thing and setting it was another. Aniline for red and indigo for blue were on the early market, and various mordants were used to set them. The pioneer woman knew that urine was a fair mordant for indigo, and an inexpensive one. Its use probably gave rise to the expression, "stinks like a blue-dye pot." Sumac yielded a purplish black, and mulberry roots or copperas produced yellow. Various tan effects were obtained by the use of blackjack bark, and a dirty-looking, purplish gray from milk purslane.

The women often held weaving contests with each other. At visiting time two would discover that they were ready to begin a new web of cloth, and one would wager the other that she could finish first. So great was their enthusiasm at a weaving race that they often sat up all night at the loom and called in other members of the family to keep the shuttle going. Holland *(The Double Log Cabin)* cites the instance in which a young lady spun and wove sixty-three yards of linsey-woolsey, using cotton instead of flax, and sold it in Fort Worth for a dollar a yard to make money for her trousseau.

Washing was strictly an outdoor industry. Tree blocks supported the whisky barrel tubs, and also served as battling blocks. The clothes were hand-rubbed and then battled with a wooden paddle until the dirt was loosened. They were boiled in iron pots over blazing coals. Soap was made from the rendered discards of hog fat saponified by ash lye. Each home had its ash hopper through which water was allowed to drip slowly to form a fairly strong lye. The soap was of the soft variety and had to be stored in troughs or gourds. After the weekly washing the chairs and benches were all scoured and allowed to bleach in the sun until they were nearly white. Puncheons were scoured regularly. Indigo was used for bluing the clothes, and starch was made either of green corn or wheat flour. If green corn was used, the grains were sliced off and the cobs were scraped carefully. The mass was well washed and strained, and left for the starch particles to settle to the bottom of a tub. The water was then drained and the starch was dried in the sun and stored for future use. To make flour starch, which could be made at any time, the flour was added to a quantity of water and beaten until the gluten was collected in a solid mass and could be lifted from the water, leaving the starch behind. In either case, the starch was boiled before it was used. Flatirons were almost as important in the household as the skillet and lid, but many housewives did without them as a sort of pet economy. In such cases they did not starch their clothes but pulled them and shook them dry with care.

In the summertime the family toilette was made outdoors. The tin or gourd washpan sat on its block of wood, and over it hung the family towel and comb. Luxurious castile soap from the stores was sometimes used for washing the face and hands, but a dipper of soft soap more frequently sufficed for everyday use. Nice people bathed on Saturdays, one at a time, using a washtub in the kitchen. If there was only one room, other members of the family found outside chores to do while one took a bath. If there was a creek handy, in the summertime it saved a lot of water carrying for baths. Some of the early women settlers were far too modest to bathe in the creek. Some of them were too modest to strip off at any time all their clothes at once. Mrs. Lucy Taylor, who at the age of eighty-six was buried in 1908 in the Erwin Cemetery, was proud that she had never been wholly naked since the mid-wife who attended her mother had washed and dressed her at birth.

Soldiers were stationed in the fort at Jacksboro during and after the Civil War, and the Parker County people were fortunate enough to get orders from the garrison for corn. The entire family would be called into action to fill these orders, and blistered hands usually followed their hurried efforts. George Taylor, young son of W. T. and Lucy Taylor, conceived the idea of a corn-sheller, but his father hooted at the idea and forbade his taking time to work out his wild notion. He was about fourteen years old and had a head of his own. When his father was away, he would slip into the woods and tinker with his invention. Sometimes he hid out at night and worked by the light of a brush fire. When his father saw that the machine really worked, he was very proud of George. Wheat was threshed by the tramping of horses over the grain, the chaff being blown away as the wheat was poured in the wind from a vessel held high over the head to one on the ground. About three miles from The Pool was the Shadle Rock, a large flat surface, to which people would come for miles around with their wheat and horses for threshing day. This selfsame rock has since been crushed and used in building the highway from Fort Worth to Jacksboro.

The first settlers fenced off their little farms with rows of brush, fences that helped protect the crops from wandering herds but wouldn't turn a cow if she were determined. Timber was scarcely heavy enough to make a practice of logrolling in clearing the land. The ground was burned off after the first clearing to kill the weed and grass seed. The burning off of the land after each harvest was strictly believed in and was practiced for years before the farmer learned that the soil was enriched by turning under the vines and stalks.

Fencing was necessary for the protection of the family and of the crops from Indians and stock. The expert rail splitter would divide a log into sixths or eighths with his maul and wedge. He was someone to be looked up to; so was the fence builder who could lay the zig-zag row so well that it would stand a half-century before falling down. Stake-and-rider fences were seldom used in the early years, as wire for lashing the stakes together at the top was virtually a necessity—and the people did not have wire.

When barbed wire fences came into vogue and the land was fenced against the wandering herds—as well as the rustlers—there was a general uproar as to the humaneness of their use, and against blocking the way for horseman or herd. The screw worm came along with the barbed wire and gave the farmers another duty to add to the daily program, which began at four in the morning and ended only late at night. The rail fences around the homes were, by the children, nearly always picked clean of bark to be used for kindling. Gates were made of small poles lashed on rough boards. Picket fences were common for use around the yard or the vegetable gardens, but when the family heard the angry lowing of bulls in the mating season, they barred the door and prayed that the animals would not meet within their picketed enclosures. These bull fights were common, at noon or night as they chanced to be, and those who happened to witness one were awed by the horror of it. Often one of the bulls was gored and stamped to death, but sometimes they fought until each was worn out and backed off peacefully from the other.

Planting was largely done in hills. Before the grubs were removed and a plow could be put in the soil, a forked stick was used to plant the seeds in hand-dug furrows. Often the planting was done on the site of burnt brush heaps before the clearing could be finished. Especially did tobacco have to be planted on a clean place. The men smoked pipes and chewed tobacco. Some of the energetic ones smoked shuck-rolled cigarettes. The older women chewed tobacco and smoked pipes. Most of the young ones dipped snuff, which they made by drying the tobacco leaves on a warm skillet lid, pounding them to a powder, and sifting to remove the stems. The growing of tobacco played out along in the eighties, because the home-grown variety proved to be inferior to that imported from Kentucky, Virginia, and the Carolinas.

Broom corn was grown for the making of round brooms, which were used at least once a day for a general sweeping of the puncheon floors and for occasional brushing up as lint and other debris accumulated. These brooms also were used injudiciously to sweep the yards down to the very clay. If she were a housekeeper at all, the pioneer woman could not stand the sight of loose dirt. As fast as sand worked up from the ground, she got out her broom and swept it far from her sight.

She built up her flower beds ridiculously high with boards or rocks, believing that was the way to plant flowers. The bordered elevation did keep little chickens from scratching up the seedlings, but it necessitated the carrying of quantities of water from the spring or creek; and when the hot weather increased this task to the breaking point, she let the beds dry up, making a new start the next spring.

Wild flowers bloomed everywhere, many varieties of which are said to be now extinct. In the woodlands and on the prairies, the bright patches of red, blue, purple, pink, and yellow flowers helped the newcomer to forget some of his hardships. There were sweet william, balmonia, blue sage, white daisies, Texas pink stars, coreopsis, gaillardia, buttercups, johnny-jump-ups, hollyhocks, sheep sorrel, primroses, wild honeysuckle, niggerheads, and many other varieties. The red and black haws, box elder, wild plums, berries and redbud bloomed along the creek banks, and in the early spring the Clear Fork and its vicinity was redolent with the fragrance of the winter grape blossoms.

There were few roses in the yards. The Hemphills at Veal Station had some bushes of the common, early-blooming variety, and while they lacked much that a rose must have today, Mrs. Wynn says she recalls how these bushes flaunted their pink and red colors and their pure rose fragrance at her when she was a small child. The flowers mostly used for yard planting were mallow, old maids, zinnias, sunflowers, hollyhocks, bouncing betty, morning-glories, four-o'clocks, rose moss, balsam vines, cypress vines, and pinks. Flowering shrubs early included the lilac, tamarisk, and bird-of-paradise. Hanging baskets of wandering jew or rose moss usually had a place, and many homes had small beds of the native cacti.

Chickens did well on the new land, and around every cabin were to be found speckled and odd-colored hens and a red rooster or two. Geese, ducks, turkeys, and some guineas were raised. Besides the oxen, cattle, horses, mules, sheep and hogs, there were always a bunch of brindle or spotted cats and a Bulger, a Joler and a Dash or two of the mongrel canine family.

Before cotton reached its heyday in the South, the people made what money they could by the sale of their livestock, corn, hides, tallow and syrup. The native grasses fattened the horses and cows, and the hogs fed on the acorn mast. Prairie hay abounded in the uplands, and almost everywhere was sage grass. The traveling grasshoppers came down several seasons from Kansas and stripped crops and grasslands to the stem. The producer was out little money; so when he did find a market his profit was almost net. He had to go often through mud and rain to reach his market, but only his labor was involved. Produce was sold in Weatherford, Fort Worth, McKinney, and Jacksboro. Buyers for the cattle kings usually rounded up the few head of livestock the average family could dispense with each year.

The Patrons of Industry was organized in 1874 with fifteen granges scattered throughout the county. On the Clear Fork there was a grange in the Central community. Its members found that it not only provided them with collective powers by which they hoped to better themselves commercially, but that it also gave them a new social diversion. The latter was probably the most important thing the grange did for the people. Its high purpose of better prices by direct selling came to naught, but there was much fun at the initiations, and the members enjoyed the curiosity they provoked among non-members.

Among other things that the Parker County soil would do was to grow watermelons, and they were raised almost from the start, although it was not until about 1900 that the nation began to learn about Parker County melons. G. A. Holland of Weatherford and Luther Lytle of Peaster took twelve Triumph melons to the World's Fair in St. Louis in 1904, and brought the gold medal back with them. The melons totaled 1,185 pounds, ranging from 96 to 106 pounds each. The sightseers at the fair were amazed at the size of the melons, and public cuttings had to be staged to assure them that the exhibit was not a fake. Long before this time Bill Sullivan of the Erwin community had made a local name for himself as a melon grower, and people in the Poolville section who had had less luck with their melons would wait anxiously until Sullivan came along the road with a wagonful of the green motley beauties which he sold for a dime or fifteen cents each.

A diversity of work went on all the time. There was the constant attention demanded by the stock, the driving of the herds to water, the hauling of water for home use if the spring or well went dry, the problem of combating the heel-fly, which created havoc among the oxen.

PIONEER FOLK WAYS

To escape the heel-flies the animals would make a wild dash for the creek, likely as not throwing down and dragging their driver. At last when the owner had located them—usually stuck in the mud—it was no easy problem to get them back into harness again. If he found them bogged down in mud, he had to throw a rope around their horns and drag them out on horseback.

House and crib raisings were held when a family saw need for more shelter for itself, its livestock, or its crops. People would be invited from the neighboring farms for an all-day get-together. The women would spend the morning at cooking, while the men ripped the bark off the new logs and built them into neat structures. The women would knit or quilt in the afternoons. Sometimes rail splittings were occasions for similar social affairs.

The abundance of red clay stimulated brick-making. Many of the early business houses and some of the homes in Weatherford were made of brick, and even the country dwellers soon were using the brick for their chimneys. John Martin built a number of kilns in the Poolville territory, and the settlers were given their first jobs as factory workers. The brick, however, was inferior, and after a few years the industry died out altogether.

In each community some men specialized in coffin-making, and when anybody died he was promptly informed and given the measurements of the dead body. He would make the coffin of boards, covering it with black velveteen or black calico and adding silvered handles, which were carried in stock at the stores. The family would bear the expenses of the coffin materials, but the maker donated his work.

Wagon roads were a problem in bad weather, but they did fairly well when it was fair. In the horse age, there were always wagon yards in Weatherford, furnished by the merchants for their country customers. It was fun for a group of neighbors to go to Weatherford the same day and put up for a night at a wagon yard. The places usually were filthy. Manure was seldom removed from the stalls provided for the teams. The yard itself was strewn with fodder stalks and debris. The houses usually had a fireplace for warmth and for cooking, a creaky table, and a bench and chairs. The floors were caked with dirt. But it was all free, and the users, who seldom had enough money to stop at a hotel, could manage for a night, and they thrilled at the opening of bought canned goods—sardines, potted ham, grapes, or peaches—and cheese and crackers which they added to their feast of coffee, freshly fried bacon, and baskets of grub they had prepared at home.

Sometimes a crowd of neighbors would venture down south of Weatherford to the Brazos River and spend a few days picking up pecans. At night they would gather around a big fire and play games and tell tales and sing songs.

The people were highly social and neighborly. In times of sickness the men would fall in and lay a neighbor's crop by, and at night they would take time about sitting up with the patient. Neighbors were always willing to help at corn shellings, house raisings, quiltings. They joined together at bee-tree cuttings. Social contacts also were provided at church, singings, baptizings, brandings, picnics, box suppers, shivarees for newlyweds, melon slicings, candy pullings, infairs, play parties, weddings, dances, funerals.

Literary and debating societies were popular after the schools were established. Many a speech was first tried out on the stumps in some new clearing. The spelling bee went hand-in-hand with the old blue-back spelling book. Many spellers knew every word in the book as well as the page number and column in which it appeared. Play parties were permitted by the church members, and a candy pulling or breaking was usually thrown in for good measure. They played snap, fruit-basket, post-office, spin-the-pan, and many marching and singing games. But dances were dances, and nothing as tame as a candy-breaking marred an all-night fling. Supper sometimes would be served by the host and hostess at midnight to give strength to their guests, who did not expect to depart until daylight. From the time the host would cry out gaily to approaching guests, "Light down!" or "Light and look at your saddle!" the revelry was on.

There was much fun when a newcomer invaded the social circles and was taken to his first badger fight or on his first snipe hunt, both of these being "sells." Physical strength was always admired. The best rail splitter, the strongest weigh lifter, the longest or highest jumper, the most accurate marksman, or the best wrestler was champion for the day. The young men sparred, pitched baseball, ran foot and horse races, and sometimes the more agile performed on horizontal bars. Swimming was uncommon, and a woman seldom knew how to swim. Riding horses well was indispensable for both men and women, but the women never raced. Under no circumstances did a lady ride astride. Even the little girls had to sit sideways behind their mothers when they were taken on horseback. The women wore long riding habits made of black calico, and if a woman's horse ran away with her, she was liable to get entangled with her stirrup and long skirt, but modesty had to be served.

Card games often enlivened the winter evenings for those who felt they could wait until summer to begin afresh with the church. Poker, euchre, casino, checkers, and dominoes were common. Among the games played by the children and adolescents were fox-and-the-goose, mumble-peg, jacks, club fist, hull gull, William Trimbletoe, base, blind-fold, one-eyed cat, ring-around-the-rosie, hide-and-seek, whip-jacket, hiding the switch, thimble, frog-in-the-middle, drop the handkerchief, bull pen and leap frog. Country children spent much time in playing house, building their make-believe homes in the woods with piles of small tree boughs, and visiting from house to house as the chief entertainment. They could always amuse themselves by searching in the woods and fields for pretty rocks, clearballs, inkballs, sunflower wax and stretchberries, for hackberries and other ripened wild fruit, popballs, elderberry shoots for making whistles, or for elm or hackberry roots to be used for toothbrushes.

The sands of the Clear Fork and of Sandy Holler were ideal for the building of toad cities. The toad house was built by scooping out damp sand, inserting a small foot in the hole, and packing the sand back around the foot, after which the foot was removed with great care lest the house fall in. The children built cabins of corn cobs while their elders shucked and shelled corn—and at other times too. They would play for hours at making mud puddles of the semi-quicksand, at crude modeling with clay, at swinging on vines of the wild grape, or at ridey-horsey on saplings they bent down. Their chewing gum of sunflower wax and stretchberry was excellent for popping, but it was never the treat that sugar-coated gum, which stores began to carry soon after the Civil War, became.

Gossip, of course, was one of the chief pastimes. Women sometimes stepped off the straight and narrow path, and wise heads nodded thereafter. If a woman separated from her husband, she usually was blamed for the marital failure, but if she were any part a lady, she would not further disgrace herself by getting a divorce. A more grievous plight than ever was for a woman to fail to get married before she was twenty-five. No one in his senses would marry an old maid of twenty-five or past. Women liked to talk about the slovens in their neighborhood——triflin', they called them. Why, they made butter with cow tracks in it, it was so vile smelling. They couldn't make an apple pie bed. They stitched their selvage seams together instead of whipping them. Their spinning rolls were bull-tails, bulky and not suitable for the making of good thread. They were the kind of people who had no turkey-red embroidery on white pillowshams, who let the fire go out, who had to borrow soft soap, who didn't keep the weevils out of their seed peas, who let their gourds get soggy.

The people were superstitious in general, and little did they dream that the finding of well water by means of a "water witch" might be a practice that scientists would one day laugh at. It was true that the switch operated better in the hands of certain persons, but many a man who was proud of his well of water would relate that he saw with his own eyes how the switch nearly twisted in two when it was brought to the coveted spot. Walking under ladders, the hearing of screech owls, the accidental donning of a garment wrong-side out—all these and many other superstitions brought the supernatural into play in the lives of the pioneers.

Back in the seventies when John Pope married Ellen Montgomery of Jacksboro, the Clear Fork neighbors all gathered at the Chelsea Pope home near The Pool for the infare. The cakes and custards were cooked and all was in readiness. Darkness fell and the guests had all assembled, but John and Ellen did not come. The guests joked about their being late to their own infare— the second day celebration after a wedding—and gossiped and milled about, and still John and Ellen did not come. Finally, Mrs. Pope picked up her broom and began to sweep.

"Don't sweep after dark, Mrs. Pope," someone advised her anxiously. "You'll sweep a member out of your family."

"One has already been swept out of this family!" she cried, sweeping all the harder, and breaking into loud sobs. John was not swept out of the family, however, but he and Ellen did not arrive until the next day.

Many of the first settlers brought the chills and fever with them, but once they were successfully combated with liberal doses of quinine they disappeared. There were few mosquitoes on the Clear Fork and probably no malaria-bearing ones. Smallpox was a dread disease, but the settlers already knew a person could be inoculated against it by the transfer of virus from the sore of another. Some member of the family took a needle and scratched the arms of the others and wiped on to the raw surface a little pus from another's sore. Considerable effort was made to keep a sore alive somewhere in the community at all times for the benefit of those who hadn't "taken." Red eyes was a common affliction because people all used the same towel in a family and even gave it to the visitor to use. They never became immune to the disease but had it time and again. A little breast milk was used to cure the babies' eyes, or rather to help them cure themselves. But the grown-ups used a medicine they made of red seal or yellow puccoon. When a woman got an attack she donned a large green calico sunbonnet which she believed gave her much relief. But head lice was something they had no cure for except hand picking. They believed the vermin dropped from the heads of Indians as they made their raids. Scabies was not very prevalent.

There were many home remedies, some tinged with superstition. They used a tea of the soft inner bark of the blackjack for the flux. A tea of the white part of chicken droppings was given to babies for the hives. Balmonia tea was a laxative as well as senna, which they grew in their gardens. Nightshade also was grown for use in poulticing boils and other forms of swelling, and poultices also were made of the root of prickly pear. A salve boiled down of the stems of the Spanish dagger was used for rubbing the breasts during pregnancy. Lobelia tea produced vomiting, and the antidote for excessive vomiting was a tea made of the pulverized lining of chicken gizzards.

Whooping cough, measles and mumps went the rounds. Visitors carried the germs to and from their homes. Every visitor was asked if he wanted to wash up before eating, and, as a courtesy to his host, he did, using the family towel and comb. He might even be too ill to leave after a night's lodging but he would never insult his host by offering to pay for the care he necessitated. Stock hunters and horse-traders would be away from their homes for days at a time, staying here and there, but they never insulted their hosts by offering to pay for a meal or a night's lodging, or for feed for their saddle horses. The latchstring did hang out.

The school houses were used for gatherings of all sorts, for church and singing on Sunday, for box suppers on Saturday nights, for Friday afternoon speeches by the children. Plays and minstrels were given frequently by the young folks, and if the memory of the old-timers is to be trusted, these amateurs were just about as good as Richard Mansfield or Al. G. Fields. Calisthenics was taken up in the nineties as a genteel art and exercise by the ladies. They became very proficient with the dumbbells, but some who ventured to put on bloomers came very near to dismissal from the church. In Weatherford some of the women dared to ride bicycles, and about the turn of the century some of them learned to swim. Holland records an item from the Weatherford *News* of 1876 which recounts the doings of a literary society. Miss Bettie Rider gave the address of welcome. Miss Fannie Goodlett offered an essay on "Whom We Should Marry." Miss Katy Lewis made "A Plea for Old Maids." Miss Susie Couts recited "The World Moves," and John O. Ford made the principal address on the topic, "Should the Bible Be Abolished from Our School?"

There was much good fiddling in Parker County, both in the homes and at dances. Henry and Joe Gilliland, Big Jim Brawley, Eck Robertson, J. E. Clifton, and Will Wynn were among those who played on the Clear Fork; Arch Bozzell was the head player on Bear Creek. "Sallie Goodin," "Old Dan Tucker," "Cotton-Eyed Joe," "Money Musk," "Soldier's Joy," "Billy in the Low Ground," "Buffalo Gals," "Eighth of January," "Turkey in the Straw," and whatever they had heard from any other fiddler at any time made up the repertoire of these musicians. As many fiddlers played as would come to a dance, and if the floors were too crowded to accommodate all the guests at once, some of the men would sit near the fiddlers and strike their strings with knitting needles, both to amplify the volume of music and to keep themselves in motion. If a dance was planned for days ahead and elaborate supper arrangements made, it was called a ball. Sometimes it was a subscription ball at which each man bore the expense of the supper eaten by himself and his partner. The bigger the home, the more in demand it was for dances, but if the hosts had but one room, the dancers were not dismayed. They moved all the furniture outside and the dance went on.

The W. T. Taylor family had grown to such proportions that it was necessary to build a four-room log and frame house in 1875, a part of which still stands in the Erwin settlement. This was one of the largest houses in the whole countryside, and when it was finished word went out that a great housewarming was to be held. The people came from up and down the hollows of the Clear Fork, from Walnut Creek, from Slipdown, and from The Pool. It was a religious family and the daughters were not allowed to dance, but the guests wanted to. Fiddlers had come expecting to play. Taylor soon sensed the wishes of the throng, and gave the word to dance. By the time the fiddlers tuned up, the men and boys had moved enough furniture out of the house for the first set. Soon they were dancing all over the new house, and it was declared one of the biggest dances the community had ever seen.

Jeff Voyles, one of the shrewdest horse traders the country ever produced, became one of the best dance callers in the section. One of his sons, Claude Voyles of Austin, delights in telling the tale that his father as a lad in Arkansas was once soundly whipped because he told on returning from a circus about a man who rode a strange, two-wheeled vehicle called a bicycle. His father tanned Jeff good, so the story runs, because he tolerated no lying in his family. Jack Holland, from Kentucky, also was expert at calling the dance. He was given to featuring his sets with the elbow swing, and ending them dramatically with the figure, trail home.

The average home allowed for sets of four or six couples in a square set. The fiddler had to have enough room in which to bend his elbows and stamp his feet. The caller did or did not dance. If more couples were present than could dance in one room, a set was made up in another room if there was one and perhaps a set or two on the porch if it wasn't too cold. Sometimes so many came to a dance that the girls had to stand against the walls or in the corners while the boys hung around outside, perhaps with a bottle to keep them company.

Thus, Dean T. U. Taylor, of the University of Texas, who was reared in Parker County, describes the dance movements and calls. The fiddlers would tune up; the boys would grab their partners; and the caller would begin, "Circle left! Honor your partner! Lady on the left! Join hands and circle left! Break, and promenade for home!"

That usually concluded the first figure, and into the second they would go to the call, "Balance all!" with all dancers doing their individual stunts. The boys usually got to the center, where some cut the pigeon-wing. Others did the back-step, the double shuffle, the hoe-down, or the clog. The girls kept time to the music as they formed a broken circle around the men until the shrill voice of the caller sang out some such doggerel as, "Toes to the center! Back to the wall! Take a chaw of tobacker, and promenade all!" Then they found partners and places again.

These were only preliminary figures to the main dance, which usually consisted of the "right and left," the "dos-a-dos," "chase the goose," and "cage the bird." As the set progressed, the caller used his ingenuity in side remarks. The dancers went through the figures with mechanical perfection, following only the general directions of the caller. When he would bellow out some remark like "Shake a leg," "Hit it up," or "All stampede," the dancers would smile, but they would keep on dancing. The calling was principally to fill in. In the dos-a-dos figure, a common call, sung out in a high pitch, "Move along! Everybody dance! The girls may skip! The boys may prance!" was enough to put everyone in a gay frame of mind.

Most sets ended with the figure, cage the bird. "First couple to the right," the caller would begin, "Hands all around! Cage the bird!" The girl of the first couple would move to the center while her partner and the boy and girl of the second couple would clasp hands and dance around her. The caller would go on, "Bird hop out and crow hop in! All hands around and once again!" Everybody would then take a turn at the dance until they got the cue, "Swing opposite lady and swing your partner on the next! Cage the bird!" The girl of the second couple would then become the bird with her partner, the boy and girl of the third couple circling about her. On the dance would go until all the girls had been the bird. Then the caller would yell his grand finale, "Swing corners and all promenade!" or "Swing corners, and trail home!"

There are fences now in Parker county, and paved roads, and old-age pensions. There are government rebuilt houses in which families have been resettled after industry in Fort Worth and Dallas shut its doors to them in 1930. There are automobiles and cream separators and silos. The big pool is a stretch of sand. No herds go thundering by.

But here and there is a remnant of an old log cabin or an old log fence. . . . Here and there a wrinkled old woman who likes to raise her eyes from her knitting and tell how many yards of thread she used to spin in a day. . . . Or an old man in an upholstered chair who remembers that time the Indians nearly got him or that day the oxen half-killed him when they dragged him across the field in heel-fly time.

WISE SAWS FROM TEXAS

By MRS. MORGAN SMITH and A. W. EDDINS

Old sayings collected in Texas have been contributed by both Mrs. Morgan Smith and Mr. A. W. Eddins. Many of the sayings in these lists are known to belong to remote antiquity; others bear marks of more recent origin, or at least of local modification. No attempt is made here, however, to deal with the difficult problem of origins. If a saying has been accepted by the Texas folk and is used by them to express their proverbial wisdom, it is a part of their folk-lore, no matter if used elsewhere and no matter what its origin.

I.

By Mrs. Morgan Smith

My interest in old proverbs dates from afar back, for many were quoted to me by my family and friends during my childhood. The old maxims were used much more then than now. Who can deny that a great deal of wisdom is passing with them?

How well do I remember when a gentle voice used to quote to me one old proverb familiar to us all:

"A whistling girl and a crowing hen
Are sure to come to some bad end."

Upon other occasions I have seen a finger pointed to the ceiling of the parlor, to the dark corners in particular, and heard the gentle voice say:

"Where cobwebs grow
No beaux go."

That old saying was alarming enough to insure the absence of cobwebs during those charmed years of anticipated romance, lurking perhaps just within reach.

One of the proverbs that I have chanced upon in Texas has been recorded among very old English sayings. It runs thus:

"A woman, a dog, and a walnut tree——
The harder you beat 'em, the better they be.

The verse may go back to the time when the custom was for the wooer to creep up from the rear and fell the object of his choice with the jawbone of a mastodon, whereupon, rubbing the stars from her delighted eyes, she arose and sweetly followed him.

A later period brought a milder tone to the proverbs pertaining to woman and her place in the home. The following saying, however, is still far from our modern viewpoint:

"A woman, a cat, and a chimney should never
leave the house."

From the border of Mexico comes this variant of the crowing hen. The story goes that a priest was ruled in his home by a most domineering sister. In his great longing to be master of his own house, he sighed:

"It is ill with the roost when the hens crow and
the cock must remain silent."

Upon one occasion I received this good advice:

"Never speak of ropes in the home of a man
whose father was hung."

This saying——said to come from the Old World——was at one time fitting in Texas. At various places over the State one may yet see trees pointed out as having been used for gallows.

Another proverb in which ropes figure is:
"A man once bitten by a snake will jump at
the sight of a rope in his path."

References to firearms, strange to say, are not frequent in the old sayings of Texas, and are confined to such mild statements as——

"You can't kill an elephant with bird-shot."
"Where the feathers fly is where the shot hit."
"Don't waste your ammunition on a dead duck."

More typical of the frontier is——

"Colonel Colt made all men equal."
"Trust in God, but keep your powder dry."

Perhaps earlier is——

"Never stir the fire with a sword,"
meaning guard against inflaming a wrathful nature.

A two-hundred-year-old china plate owned by a Texan bears a picture of a pompous gentleman in a three-cornered hat and knee breeches, leading a cow and a sheep through the street. From the windows of the houses, faces smile and hands wave. Beneath the picture is printed this ancient maxim:

"Now that I own a cow and a sheep, my
 neighbors bid me good-morning."

Occasionally the negro will quote some saying characteristic of his race and intelligence. One old colored man once said to me:

"Every sausage knows if it is mek outer cow or
 dorg."

The meaning is none too clear, but the explanation ran something like this: "Everybody has their troubles: you has yours, I has mine. Some is real, and some is made outer nothin' at all."

Other sayings contributed by negroes include:

"What goes over the debbil's back buckles under
 his belly."
"A melon spiled early won't grow no better with
 age."
"All is lovely and the goose hangs high."

This last saying is said by a contributor to *Harper's Magazine* to have originated with the negro slaves. When the affairs of the plantation were prosperous, they were allowed roast goose. When the goose was dressed and hung up, all was lovely.

One of our old and much used sayings——
"I saved my meat and manners,"
has been changed by the negroes to——
"I saved my mannahs and my possum too."

From old-time West Texans I have gathered the following:

"Life ain't in holding a good hand but in playing a poor hand well."
"A fool talks with his ears stuffed up."
"You can never get knowledge by riding a goat."
"Let every man skin his own eel."
"Every man has got to kill his own snakes."

Of a stingy man it is said that——
"He would skin a flea for the hide and tallow."

Appropriate to West Texas also is——
"Never leave the mark of the pot upon the ashes."

Cowboys of the old day have been known to say of a vindictive man:

"He is like the Pope's mule, that keeps her kick for seven years."

A prominent West Texas ranchman gave me the following lines to be kept in mind when buying a horse:

"One white foot, *buy* him.
Two white feet, *try* him.
Three white feet, *deny* him.
Four white feet and white nose,
Cut off his head and throw him to the crows."

I have made no mention of those old and wise and well-meaning proverbs which we as children so patiently and diligently copied, page upon page, for the improvement of our penmanship. As I look back, I am quite sure that most of those rare bits of wisdom passed over our heads. We little knew and little cared that——

"Eternal vigilance is the price of supremacy,"

or that——
"Procrastination is the thief of time."

One copy-book proverb, however, we did understand too well——
"Early to bed, early to rise
Makes one healthy, wealthy, and wise."

I am quite sure that this old saying has now vanished and that the present generation knows it not. And were I to quote another of the copy-book maxims——
"It's the early bird that catches the worm,"
no doubt the innocent inquiry would come: "Why should the little birdies want to get up so early anyhow, just for a mere worm?" Or, "It served the worm right for getting out so early."

II.

By A. W. Eddins

Grandmother was a pioneer Texan, who came to Blue Ridge in the early forties. Left a widow by the war, she was sustained in her hard struggle to raise her large family by many quaint sayings full of wisdom and knowledge of life.

Here are some of them:

> If you make your bed hard, you can turn over oftener.
>
> You can never get all the possums up the same tree.
>
> There was never a persimmon except there was a possum to eat it.
>
> Leave her alone and she'll come home to her milk.
>
> Lick by lick the cow ate the grindstone.
>
> The higher they go, the lower they fall.
>
> She will soon wish she was back under her mammy's bed playing with the cats.
>
> Cut your peaches, gals; thunder ain't rain.
>
> Come light, go light.

Nothing ever went over the devil's back that didn't come back under his belly.

Fox is the finder; the stench lies behind her.

The hit dog is always the one that howls.

Before my face, honey and sugar; behind my back, you old wooden-legged devil.

Short visits make long friends.

The polecat can't tell the buzzard that he stinks.

Big talker, little doer.

There are more ways to kill a dog than by choking him to death on hot butter.

The man who dances pays the fiddler.

Let sleeping dogs lie.

Don't dig up more snakes than you can kill.

Enough of a good thing is enough; too much is a dog's bait.

What can't be cured must be endured.

The morning rain is like an old woman's dance, soon over.

Talk is cheap, but it takes money to buy whiskey.

It's not what you want that makes you fat, but what you get.

More cotton will grow in a crooked row than in a straight one.

Lots of hands make light work, but many mouths make empty dishes.

COLLOQUIALISMS ALONG THE SABINE

By TRUEMAN E. O'QUINN

Besides being partial in coverage, this list does not purport to be of words and phrases used exclusively in the Sabine River country. It must be remembered that many of the early settlers in East Texas and Western Louisiana, along the Sabine River, were immigrants from other Southern States where the same expressions, or variants, were used and yet survive in some form. But the particular colloquialisms of this list were gathered in the Sabine River sector and are chosen from a dialect I have spoken all my life. Of Vernon Parish, Louisiana, where I was born, it was often said by Louisianians living in a more prosperous section that you could "tell a fellow from Vernon Parish by the rattle of his wagon." This imperfect list of colloquialisms presents a few rattles from the Sabine bottom wagon.

Coon, *v.* The act of crossing a creek or a gulley on all-fours, usually on a log. "I *cooned* the foot-log on Castor Creek last night."

Cabbage, *v.* To take hold, to grab. "I *cabbaged* on to it right then and there."

Break a trace chain, *v. phr.* To perform the supreme act, making the greatest effort. The same as "breaking a leg" or "straining a point" to accommodate someone.

Act white, *v.* To do the right thing. "The least he could do would be to *act white* about the thing."

Adam's off ox, *n. phr.* "I wouldn't know him from *Adam's off ox.*" Usually sounds like "Adam's au fox." Variants are: Adam's off mule, Adam's house cat.

Joobus, *adj.* Doubtful, dubious, skeptical. "I was *joobus* of him from the start."

Rozzum, *n.* Resin. Gum from pine trees; often mixed with sweet gum and chewed; when treated and hardened, used on fiddle bows.

Wash hole, *n.* Swimming hole. "The gals have went a-washing down at the *wash hole.*"

Tote yore own skillet, *v. phr.* Make your way independently, or "paddle your own canoe."

Let the cat out of the wallet, *v. phr.* To disclose a secret, or to "spill the beans." Sometimes distorted to "let the cat out of the water." Variant: let the cat out of the bag.

Dew claw, *n.* Imperfect toe on dog's leg. A superstition exists that a dog with dew claws will not be subject to fits.

Yaller janders, *n.* Yellow jaundice. Malaria, treated with quinine.

Cupping, *v.* To bleed a person by using a quinine bottle heated with coals of fire inside. As the bottle cooled, with its opening pressed against the lanced flesh, blood was drawn from the patient. Used in lieu of lancet bleeding. Sometimes employed to cure "fits."

Had it in me big as a horse, *v. phr.* "I got so mad at that lay-out, I got me a hog-leg that'd shoot a bullet like a nubbin o' corn and went over there to smoke 'em out. Why, *I had it in me as big as a horse* and couldn't stand it no longer!"

Butt his brains out on a stooping post oak, *v. phr.* To end a worthless existence in ignoble style. Post oak trees are regarded as useful only for posts, and if such an oak is stooping, it is not useful even as a post. "I'd rather *butt my brains out on a stooping post oak.*" A man who isn't worth the powder and lead it would take to kill him "ought to *butt his brains out on a stooping post oak*."

Big enough to go to mill, *adj. phr.* Descriptive of a boy old enough to bear the responsibility of being sent to grist mill with corn to be ground into meal.

Independent as a wood-sawyer, *adj. phr.* Very independent, self-reliant. Wood-sawyers burrow into pine logs, cutting channels with distinct, clipping noises, and, like the barber who kept on shaving, continue their work without interruption.

Stump water, *n.* Water accumulating in hollow of stumps, usually the color of coffee. A thing that "tastes like *stump water*" is very foul.

As soon owe a nigger for a basket, *v. phr.* Same meaning as, "I'd as soon be in hell with my back broke," used to describe an unpleasant situation. Bottom Negroes make extra money by selling hand-made cotton baskets constructed of split white oak, and the supply is always greater than the demand; therefore, most sales are "on a credit," and the maker usually continues to call every day until he finds the purchaser (usually a white man) with fifty cents in his pocket to pay for the basket.

Shell down the corn, *v. phr.* To confess. Variants: acknowledge the corn, own the corn.

Walking for a wagon, *v. phr.* To hurry, walk rapidly. "I saw Jim Driver pass the gate this morning like he was *walking for a wagon*." Walking as if to overtake a wagon.

Come through by Brister's, *v. phr.* Take a short cut, to arrive "across lots."

Whack, *v.* To lie. A "whacky" is a lie.

Clever, *adj.* Hospitable, cordial. A host is clever who is entertaining and makes his guests "feel at home."

Across the peach orchard, *adv. phr.* Direction of the wind, used to describe a cold, northwest wind. "She's coming *across the peach orchard* this morning!" means the wind is cold and out of the northwest. Most orchards once were planted on the northwest side of the farm buildings in the belief that exposure to the northern elements prevents fruit trees from coming into blossom too early in the spring.

Dipped, *adj.* Mix-blooded, one who has Negro or Indian blood.

Greasy year, *n. phr.* A prosperous year, plenty of lard and bacon in the smoke-house.

Cake bread, *n. phr.* Bread made of flour, instead of corn meal. A delicacy.

Brought on, *adj. phr.* Something bought at a store. "The fish wouldn't bite, so we got *brought on* trout for supper." "Brought on bread" is "lightbread." Perhaps a corruption of "boughten," bought.

Tush hog, *n. phr.* A leader, usually a bully. The "tush hog" of a herd is usually the biggest, most vicious male, and has large tusks. "He roars like a *tush hog.*"

Shack bully, *n. phr.* A bully in the saw-mill town section. Most early saw-mills were portable, and workers' living quarters were mere shanties or shacks; hence, the "shack bully" ruled the saw-mill shack sector.

Dry so, *adv. phr.* "I'll just take it *dry so,*" means to take liquor straight. To do anything without ceremony, without preparation.

Saw-mill license, *n. phr.* Similar to "cotton patch license." State of living with a mate without being married (to the mate). "I lived with her under a *saw-mill license* till we busted up and she went back to her husband."

Back a letter, *v. phr.* To address a letter.

Make out your meal, *v. phr.* Eat enough. The "clever" host or hostess will say, "Now, Mr. Blank, *make out your meal!* What can I pass you?"

You set handy, *adj. phr.* "You are handy [to a dish at the table]. Help yourself to the fried chicken and pass it down the table, please."

Finding tracks in the yard, *n. phr.* (Negro). Discovery that one's spouse is unfaithful.

Long way from my Chloe's houses, *adj. phr.* (Negro). A long way from home. Chloe is a universal name applied in some sections by Negro men to their wives.

Tote level, *v. phr.* A man who "won't tote level" will cheat, will shirk his work, is unreliable or dishonest.

So lazy he wouldn't count money on the halves, *adj. phr.* Tenant farmers rent on the basis of "thirds and fourths"; that is, the landlord gets one-third of the feed crops and one-fourth of the cotton; so a man who wouldn't count money "on the halves" is about the laziest man in the world.

Boge off, *v. phr.* To wander away. "He *boged off* down town just at meal-time!"

"OLD OBADIAH" AND "MY JUANITA"

By ALICE ATKINSON NEIGHBORS

OLD OBADIAH

I cannot remember when the rhyme of "Old Obadiah" was not known to me. The version in our family, exceedingly popular with us children, probably came from my great-grandmother Nancy Moore, of South Carolina, who married George Claver Brightman and came to Texas in 1843, by way of Indiana and a flat-boat voyage down the Mississippi.

Numerous other characters must, in the widespread popularity of this rhyme, have taken the Biblical Obadiah's jump "in the fire." Mrs. J. E. (Ruth Eubank) Page of San Antonio says that in her childhood Hannah Mariah was the heroine of the rhyme. "Hannah Mariah," she says, "was an actual character of the neighborhood, and a very unusual one. One day my brother and I, as children, were shouting the lines of the jingle to each other when in walked the actual Hannah Mariah in person, her eyes flashing fire. My father, Jesse T. Eubank, brought the jingle with him to Texas from Kentucky, his ancestors being from Virginia." Another friend of San Antonio, Miss Annie Charlotte Terrill, as a child learned the rhyme with *Henry McGuire* jumping "in the fire." The version in her family came from Mississippi.

"OLD OBADIAH" AND "MY JUANITA"   251

The use of cotton at the conclusion of the jingle marks it of Southern adaptation, whatever its origin. In reciting it the chief rule for children to follow, with voices increasingly high, is the law of acceleration, imitating the upward zip of a sky rocket and neglecting not to shriek, shout, and whir the tongue.

> Old Obadiah jumped in the fire;
> The fire was so hot, he jumped in the pot;
> The pot was so black, he jumped in the crack;
> The crack was so high, he jumped in the sky;
> The sky was so blue, he jumped in the canoe;
> The canoe was so deep, he jumped in the creek;
> The creek was so shallow, he jumped in the tallow;
> The tallow was so soft, he jumped in the loft;
> The loft was so rotten, he jumped in the cotton;
> The cotton was so white, he jumped out of sight;
> And there he stayed until broad daylight.

ONCE THERE WAS A MAN, HE CAME FROM THE WEST

My father, the late E. S. Atkinson, who was born and bred in Brooklyn, New York, and who was a captain in the United States Army during the Civil War, probably learned this ditty during his campaign days. He made no pretense of having vocal attainments, but, to help his wife with the large family of children, he would in the evenings sing and rock the youngest to sleep while the older children would hang around entranced.

The putting to sleep process began with "Once There Was a Man, He Came from the West." We children did not call the song by that title, however. We'd say, "Sing 'Mushie Doodle'," that being not only a shorter but a better title. At first each accent of the music was further accented by a jarring thump of the foot on the floor, accompanied by an equally jarring thwack on the shoulder of the heavy-eyed youngster. After several renditions the thwack became a gentle caress, and the tune was changed to "The Low-Backed Car." How sweet Peggy's adventure ended on that market day remained, however, a mystery to this particular youngster for many years, for always the next thing she knew it was broad daylight and the birds were singing. I have never heard "Once There Was a Man, He Came from the West" except when sung by my father.

Once there was a man, he came from the west.
    1st Cho.: Mush-i-doo-dle, dink-tum-doo-dle, Doo-oo—
He lay on the grass till he caught the croup.
    1st Cho.:
Then they dressed him up in some soldiers' clothes.
    1st Cho.:
    And he had a wife which was none the best.
    And they made a tent out of her hoop.
    And it's down to Harper's Ferry she goes.
    And he loved her best of all the rest.
    2nd Cho.: For her name was Boo-dle, Bid-die, Boo-dle,
        Shin-nack Doo-dle. Shake her up.
And they brought her to with some soup.
    2nd Cho.:
For she's wanted there to fight the foes.
    2nd Cho.:

"OLD OBADIAH" AND "MY JUANITA"   253

THE LOW-BACKED CAR

This song, known also as "When First I Saw Sweet Peggy," is an Irish composition ascribed to Samuel Lover; my father always sang it with lullaby intent. It is to be found in William Cullen Bryant's *Library of Poetry and Song,* New York, 1886 (revised and enlarged edition), and in *The Listening Child,* compiled by L. W. Thrasher. The music here given may not be according to to Irish folk music, but it is exactly as it was sung to me. That is, the tune is correct, but in writing out the score I have had to guess at the key. One note looks appallingly high, but that is the way it sounded.

THE LOW-BACKED CAR

1. When first I saw sweet Peggy,
   'Twas on a market day;
   Within a low-backed car she sat
   Upon a truss of hay;
   But when that hay was blooming grass,
   And decked with flowers of spring,
   No flower was there that could compare
   With the blooming girl I sing.
   As she sat in the low-backed car,
   The man at the turnpike bar
   Never asked for the toll,
   But rubbed his old poll,
   And looked after the low-backed car.

2. In battle's wild commotion,
   The proud and mighty Mars
   With hostile scythes demands his tithes
   Of death in warlike cars;
   While Peggy, peaceful goddess,
   Has darts in her bright eye
   That knock men down in the market town,
   As right and left they fly;
   While she sits in her low-backed car,
   Than battle more dangerous far,—
   For the doctor's art
   Cannot cure the heart
   That is hit from the low-backed car.

3. Sweet Peggy round her car, sir,
   Has strings of ducks and geese,
   But the scores of hearts she slaughters
   By far outnumber these;
   While she among her poultry sits,
   Just like a turtle-dove,
   Well worth the cage, I do engage,
   Of the blooming god of Love!
   While she sits in her low-backed car,
   The lovers come near and far,
   And envy the chicken
   That Peggy is pickin',
   As she sits in her low-backed car.

"OLD OBADIAH" AND "MY JUANITA"   255

4. O, I'd rather own that car, sir,
   With Peggy by my side,
   Than a coach and four, and gold galore,
   And a lady for my bride;
   For the lady would sit fornenst me,
   On a cushion made with taste,—
   While Peggy would sit beside me
   With my arm around her waist,
   While we drove in the low-backed car,
   To be married by Father Mahar;
   O, my heart would beat high
   At her glance and her sigh,—
   Though it beat in a low-backed car!

MY JUANITA, I MUST LEAVE YOU

"My Juanita, I Must Leave You" was learned by my brother, E. S. (Ted) Atkinson, Jr., while he was a member of the surveying party laying out the route for the Kansas City, Mexico and Orient Railroad in Mexico. This was in the early nineteen hundreds. The language itself, aside from the story, would mark the ballad's locale. Miss Annie Terrill, of San Antonio, says that as a child she heard some white transient cotton pickers sing the song on her father's farm in Wilson County.

Slow tempo—moonlight night—guitar. Handkerchief.

MY JUANITA, I MUST LEAVE YOU

"My Jua-ni-ta, I must leave you. I have come to say fare-well."
They were stand-ing by the ru-ins where the som-ber sha-dows fell.
"You will miss me, Al-ma Mi-a, for a day and then for-get,
and this part-ing kiss I give you. Jua-ni-ta, your eyes are wet."

1. "My Juanita, I must leave you;
   I have come to say farewell."
   They were standing by the ruins
   Where the somber shadows fell.

2. "You will miss me, alma mia,
   For a day and then forget,
   And this parting kiss I give you—
   Juanita, your eyes are wet.

3. "Crying? Why, my babe, Juanita,
   Do not weep because I go.
   I'm not worthy—there's a good girl!"
   "But, Señor, I love you so!"

4. "Love me! Why, of course, Juanita,
   And I love you; so do not weep."
   "But, Señor, if you did love me,
   You would never, never leave."

5. "One more kiss? I'll give you fifty."
   Round her form his arms entwined.
   They were standing near the ruins
   Almost hid by clustering vines.

6. "Don't be angry, *dulce mia*.
   How your cheeks like roses glow,
   And your dark eyes flash like jewels,
   Fairest maid in Mexico.

7. "I never thought that my flirtation
   Would leave an impress on your heart—
   For I leave to wed a maiden
   Of my country——we must part."

8. They have parted now forever;
   Juanita leaves the place alone;
   In her eyes no tear-drops glisten,
   From her heart all love has flown.

9. In the morning two *vaqueros*
   Paused to rest there in the shade,
   Para descansarse[1], sought the shelter
   By the shadows foliage made.

10. "Por Dios!" cried *un vaquero*,
    As he pushed the vines apart,
    "There lies a *'Mericano*
    With a dagger in his heart!"

---
[1] To rest themselves.

SILVER DREAMS AND COPPER PLATES

By MAE FEATHERSTONE

The storied land of the Southwest contains no place where more romance and legend can be found than the hills of Mills County, Texas. From the cliff-lined banks of the Colorado River, the brush-covered hills stretch northward, among them tradition and folk-lore thriving as freely and abundantly as the bluebonnet in the spring.

In the dawn of Texas history, legions of pack trains, carrying gold and silver from mines in the mountains of Mexico and from the hidden shafts of the Lost San Saba Mine, moved slowly up the trail which crossed this land rich in natural scenic beauty and led by the Epley Spring. At least that is what the treasure-seekers say. Here the weary travelers drank the cool waters of the spring, rested in the shade of the pecan and elm trees, and then resumed their northward journey, leaving behind strange and fantastic stories about the contents of their packs.

But not all of the gold and silver laden burros which camped by Epley Spring ever reached their destinations somewhere to the north. Roving bands of Indians charged back and forth among the brushy slopes around Epley Spring and spread panic among numerous pack trains. As a result, some of the gold and silver from the Aztec mines still lies buried in the hills of Mills County.

SILVER DREAMS AND COPPER PLATES 259

With the advent of the cattle industry in the brush country of Southwest Texas, Epley Spring became a famous watering place on the western branch of the Chisholm Trail. Then thousands of cattle on their way to markets in Denver stopped here for water, and the whispering voices of the fleeing miners and the attacking Indians were stilled by the angry milling and bawling of the cattle and the incessant shouting of the trail drivers.

The voices, though stilled, were not dead. As the country around the spring became settled, the whispering spirits walked and talked again. They started a long line of treasure-seekers, which still continues, on a quest which is still unfinished.

Dozens of men have hunted for buried treasure in the hills around Epley Spring; a few of them whose stories have never been told are Uncle Jimmie Guthrie, Wiley Wall, Dutch Hollenback, and Monte Henderson.

In 1884, a man named Shultz bought the farm on which Epley Spring is located and moved his family there. The following May two men and three boys, who were traveling west in a covered wagon, stopped at the Shultz home. They had several charts which, they said, were supposed to lead to the place where fifteen jack loads of silver bullion were buried. Their story ran as follows:

Years ago, a band of men, some Americans and some Mexicans, were traveling from Mexico to some part of the United States with a pack train of silver bullion. They had taken the ore from silver mines in Mexico and were going home. In the group was a Roman Catholic priest.

The Indians bothered them in the San Saba country, but they became more menacing as soon as the Colorado River was crossed. Late one afternoon, the pack train camped by Epley Spring. As soon as darkness came, the weary travelers took the fifteen jack loads of silver out in the hills and buried it. The priest made four charts showing the location of the treasure, placed one in each of three copper boxes, and buried them in three different places some distance from the silver. He kept the fourth chart. Then he made several charts showing the location of the copper boxes. The charts in the boxes were so arranged that each one had to be found before the silver could be located.

With their silver thus secured, the men continued their journey under the cover of darkness, but before morning the Indians made a severe attack on them. A few escaped, but most of the miners were killed there in the lonely hills under the paling stars. Whether the priest escaped no one knows, but the prospectors who stopped at the Shultz home claimed that they had the original chart which he had made and kept with him.

Their chart called for a large pecan tree a given distance and direction from the Epley Spring. The tree was supposed to have a limb cut off and a spike driven in the remaining part and pointing toward the treasure. Doubtless the chart was more definite, but the daughter of Mr. Shultz, who told this story to me, had forgotten many of the details.

No tree fitting the description could be found, but the men easily located a large pecan stump about one hundred yards east of the spring. They thought that the spike must have pointed northwest, as the nearest hills lay in that direction.

The prospectors stayed around and searched for several months, and then all of them except one man, a Mr. Brooks, left. He hunted among the near-by hills for several years before he finally left, too.

The treasure-seekers left, but their story remained— burned in the minds and hearts of several children of the adventurous Coronado.

Chief among these was Uncle Jimmie Guthrie. Uncle Jimmie became interested in buried treasure about 1887, while Mr. Brooks was still prospecting. He left his home in Mullin and worked with Mr. Brooks and the two Urbach brothers of Goldthwaite for several years. When

SILVER DREAMS AND COPPER PLATES 261

Mr. Brooks left, he sold his mineral rights, cabin, and equipment to Mr. Guthrie for four hundred dollars. The cabin was located about a quarter of a mile north of the Epley Spring. Here Uncle Jimmie lived for almost thirty years digging and prospecting among the neighboring hills. Out on a hillside one day he discovered a large flat rock on which was crudely drawn a long curved line of jacks headed for the mouth of a cave, but the rock was map-side-down; so it did not help him so far as guidance was concerned. This was not the same rock which Dr. Jim Kirkpatrick's men found.[1] Dr. Jim's men found their rock some time earlier.

In his long siege of digging, Uncle Jimmie dug a vast labyrinth of caves into several hills north of the spring, and these are still called the Guthrie Caves.

Uncle Jimmie was a great talker. He had a shrill, sing-song voice, and he talked to anyone who would listen. He loved nothing better than to get a crowd of people around him and tell stories about the Mexican silver for which he was seeking. He always carried a number of Indian arrowheads with him, and he amused many children and older people as well by holding up an arrowhead and relating its history from the time it was chiseled by some dusky brave until it fell into his hands. Many a buffalo and many a savage Indian had been killed by the flint points which he carried.

Uncle Jimmie knew the Bible from cover to cover, and he always attended church and Sunday School at Bethel, a small church several miles from his cabin.

My father and mother, Charles G. and Blanche Moreland Featherstone, moved to a farm about two miles east of Epley Spring in 1907, and for many years Mr. Guthrie was a constant visitor in their home. He whiled away many long winter evenings sitting by their fireside and telling stories to my older sisters. Naturally Uncle Jimmie was a great favorite with them.

Many public picnics were held at the Guthrie Caves, to Uncle Jimmie's great delight. Besides the picnic

---
[1] J. Frank Dobie, *Coronado's Children*, p. 45.

crowds, random bands of pleasure seekers frequented the chalky hillsides; so what time Uncle Jimmie was not actually digging, he was guiding people through the intricate passages and tunnels he had made.

Although Mr. Guthrie carried on most of his operations alone, he worked for a while with Dr. Jim Kirkpatrick and Bob Urbach, who were making an extensive search in some hills west of the spring. It was they, and not Uncle Jimmie, who unearthed the first of the priest's copper boxes. On the lid of this box was etched a long string of pack burros headed for the mouth of a cave, and beneath that was the name Padre Lopez and the date 1762. Unquestionably they were on the trail of the buried Aztec treasure, but the story of Dr. Jim has already been told.[2]

Uncle Jimmie continued to work, sometimes with some interested party but most often alone, until age began to claim him, and his health began to fail. About 1917 his sons came and took him back to Mullin, where he died several years later.

But Uncle Jimmie's spirit still lives, and, hand in hand with the lure of buried treasure, still haunts the hillsides where he worked. The Guthrie Caves are now crumbling ruins. Only a few look safe enough for one to venture into their dark, uncertain depths, and they are the home of innumerable cave rats and rattlesnakes. But Uncle Jimmie's spirit moves restlessly back and forth among the musty obscure tunnels—still pursuing his dream, still seeking.

A man who prospected for several years near the site of Mr. Guthrie's digging was Wiley Wall, an Indian. When my father moved to Mills County in 1893, Wiley lived with his Indian mother and his sister, Landonia, on a farm about five miles north of Epley Spring. But Wiley became interested in buried treasure, and in 1901 he sold his farm and bought a large tract of land just west of Epley which included the site of Mr. Guthrie's excavations. The two became steadfast friends, but they

---

[2] J. Frank Dobie, *Coronado's Children*, pp. 43-49.

did not work together. As a Mills County pioneer expresses it, "They did not see things alike." Wiley explored in other places on his land, but he never discovered anything unusual except some strange writing—probably Indian pictographs—on the walls of two or three natural rock caves.

The Walls were typical Indians who, due to circumstances, were living among civilized people. For several years after they moved to their new farm, they did not build a house but lived in a dug-out cellar. Even after the house was built, Grandma Wall continued to live in the cellar most of the time.

Many stories were told about their queer way of living. One was that the Walls did not have a comb and that Landonia's hair had not been combed for seven years. Another was that, on cold winter nights, they often brought their whole flock of goats in the house, and sometimes Landonia slept with the little kids.

The Walls were very silent and reticent about their affairs. They were, also, very devout and religious, and Wiley knew the Bible as well as Uncle Jimmie Guthrie. Moved by the spirit of God, Wiley overcame his taciturnity enough to take up preaching. He preached at Bethel one windy Easter Sunday, and I well remember hearing my father tell about it.

He said that the church swayed like a tall pine in the wind. As the sermon progressed, the congregation became more and more restless. Numbers of people got up and walked out, but Wiley preached on undisturbed. Later Uncle Jimmie, who had not been at church that windy morning, remarked that he thought things were coming to a pretty pass when Wiley Wall tried to preach —no wonder the Lord had tried to destroy the church.

Time went on, and the story of the Mexican treasure was almost forgotten. Epley Spring was no longer on a road but was hidden in a tangle of brush in the corner of an isolated field. But in 1932 Dutch Hollenback came to Mills County prospecting for buried treasure. He had a machine which was supposed to locate buried metal to the depth of fifteen or twenty feet. Two men were needed to operate the machine, one to carry the device itself and another to carry the batteries by which it was run. As it was carried along near the ground, the machine made a slight buzzing noise, but when it was near buried metal, it buzzed loudly.

Some local boys became very much interested. They went with Mr. Hollenback on many of his exploring trips and carried the digging implements. One day, while they were walking across an open meadow, the machine set up a loud buzzing.

"Here!" said Dutch. "Dig here!"

The boys began to dig furiously, and in a few minutes they unearthed an old broken teakettle.

Mr. Hollenback and Doc, his battery man, prospected over all the hills around Epley and explored many natural rock caves, with which this vicinity abounds. They searched extensively around the Dry Pond, the dry bed of an old dirt tank located in a tangle of brush on a hill about two miles west of Epley Spring. On the west side of the Pond stands a great live oak tree on the rugged bark of which are cut two indistinct maps. On the eastern edge of the Pond, directly opposite the regal oak, stand several elm trees, and it was beneath one of these elms that Dutch Hollenback, in July of 1932, unearthed a small copper box, the second of the boxes buried by Padre Lopez to be found. On top of the box was a Catholic Cross and some Spanish writing. Inside was a single piece of paper with the same cross and writing on it. But the writing on the paper was so dim that it could not easily be read.

Dutch talked very little after he found the box. He only said, "That's what I'm looking for," and he seemed satisfied. He kept the chart, but he gave the copper box to Roach Fox, a local man who was helping him that day and who had actually dug the box up.

The writing on the box was in the form here given:

SILVER DREAMS AND COPPER PLATES 265

Mapa
Oriental Sudeste
2500
Caja Fuerte mucho dinero
doblon de oro
Jeados escudos vaja
Bjondea cuatro
bjondea ocho

┼

Deigratia Peated
Padre Lopes
1762

One day in August, several weeks after the discovery of the copper box, I and some friends of mine, laughingly calling ourselves Coronado's grandchildren, spent an entire day exploring places of legendary interest near our homes. We crawled through some of the Guthrie Caves, killed a rattlesnake, drank from the icy waters of Epley Spring, and visited the Dry Pond. The bed of the Pond was ridged and uneven, showing traces of former diggings. The aged live oak stood stately and silent, and across the Pond, at the foot of an elm, was a shallow hole. The August sun smiled tolerantly down upon us, and a faint breeze which stirred lightly in the brush seemed to whisper, "Not far away Dr. Jim Kirkpatrick dug up the first copper box; over there Dutch Hollenback dug up the second; the third is somewhere close by."

According to Monte Henderson, he knows where the third copper box is buried; three different fortune tellers have told him its exact location.

For a number of years the Hendersons have lived at the foot of the hill on which the Dry Pond is located. Their home is composed of three large caves dug in the hillside, and a tent. Aside from tending their flocks of goats, Mr. Henderson and Monte spend a great deal of time searching for clues to the buried Mexican treasure.

One day while herding his goats, Mr. Henderson found a flat rock map half-buried in a dense brush thicket. On it were drawn two lines forming an acute triangle near the center of the rock and extending to the right side. Between the two lines was a large figure 3. In the upper right-hand corner was crudely drawn an Indian woman in the act of shooting an arrow from a large bow, and in the opposite corner was a mountain goat. The rock was broken off sharply at one side; so Mr. Henderson did not know whether he had all of the original map or whether part of it was still undiscovered.

One Sunday afternoon during the Christmas holidays of 1934, I went hiking with a crowd of boys and girls, and our rambling walk eventually led to the Henderson homestead. We found Monte at home alone. Scarcely had we taken a drink of water from the tin dipper which hung by the well in front of the tent until we began to question him about his treasure hunting experiences. Aside from showing us the map that his father had found, Monte said very little at first, but when we convinced him that we wanted a story about his own experiences and were not trying to find the buried silver, he talked freely and fluently.

He took us through an old rock cave he had recently reopened and showed us some curious-looking but indistinct writing on its walls. Then we went to the Dry Pond. On our way there we passed a small tent made of green burlap curtains—curtains like those recently stolen from the nearby Live Oak School. Monte told us that it was the camp of a prospector named Brown who had acquired the mineral rights to the land on which all of them were searching.

The Dry Pond had changed greatly since 1932. Much of the brush had been cleared away, and scattered over the bed of the Pond were several huge mounds of dirt. Water stood in some of the deep holes, and the whole place showed that it had been the scene of recent activity.

SILVER DREAMS AND COPPER PLATES 267

Monte led us to a place some distance south of the Dry Pond and said that here Dr. Jim Kirkpatrick had dug up the first copper box about 1902. We already knew where Dutch Hollenback had found the second box east of the Pond. Then he stepped off twenty good paces directly north of the majestic live oak and pointed to a slightly sunken spot of ground.

"Here," he said, "the third copper box is buried. I know, for three fortune tellers have told me so."

We asked him why he did not dig it up, and he replied that he was only waiting for Brown's mineral rights to expire. Then he would file mineral rights and unearth the box.

Each time Monte's conversation lagged, a few tactful questions or exclamations of wonder started him afresh. He told us a strange story about two Mexican prospectors from Monterrey who had been there a short time ago. It ran something like this:

It was night, and a pale moon was shining. Monte was standing on the west side of the Pond beneath the huge live oak, and the two Mexicans from Monterrey were standing across the Pond beneath an elm tree. As they watched, two spirits arose from the center of the Pond and moved silently toward the two Mexicans. When then reached the edge of the Pond, they stopped between two young elms, and, after standing there several seconds, they disappeared into the ground. The Mexicans immediately began to dig on the spot where the spirits had disappeared. Monte watched them for a while, but, fearing discovery, he soon went home. The next morning the Mexicans and their camp were gone. As yet no one knows where they went, but between the young elms a cross was dug, five feet long with arms three feet wide.

We crossed the Pond, and, sure enough, there between two elms was the freshly dug cross. It was about eighteen inches deep. As we stood looking down at the shallow cross, I suggested to Monte that perhaps the Mexicans had discovered the third copper box, but he shook his head. They might have found gold or silver, but they did not find the box. He knew where it was buried.

On our return, we stopped at Henderson's well for another drink, and Monte brought out a number of his father's maps and showed them to us. But they were all copies; Mr. Henderson would let no one see the originals. In explaining the maps, Monte grew very eloquent. He retold the story of the fifteen jack loads of silver, told us all about the fight with the Indians, and about Dr. Kirkpatrick and Uncle Jimmie Guthrie. Then he gave us the whole history of Epley Spring and was closing with a complete account of the Chisholm Trail when my sister Fay, who had been only half listening, broke the magic spell by turning to another member of the hiking party and casually asking, "Dick, who is Jack Loads?"

In the late summer of 1936, several local men entered into an agreement with W. P. (Prock) McCulloch, a prominent business man of Goldthwaite and owner of the land on which the Dry Pond is located. Their plan was to lease the land and begin prospecting on a large scale. When they were almost ready to begin operations, a prospector named Woods from Wichita Falls came to Mr. McCulloch and wanted to lease the land. He was told that the land was leased for a certain period of time. Mr. Woods then went out to the Dry Pond to see what the other men were doing. They were digging north of the Pond. Mr. Woods told them that they were wrong, and then he pointed out a place east of the Pond. He said that if they would sink a shaft thirty feet deep there, they would strike the intersection of three tunnels that in reality were old mining shafts.

One place seemed as good as another to the men who held the lease; so they sank the shaft. And at a depth of between twenty and thirty feet they really did strike a point where three tunnels intersected. The dirt roofs of all three tunnels were supported by old worm-eaten log rafters, supported at regular intervals along the sides by log posts. Mr. Woods said that this was a gold instead of

SILVER DREAMS AND COPPER PLATES 269

a silver mine and that it was also a depository of a fabulous fortune in gold doubloons, but he refused to give any further specific information. He said that his information came from an old book that he got from Spain through the Spanish Government.

Excitement ran high after the old tunnels were discovered, and the men worked feverishly at cleaning out the tunnels and clearing away the debris that had been accumulating for no one knew how many years. Then came the early fall flood season. Heavy rains fell all during September. The nearby Colorado River reached an unprecedented flood level of sixty-one feet, and the Dry Pond became a small lake. The old mine filled with water; so operations ceased and have not yet been resumed.

I visited the Dry Pond in December of 1936 and found only a picture of desolation. All operations were standing still, waiting for the water and mud to dry up. And nailed to a Spanish oak by the yawning shaft was a rudely pencilled sign: "Keep Out."

THE ALABAMA INDIANS AND THEIR MUSIC

By FRANCES DENSMORE

This article is based upon unpublished material of my own collecting in possession of the Bureau of American Ethnology, and is used by permission of the Bureau.

The chief, and almost the sole, worker in the field of the Alabama Indians, so far as their ethnology and folklore is concerned, has been John R. Swanton. The historical résumé of my paper is derived from his *Early History of the Creek Indians and Their Neighbors*, Bulletin 73, Bureau of American Ethnology, Washington, 1922, pp. 191-201.

A much fuller and more extensive historical treatment of the Alabama Indians, however, is by Harriet Smither, "The Alabama Indians in Texas," *Southwestern Historical Quarterly*, Austin, Oct., 1932, Vol. XXXVI, pages 83-108. This very scholarly, and also sympathetic, treatise carries references to virtually everything that has been written on the Alabamas. It may be regarded as the final word on this tribe. A supplementary pamphlet, good for description of present day ways and conditions of the tribe, is by Mary Donaldson Wade, *The Alabama Indians of East Texas*, Livingston, Texas, 1936.

Dr. John R. Swanton's recordings on the Alabamas are contained in his *Myths and Tales of the Southeastern Indians*, Bulletin 88, Bureau of American Ethnology,

THE ALABAMA INDIANS 271

Washington, 1922, and in three papers in the *Forty-second Annual Report of the Bureau of American Ethnology, 1924-1925,* Washington, 1928, the titles of the papers being as follows: "Social Organization and Social Usages of the Indians of the Creek Confederacy," "Religious Beliefs and Medical Practices of the Creek Indians," and "Aboriginal Culture of the Southeast."

THE ALABAMA TRIBE

In common with many Indian tribes, the Alabama have a tradition that they ascended out of the earth. An origin-legend published by Schoolcraft[1] tells how they appeared between the Cahawba and Alabama rivers, and an old Indian related to Dr. John R. Swanton a story in which he said: "The Alabama and Koasati came out of the earth on opposite sides of the root of a certain tree and settled there in two bodies. Consequently these differed somewhat in speech, though they always kept near each other."

The Alabama were the most conspicuous tribe of the Upper Creeks except the Muskogee, the old forms of the tribal name being Albamo and Alibamu. Some of their traditions show a closer connection with the Choctaw and Chickasaw than with the Creek. The languages of the Alabama, Choctaw and Chickasaw, as well as of the Hitchiti and Koasati, were mutually understood, and the histories of the tribes have many points of contact.

The history of the Alabama tribe is uncertain prior to 1541, when De Soto and his companions, having been severely handled by the Chickasaw, set out toward the northwest for a province called Alibamo. The chronicle of the De Soto expedition describes the meeting with this tribe thus: "So soon as they saw the Christians draw nigh they beat drums, and, with loud yells, in great fury came forth to meet them."

---
[1] Schoolcraft, Henry R., *Indian Tribes*, Pt. 1, pp. 266-267. Philadelphia, 1851.

After this episode the Alabama disappear from sight until the settlement of Louisiana by the French, when they were located on the upper course of the Alabama River. In March, 1702, they are mentioned as successful enemies of the Mobile tribes, and in May, 1703, the English induced the Alabama to declare war against the French. Deceived by pleasant promises, the French sent five messengers, who were received by twelve Alabama bringing a peace calumet. That night, however, the Alabama killed all the party except one, who escaped with a broken arm and carried the news to Mobile. Bienville undertook an early revenge but was deserted by his Mobile and other allies, who were secretly in sympathy with the Alabama. His punitive expedition failed, but two years later La Harpe records that a bounty was placed on Alabama scalps, the Chickasaw bringing in five such scalps and receiving guns, powder, and ball in exchange for them.

Fort Toulouse, commonly called the Alabama Fort, was established in 1717, and Pénicaut mentions the Alabama among the tribes which came to "sing the calumet" before M. de l'Epinay in that year. Tranquillity reigned until the close of the French domination.

Changes came rapidly after the English accession in 1763. Fort Jackson was established on the former site of Fort Toulouse. According to the terms of a treaty made here in 1814, the Alabama ceded all their land to the white men. Meantime a portion of the tribe had moved across the Mississippi River into Louisiana, attracted by the fresh hunting grounds in that colony. One settlement was located on the Red River, about sixteen miles above Bayou Rapide, and a village of about forty men was situated "on a small creek, in the Appelousa district, about thirty miles northwest from the church of Appelousa. . . . They raise corn, have horses, hogs and cattle, and are harmless, quiet people." Other villages are mentioned by writers of this period. From Opelousas the Alabama moved to the Sabine River, where they formed a new town the name of which is not known.

Dr. J. R. Swanton received the following information in 1912 from John Scott, chief of the Alabama and the oldest member of the tribe: "There was an Alabama village in Texas called Fenced-in-village a short distance west by south of a mill and former postoffice called Mobile, Tyler County, Texas. Next they settled in . . . Tak' o' sha-o' la ('Peach-tree Town'). This was about two miles due north of Chester or twenty miles north of Woodville, Texas. Their next town was three miles from Peach-tree Town and contained a 'big house' . . . and a dance ground, but was unnamed. After a time the Alabama chief decided to move to Pat' ala' ka (said to mean 'Cane Place'), where the Biloxi and Pascagoula lived, and some other Indians went with him. A part, however, returned to Louisiana, where they remained three years. At the end of that time they came back to Texas and formed a village which took its name from a white man, Jim Barclay. They moved from there to the village which they now occupy, which is called Big Sandy village from the name of a creek, although it took some time for the families scattered in Texas to come in."

A few families still remain in Calcasieu and St. Landry Parishes in Louisiana. A small portion of the tribe is located near Wcleetka, Oklahoma. A station on the St. Louis - San Francisco Railroad south of Weleetka bears the tribal name, but the large majority of the Alabama are now living in Big Sandy village, in Texas.

THE ALABAMA IN TEXAS

Big Sandy village is located in Polk County, about seventeen miles east of Livingston, at the edge of the Big Thicket in the long-leaf pine region. After being bandied about for years, the Alabamas were in 1854 deeded 1280 acres of land, by the State of Texas, to be held "tax free." Sam Houston was instrumental in getting it for them. Situated near the Big Thicket, then lush with game, the location was particularly favorable to the Indian mode of life. In 1928 the United States government purchased 3071 acres of adjoining land and turned it over to the Alabamas and Koasatis, who live with them. Their game has largely disappeared; the soil of their land, never fertile, has been depleted; but they are better housed, have better schools, and enjoy more security than formerly. In 1910, according to the census, there were 202 Indians in Polk County; in 1930, 245, of which 202 were Alabamas.

The Presbyterian Church has maintained missionaries in this village ever since the Curry family took up residence there in 1882. Previously the village had been visited by Rev. Tenny Crockett and Rev. Jones, of Woodville. The present missionaries, Rev. and Mrs. C. W. Chambers, came to the village in 1899. In writing of the Alabama, Mrs. Chambers said: "They are fine folks, learn quickly, and are honest. They have never had war nor any sort of trouble with the white men. They are intensely religious. There has never been a divorce in the village." Beside the large church edifice there are several mission residences.

The Indians are under a combination of Federal and State administration. The nearest Federal superintendency is that of the Choctaw at Philadelphia, Mississippi. The general affairs of the Alabama are in charge of an Indian Agent appointed by the Texas State Board of Control. The United States Government built a house for this official in the village, also a four-room schoolhouse and a hospital. A gymnasium was in process of construction in 1933. The Government built four-room houses for the Indians many years ago; but as these houses contained no provision for cooking or heating, the Indians preferred to live in their old houses. Then the Government gave them cookstoves, but they found difficulty in using them. Heating stoves were next provided, but the houses were so small that a portion of the family still occupied the old dwelling.

The Alabama living in Oklahoma are rapidly giving up their own language and speaking either Creek or English, but the Alabama in Texas still use the native language in their homes. The children attend school but hear the Alabama spoken at home. There has been some marriage with the Koasati, which has affected the language, and it is said that both tribes now use a "trade language" understood by several tribes. Mrs. Dorothy Schlotter of Dallas, Texas, daughter of the Rev. Mr. Chambers, is probably the only white person who can speak the old Alabama language. There has been no intermarriage between the Alabama and the white race; nor have negroes mingled with the tribe.

Many of these Indians find employment in the autumn picking cotton for neighboring farmers, and some are employed in the lumber industry, which is extensive in the region.

After the death of John Scott, the Alabama were without a chief until Charles Martin Thompson was elected to that office in 1928. A formal installation took place in January of that year and was attended by many white men from Houston and other cities; but something about the election was unsatisfactory to the Indians and another was held in March. Since that time Charles Thompson has been recognized as the chief. His Indian name is Son′ ke mĭ′ kko (popularly spelled and called Sun-Kee), the word "mikko" meaning chief. He said that he did not know the English equivalent of the first part of his name.

A prominent member of the tribe at the present time is Harden Silistine, probably descended from Cylestine, a chief in the old days. The name is derived from the French *Celestine* and has been spelled in various ways. Mention should be made of an old Alabama named Petigo, after Judge Petigo of Woodville. He never cut his hair but wore it in long braids. His death occurred about 1923. Hickman Chambers, son of the missionaries, remembered going hunting with Petigo when a boy and hearing him sing about the deer and other animals that they hunted. All such songs have been forgotten.

Basketry was formerly an important art of the Alabama. The baskets were woven of narrow strips of cane, the portion comprising the pattern being colored with native dyes. Thompson said that black dye was obtained by boiling the bark of the sumac and that red dye was made from the bark of the wild peach tree. Many styles of baskets were made, including a square basket that was smaller at the top than at the bottom, and an oblong basket. Both were peculiar in that the pattern on the bottom of the basket was different from that on the sides. A large square basket, formerly used for storing corn or other food, was obtained from Thompson. The cane used in basketry was abundant in former times but can now be obtained only at a distance of about twenty miles. For this reason few baskets are made at the present time.

Charles M. Thompson is an expert worker in wood, and excels in the making of bows and arrows. His bows are from two and a half to six feet long and are of ironwood or hickory; for his arrows he uses "possum haw."[2]

"THE VISIT TO THE SKY"[3]

The following story was related to me by the chief of the Alabama, Charles M. Thompson.

In the beginning four old men walked toward the west. They heard a sound—*boom, boom.* The sky opened and they went up. One after another they ran through the sky.

One said, "I am the panther, running through." Another said, "I am the wolf, running through." Another said, "I am the wildcat, running through." The last one said nothing, but he got caught and was killed. The others went on until they came to a place where an old woman lived by herself. There was a river near by.

---

[2] Since this article was written Chief Sun-Kee died, September 8, 1935.

[3] Three versions of this story are presented by Dr. John R. Swanton in *Myths and Tales of the Southeastern Indians*, Bulletin 88, Bureau of American Ethnology, a work containing 64 Alabama and 65 Koasati stories, together with large collections from other tribes. The narrative here presented resembles chiefly the first version (pp. 139-141), in which the men, on awaking at home, found seed of corn, watermelon and beans beside them. Previously they had been without these vegetables. The incident of looking down from the sky and seeing their home occurs in all the versions, though only the first mentions "something that moved around like a telescope." The third version (p. 143) states that "God took the cover off from something and let them look inside. They saw the house from which they had come just beneath."

The old woman told a boy to make a dipper and give it to these men. One after another they dipped up water and threw it in different directions. Then they crossed the river on dry ground.

They went a long way and found some people fighting; so they could not pass. The three men made cigarettes and smoked, and blew the smoke all over the land. It became such a thick fog that the people could not see to fight, and the men passed through.

They came to a great many snakes piled up—about a mile of them. The men tied slippery elm bark all over their legs and then they could walk among the snakes. Afterward they took off the slippery elm bark and threw it away.

They went on and on. At last they came to another old woman. They had eaten nothing and were hungry. The old woman cooked squashes and put three on each plate. As soon as a man had eaten these squashes three more appeared on his plate.

The woman said, "You are dirty." She said, "Go fill a bucket with water and put it on the fire." When the water was boiling, she made them stand in a row with their backs to her, and she poured the boiling water on their backs and scrubbed them hard. They felt *light* after this and went on and on.

They went up on high to the Lord's place. The Lord asked, "Do you think you came a long way?" The Lord had a big telescope and said, "Come, look in here." They looked and saw their old home down below. The Lord said, "Do you want to go back?" They said, "Yes." The Lord gave them all kinds of seed——corn, sweet potato, and so forth, and made them sleep that night. In the morning they waked up in their old home and had all this seed with them.

MUSICAL INSTRUMENTS

A drum, rattle, and flute were formerly used by the Alabama. The drum was made of a cypress knee hollowed out, with a top of deerskin fastened in place with deerhide thongs. For making a drum, they selected a cypress knee about eight inches deep that was rotted inside, so that the wood could be removed with comparative ease. The deerhide top was removed, moistened and replaced when necessary. This drum was carried by means of a deerhide handle and was held high by the drummer. The drumstick consisted of a stick with rags wound at one end to form a "head."

A gourd rattle, obtained from Thompson, has a handle of cedar, and the gourd is of a variety that grows in the vicinity. It was said the rattle contained dried red berries of a sort that grow in the vicinity, but when the handle became loosened some beads fell out. These were rather large dull-white beads and apparently very old. Probably more than one sort of small object was placed in a rattle to produce the sound.

Thompson is an expert maker of flutes, and he made one of these instruments for the writer. It is of red cedar, with six finger-holes and the usual whistle opening, with a tapering mouth-end. The two halves of the cylinder are tied at intervals with narrow strips of thong, and the "block" is larger than on a majority of such Indian flutes. Thompson said the proper length of a flute was three "hand-widths," such a width being that of the hand with the thumb extended. The length of this flute is eighteen and a quarter inches. The writer did not hear the instrument played, as it was completed after her departure; but Mr. Hobby Galloway said he had heard Thompson play on his flutes and that the sound was very pleasing. The construction of the instrument is similar to that of the flutes used by the Plains tribes.

THE RECORDING OF SONGS

In January, 1933, the writer went to Livingston, Texas, to record Alabama songs, this being part of a comparative study of Indian songs in the Gulf States. Unfortunately the weather was the coldest in many years. Snow, rain and ice prevailed and the road to Big Sandy Village was practically impassable for an automobile.

THE ALABAMA INDIANS 279

While waiting for conditions to moderate, the writer obtained information from residents of Livingston and especially from Hickman Chambers, son of the missionaries to the Alabama.

Grateful acknowledgment is made of the assistance of Mr. Hobby Galloway, State Indian Agent, who went out to the Indian village on the fifth day of this period of waiting and brought Charles Thompson to town; he also secured a place in the County Courthouse where the work could be done quietly and efficiently. His courtesy made possible a valuable contribution to the study of Indian music.

Charles Martin Thompson, Chief of the Alabama, was seventy-one years of age when recording the songs of his tribe. He was born in Polk County and both his parents were Alabama. For many years he has been prominent at the mission and is a deacon in the Presbyterian Church. Although his vocabulary is limited, he spoke sufficient English for me to work without an interpreter and his information proved to be definite and clear. Sixty-two songs were recorded and he said that he knew "more than a hundred others." Each song was carefully selected from the large number held in his memory. The songs of thirteen dances were recorded by Thompson, many customs were described, and the legend of "The Visit to the Sky" was related. If conditions had been more favorable, he could have added extensively to this data.

He named five or six old men in the village who remember the songs but said the young men do not learn them. The dances of the Alabama were discontinued in 1898 and the old customs have rapidly given way to the customs of civilization. Thompson said, however, that a man named Palmer and some of his relatives still treat the sick by the old method and that the medicinal use of plants is known to many in the tribe. He said that he had seen the treatment of the sick in the old manner, songs being sung and the medicine made effective by blowing into it through a tube. The songs had been forgotten. In this treatment a decoction of herbs is placed in a pail, the medicine man sings four times, and between the songs he blows through a slender cane having a hole near the end, which is submerged in the water. This causes the liquid to "foam like soap-bubbles." Having thus vitalized the medicine and made it effective, the medicine man causes the patient to drink it, or sprays it from his mouth on the patient's body.

On being asked whether his songs had any words, Thompson replied, "If there are words, the meaning is not known." His songs are very old, and in such songs there often are obsolete words, so broken up and mispronounced that they resemble meaningless syllables. The Indians learn these syllables by rote and repeat them in all renditions of the song. Occasionally they know the general meaning of the words, but even this had been lost in the songs recorded by Thompson. Indian songs differ from ballads, cowboy songs and other types of early American music in the fact that words are not always used. Some Indian songs have words continuous throughout the melody; a larger number contain a few words, occurring in part of the melody; and a still larger number have no words at all, the tones being separated by a peculiar action of the throat and tongue. It is impossible to express by our alphabet this vocalization, which the Indians call "just singing."

DANCE ACTION AND MUSIC

Green Corn Dance

It is many years since the Green Corn Dance (busk) has been celebrated by the Alabama. This festival of the Creeks was formerly held when the crops came to maturity in late July or in August, taking place in the ceremonial "square ground" and lasting eight days. The "new fire" was kindled on the first day and from this fire, on the fourth day, the women kindled the fires on their freshly cleaned hearths. A feast of new corn took place on the second day of the gathering, and each day had its designated ceremonial action and dances.

"The new fire meant the new life, physical and moral, which had to begin with the new year. Everything had to be new or renewed—even the garments hitherto worn. Taken altogether, the busk was one of the most remarkable ceremonial institutions of the American Indians."[4]

No study of the Corn Dance was attempted and the songs are presented with only incidental details. Songs of this dance were recorded among the Seminole in Florida, the songs of the Buffalo Dance preceding those of the Corn Dance in that tribe as among the Alabama. Alligator dance songs were also used by the Alabama, one being recorded but not transcribed.

Buffalo Dance

On the first night of a Corn Dance the Alabama danced until daybreak, and just as the light showed in the east they danced the Buffalo Dance. Men and women joined in the dancing, and the men sang with the leader. The Buffalo Dance songs were followed by loud *halloos*, which were given by Thompson when recording them.

Two sets of Buffalo Dance songs were recorded, a portion of each set being here presented. During the first series the leader pounded on a cypress-knee drum, and during the second series he shook a gourd rattle.

The first song (not presented) was monotonous, somewhat suggesting the tramp of the herd in its repetitions of one tone, in eighth and sixteenth notes. The second of the series (No. 1) contains short phrases with a descending fourth as a prominent interval. The same tempo occurs in No. 2, which has the same keynote but is minor instead of major in tonality. (Cf. Nos. 10 and 11.) This melody is in three sections, each having its own rhythm, and the third section is in a more rapid tempo. The renditions are alike in every respect.

During the first two songs of the second series (not presented) the dancers stood still and the leader, in the

---

[4] Alice C. Fletcher in article on "Busk," *Handbook of American Indians North of Mexico*, Bulletin 30, Bureau of American Ethnology, pp. 176-178. Washington, 1907. See also Swanton in *Forty-second Annual Report*, Bur. Amer. Ethn., pp. 225, 263, 264.

middle of the circle, shook his gourd rattle; then the men moved around the circle in couples, imitating the actions of buffalo. No. 3, the last song of this series, is based on the major pentatonic scale and has the unusual compass of ten tones.

Corn Dance

In the olden days more than a hundred men and women took part in the Corn Dance. The leader took his position inside the circle and started the songs, singing the first phrase, being silent while the singers repeated the phrase, and then joining them, all continuing together to the end of the singing. In all recorded songs the accented stroke of the rattle was exactly with the voice and was followed by a lighter stroke of equal duration; the tempo of the rattle was thus equivalent to quarter notes of the song and the strokes corresponded to eighth notes. A shaking of the rattle preceded the songs for the space of two or three measures. No words occur in the Corn Dance songs. If the syllables are parts of obsolete words, their meaning has been forgotten.

According to oral descriptions of the costumes of the dancers, the men wore buckskin leggings, a beaded belt and silver armlets, sometimes two of these ornaments on one arm, one above and the other below the elbow. Each man carried a turkey-tail fan and made gestures with it as he danced. The ornaments of the women consisted of rings in their ears and large quantities of beads around their necks. On these chains might be as many as ten silver half-dollars, which jingled with a pleasing sound. Hanging from a woman's head, in the back, were many long streamers of braid and bright ribbons. Around her arm was tied a scarf or kerchief, the ends hanging down to her knees, and she carried a handkerchief in her hand, making gestures with it to harmonize with those made by the men with turkey-tail fans. The faces of both men and women were painted with a large dot of red on each cheek just below the eye. To this the men added a line of red down the nose.

Fourteen Corn Dance songs were recorded, six being presented. The simplicity of the first (No. 4) is typical of the entire group. This melody consists of five repetitions of a short phrase and has a steadily descending trend. The rhythm of the next song (No. 5) is more vigorous, but the form is simple, consisting of four phrases with a change of rhythm in the third phrase. This pattern has been found chiefly in songs of the Plains tribes. Rests occur less frequently in Indian songs than in our own, which adds to the interest of No. 6. These rests were given clearly in the five renditions of this song.

In contrast to the preceding songs, No. 7 is a smoothly flowing melody, though admirably adapted to dancing. Smaller count-divisions occur in No. 8, and the group closes with a vigorous melody (No. 9), which is framed, in part, on two descending triads, one major and the other minor. A descending fourth is also prominent in the structure of the melody. The accents, by which the song is divided into measures, were given distinctly throughout the performance.

Social Dances

The Alabama held social dances at any time, many of these dances imitating birds and animals, a custom common to many Indian tribes. A large number of such songs were recorded.

Duck Dance

Dancers moved in alternating couples of two men and two women, all imitating the actions of ducks. As in other Alabama dances, they moved around the fire, "with the sun," and they *zig-zagged* from one side to the other. The women wore ribbons on their heads, and each man had a handkerchief tied around his arm. The leader of the singing, with his drum, was stationed east of the fire.

Only two songs were used with this dance, both of which are here presented. The rhythm of the first (No. 10) is simple but effective and was well sustained.

This song is major in tonality, with a compass of five tones. The second (No. 11) is minor in tonality, with a keynote only a semitone different from that of the preceding melody. (Cf. Nos. 1 and 2.) The rhythm is made emphatic by short rests and an accent upon the recurrent tone B in the latter portion. The triple measure in this part of the song is characteristic of Alabama melodies.

Chicken Dance

Six songs of this dance were recorded. During the first four songs the men and women stood still; during the fifth the women chose partners, and during the sixth they danced in couples, facing each other, with hands on partner's elbows. For a time the men led the motion; then they swung around and the women led. Such dancing resembles a rhythmic walk, with one dancer going backward.

The Chicken Dance song (No. 12) was sung when the women took their partners. The rise and fall of the melody suggests the graceful swaying of the couples before they began to dance. The melody lies partly above and partly below the keynote, the opening measure being framed on two consecutive descending fourths—— C–G, and F–C.

Frog Dance

Both men and women took part in this dance, the women being close to the fire and the men in a compact group outside the circle of women. The leader, with a drum, sang the following song four times, after which the men and women danced around the drum. Six renditions of this song (No. 13) were recorded and are alike in every respect. Although the song is framed largely on a descending minor triad, the most prominent interval is the major third between G and B. The melody tones are those of the minor pentatonic scale.

Rabbit Dance

Only one song was used with this dance. The first portion of the song (No. 14) is framed on a minor triad and minor seventh, the tones occurring in descending order. The second portion is monotonous, and consists only of the tones A, G, and E, in descending progression. The last three measures were sung six times. It is an unusual melody, in both rhythm and melodic structure. The action of the dance was not ascertained.

Terrapin Dance

Men and women took part in this dance, folding their hands and moving them up and down in time with the song. There were two singers, one of whom beat a drum. The leader of the dancers said *"Kwee, kwee,"* and the last man responded with the same syllable.

Only two songs of this dance were recorded, both being here presented. The opening phrases of the first (No. 15) are characterized by the descending fourths C–G, and B flat–F, the song closing with the minor third G–B flat. The tone below the keynote is used effectively. The half notes were sung with a clinging tone which seemed to prolong them beyond the indicated time. The second song (No. 16) contains many small intervals, which the Indian usually sings with uncertain intonation. The tone transcribed as B flat was sometimes sung almost a semitone higher, becoming what is termed an "indeterminate third" above the keynote. This is regarded as a characteristic of primitive singing. The melody tones are more abundant than in a majority of Alabama songs, comprising all the tones of the octave except the fourth and sixth.

Horse Dance

Only five songs were used with the Horse Dance. During the first song the dancers stood still, the women in a circle and the men back of them. During the next two songs the women "danced standing still" and the men moved in two circles back of them, one circle going in each direction. The action with the last two songs of the series was not described. The "dancing" of the women was undoubtedly a flexing of the knees, causing the body to move up and down with a rhythmic motion.

The Horse Dance songs presented are the second and fourth of the series. The framework of No. 17, like that of No. 14, consists of a minor triad and minor seventh, the tones occurring in descending order. Many renditions were recorded, the differences being unimportant and probably connected with changes in the words. A different structure is found in No. 18, the principal intervals being whole tones and the melody being based on the major pentatonic scale. The rhythm of both songs suggests the motion of a galloping horse.

Woman's Dance

A very old dance was described by Thompson, who said it was danced by women walking in single file around the fire. The women did not carry anything in their hands, and they stood in their places between the singing of the songs. They did not sing, the songs being sung by two men who sat on a bench, east of the fire, one man pounding a drum and the other shaking a rattle. There were only four songs with this dance. It was customary to dance this on four nights until midnight, after which the men and women danced together, in various social dances.

Four songs of this dance were recorded but only one is presented (No. 19). Several intervals of a fourth, in descending progression, form the framework of this melody, the descent being usually broken by a passing tone. These are shown with the transcription of the song. The third and seventh above the keynote do not occur, and the melody progresses chiefly by whole tones.

Nateka Dance

Another dance by women was called Nateka. Eleven songs of this dance were recorded, a peculiarity of all the songs being a gradual increase in time during a rendition, the original time being resumed with the repetition of the song. This increase in time took place during the first half of the song, after which the rapid time was maintained to the close of the rendition. The accompaniment was provided by a man with a gourd rattle, seated on a bench inside the circle of dancers. During the first song of the series the women stood still and did not sing, the songs being given by the man with the rattle. During the second song the women sang and "danced up and down." During the third song they danced around the fire, one behind another, stopping at the east side of the fire after each song. Several sharp strokes of the rattle were given at the end of each song. The dance was held in connection with the Corn Dance.

The Nateka song (No. 20) was fifth in the songs of this dance recorded by Thompson. The tones are those of a major triad with the fourth as a passing tone. Two rhythmic units occur, and differ only in the opening tones. The increase in tempo is not indicated in the transcription.

SUMMARY OF ANALYSIS OF SONGS

The following observations are made concerning the entire group of sixty-two recorded songs. More than forty were transcribed, either wholly or in part, and the remainder were studied without transcription. A portion of the latter were practically duplications of transcribed songs, others were without musical value, and a few were uncertain in their intonation.

The purpose of this work was to ascertain whether the songs of the Alabama had a period formation which had been observed in the songs of the Yuma, the Pueblo and the Florida Seminole, as well as among the Tule Indians of Panama. No occurrence of this formation was found in the Alabama songs. On the other hand, the songs are of a distinct type, quite uniform in structure, and of a sort not hitherto found as a tribal group. Many renditions of each song were recorded and are uniform except for occasional variations of no importance. The intonation of the singer was not particularly good, perhaps due to the fact that he is accustomed to singing with piano or organ accompaniment.

The repetitions of a rhythmic unit constitute a larger part of the melody in Alabama songs than in the songs of other tribes, and there is less thematic working out of phrases. The rhythmic unit is generally kept intact and, in some instances, the rhythm of the melody as a whole constitutes a unit which can not be divided.

The rhythms of these songs are dancing rhythms, not the sort of rhythm that characterizes the songs used by medicine men in treating the sick or working magic. The Alabama songs under consideration are composed songs and the rhythms suggest ingenuity in combining durations of tone. The songs of medicine men are said to be received in dreams, and the rhythms have an individuality lacking in composed melodies. Frequently the rhythm of the entire song constitutes a unit. Such rhythms might become hypnotic in effect, if repeated for a long period of time. The rhythms of the Alabama songs are cheerful and lively, as well as simple.

Among the interesting peculiarities of the melodic structure of Alabama songs is the use of the minor triad and minor seventh, the tones occurring in descending order. (See Nos. 9, 14, and 17.) This structure, or framework, occurs in the songs of primitive races other than the Indian, and appears occasionally in the songs of other Indian tribes.

The fourth is a prominent interval in the framework of several songs, suggesting a tetrachord formation in contrast to the triad formation which prevails in many other songs. The intervals of a fourth sometimes overlap, as shown in the analysis of No. 19.

One song (No. 20) contains a gradual increase of tempo in each rendition. This mannerism was found in a Tick Dance song recorded by a reliable Choctaw singer. It also occurred in songs of the Hunci Dance of the Isleta pueblo and Buffalo Dance songs of the Cochiti, the singers stating it was customary to increase the time in songs of these dances. This gradual accelerando differed from the abrupt change of time occurring in songs with period formation, and from changes of time coincident with the words of a song or with some action of the dance. The writer does not recall an instance of this mannerism in the songs of other tribes under observation.

No. 1. BUFFALO DANCE SONG (a)

No. 2. BUFFALO DANCE SONG (b)

No. 3. BUFFALO DANCE SONG (c)

No 4 CORN DANCE SONG (a)

THE ALABAMA INDIANS

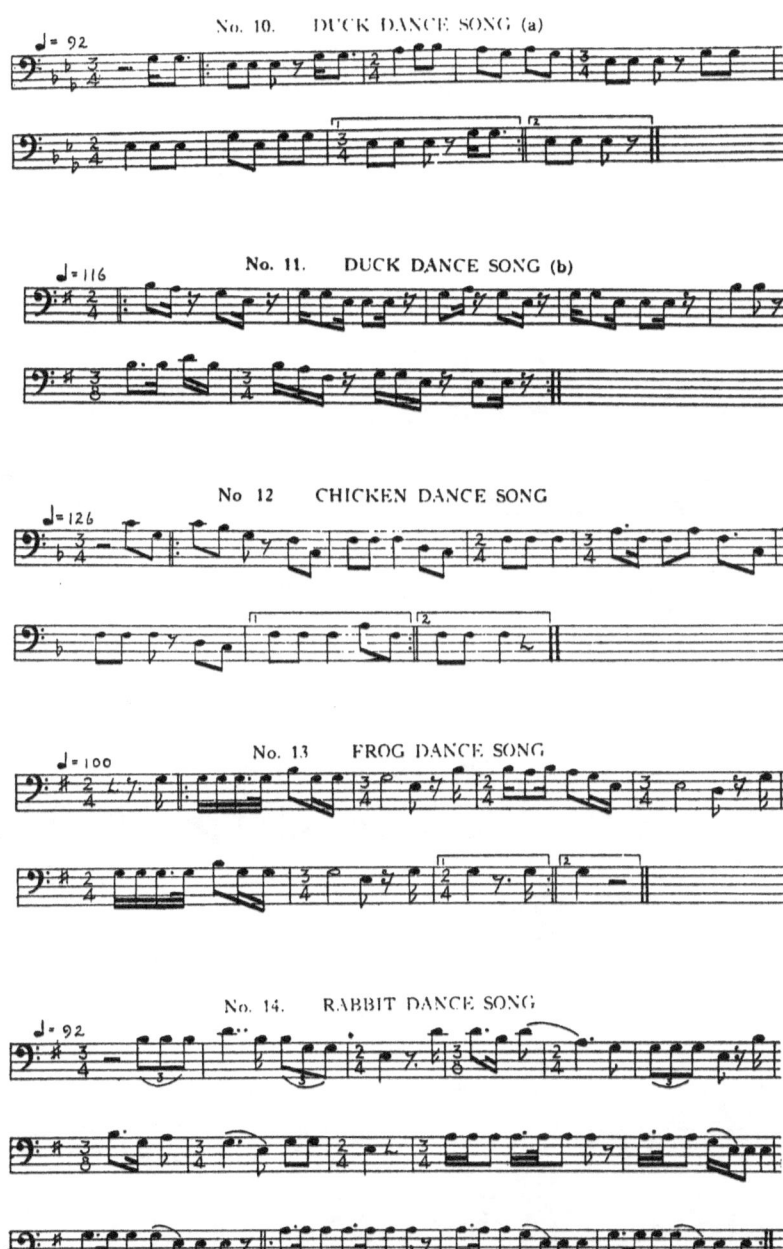

STRAIGHT TEXAS

No. 15. TERRAPIN DANCE SONG (a)

No. 16. TERRAPIN DANCE SONG (b)

No. 17. HORSE DANCE SONG (a)

No. 18. HORSE DANCE SONG (b)

THE ALABAMA INDIANS

Analysis of melody showing descending fourths

TWO TALES FROM THE ALABAMAS

By ELMA HEARD

Sun-Kee, his Indian name, seems to be preferred by its possessor, Chief Charlie Thompson, to the more commonly used English appellation. As a man he is gentle, amiable and cultured. His favorite sport is Indian ball. He is a great story-teller. In attempting to reproduce two stories he told to me, I regret that I cannot convey the charm of his accent and simplicity.[1]

HOW THE INDIANS FIRST GOT SEED

Long before the white men ever came to this country the Indians lived here. One day four Indian braves were sent out by the chief to look for seed. They were told to go west, and to go up and on. After they had traveled for a long, long time, the sky opened up in front of them, and a voice said, "Who are you?" The first Indian answered, "I am a panther," and he ran just as fast as he could and he got through.

The next one came up, and the voice asked, "Who are you?" The Indian answered, "I am a wolf," and he ran just as fast as he could and he got through.

---

[1] The first of these tales is contained in Miss Densmore's article on the Alabama Indians. She describes the conditions under which she heard Chief Charles Martin Thompson, or Sun-Kee, tell it. The variations illustrate very well not so much the inevitable mutations that tales undergo through migration as those they undergo according to the mood of the teller.—Ed.

The third one came up, and the voice asked, "Who are you?" The Indian answered, "I am a wild cat," and he ran just as fast as he could and he got through.

The fourth one came up, and the voice said, "Who are you?" He would not answer; so the heavens closed in on him and killed him.

These three traveled on and on, looking for seed, but "they no get 'um." They came to a big river that they could not cross and so they stopped. Near here there lived an old woman who told them to take a gourd and dip the water, throwing it first this way and then that way, first this way and then that way. They did this for a long while, and then the river parted and they ran through just as fast as they could. When they had passed through safely, the river went back together. They kept going on and on, looking for seed, but "they no get 'um."

Then they came to a wood where there were lots and lots of snakes. They were this deep [Here the narrator made a sign of about one foot.], and they were this big around. [He made a circle about the size of a young pine tree.] They knew they could not get through all those snakes, and so they stopped. Then they skinned some slippery elm trees and wrapped the bark around their legs, around and around. They starting wading through, and when the snakes would strike they would not even feel it. So they waded on through and got to the other side of the wood. They kept going on and on and on and on, looking for seed, but "they no get 'um."

Then they came to a big wall which they could not get through. They smoked and puffed and blew the smoke on the wall, *whoo!* and they smoked and puffed and blew the smoke on the wall, *whoo!* and they smoked and puffed and blew the smoke on the wall, *whoo!* All of a sudden it opened, and they ran through as fast as they could. They kept going on and on and on and on, looking for seed, but "they no get 'um."

Now they were very hungry; so they set out to look for food. They came to a house where there lived an old woman. She gave them a plate on which were three squashes the size of a biscuit, little squashes. They ate these and she gave them some more. They ate these and she gave them some more. They ate these and she gave them some more, and more, and more, until they were no longer hungry.

Then they went on toward the west and upward, looking for seed, but "they no get 'um." By now they were very dirty. They came to a house where lived an old woman. She got a big pot and filled it full of water and boiled it. Then she poured it on the three men and washed them and scraped them with a knife because they were very dirty. She washed and scraped them until they were clean and light,[2] and then they left.

Then they went on toward the west and upward, looking for seed, but "they no get 'um." Finally they came to the Lord's place. He showed them a big glass and let them look down through it. They saw the place on earth from which they had come. The Lord asked them if they would like to go back, and they answered, "Yes, we would like to go back and take our people some seed." That night they went to sleep and when they awoke next morning Heaven had been brought down to earth with seeds of all kinds. And this is how the Indians first got seed.

THE DICE GAME[3]

Two Indian braves were in a dice game. One would bait the other one with his horse, money, weapons, anything, and the second one lost. He bet everything he had of his own and lost. Then he started betting other things. Last of all he bet all the water in the land,—rivers, lakes, creeks, ponds, *all*. And he lost that too.

---
[2] This cleansing represents a spiritual purification.
[3] The similarity between this story and the Biblical account of how Moses smote the rock for water instead of speaking to it as God had commanded is readily apparent.

Then there was no water. All the cattle and horses and people were starving for water. He felt so sad because he had bet all the water that he went to God and asked forgiveness. God told him to go out into a canebrake and to get the biggest one of the switch canes, the kind used for fishing but larger, very large, and break it. He did as God told him to do, and from the cane water began to flow,—into the lakes, the rivers, the creeks, the ponds, and everywhere. There was again plenty of water.

HOW THE ALABAMAS CAME SOUTHWARD

By G. T. BLUDWORTH

This tribal tradition came to me, through John Lee Smith, of Throckmorton, Texas, from a Cherokee Indian named Colberta. The Cherokees and Alabamas were once closely associated with each other in Texas.

The Alabamas long ago dwelt in peace in the cold land of the Northwest, perhaps in the region of Saskatchewan. For them there was a great plenty of bear, elk, moose and other flesh as well as fish and seal that frequented the waters. But the bitter, bitter north wind often made it next to impossible for them to hunt, and then they suffered. They had heard through other tribes of a country far to the south where the Sun God the year around shed his rays upon the forests, mountains and streams, giving warmth to both the animals hunted and the hunters. Here also men could grow crops of grain and gather fruits.

The Chief of the Alabamas, desirous of bettering the conditions of his people, took the matter to Abba Mingo, "Chief of the Sky." In response he received the mandate in the form of a vision that if he would proceed with his tribe towards the south, the Great Chief of the Sky would guide his travels into a better hunting ground. The vision further instructed the Alabamas to carry with them all their possessions, including their totem pole, which was to be planted every night in an upright position directly south of their camps. Each morning they were to proceed in the direction their totem pole pointed.

The Alabamas made preparations and began their long journey. Every morning their totem pole would be leaning southward but veering a little to the east. On they marched, finding ample game for their subsistence and coming into lands warmed by the Sun God and replenished by the Rain God, where flowers and fruits were profuse. At last they arrived at the bank of a great river the like of which they had never beheld. This to them was an insurmountable barrier, and they understood not why the Chief of the Sky should have guided them such a weary way to such a blockade. True to their belief, however, they camped on the very banks of the stream, its turbid waters swishing at their feet. The Chief and his braves scarcely slept that night.

Upon arising the next day they found their faithful totem pole leaning more than was its usual custom, but this time directly to the east. Nothing remained but to cross the wide, wide stream. Undaunted, they spent several days making canoes from timbers found in the vicinity. Then they took from its moorings their totem pole, which all the time had maintained its posture, pointing directly across the river. Their crossing was safe and, after returning thanks to Abba Mingo, Chief of the Sky, for directing them safely, they continued their travels. The totem pole now pointed eastward each day until they arrived in the country that later took their name—Alabama.

THE PLAY PARTY IN VICTORIA COUNTY

By HELEN ASHWORTH MOORE

I. I MAKE MY LIVING IN THE SANDY LAND

In the eastern part of Victoria County, Texas, there is a large tract of land which originally comprised the William A. Wood Ranch, but which has, since the early part of this century, been cut up into a number of small farms in order that every available acre may be made to produce cotton. Very few of the owners of these farms work their own land; in consequence, the Wood Community, as it is called, has become predominantly a community of tenant farmers. The people are of many nationalities, of many creeds, and of widely differing customs and habits. There are Anglo-Americans, who came originally from the Old South and from the mountains of Tennessee and Kentucky; there are Bohemians, Poles, Germans, and Swedes whose fathers came to Texas in the days when boatloads of immigrants landed at Indianola and from there spread through the state, patterning their settlements on those so recently left behind; there are Italians, who came as pioneers in railroad building when the "Macaroni" lines were run through the county; there are the Irish, whose ancestors came in with the O'Connors, the Woods, the McFaddins, and others from the Old Country—known wherever cattlemen swap yarns about the old days on the trail; there are the Mexicans, too, but countless tabus on both sides prevent to such an extent social contact between them and the other nationalities that they have become a community within a community and have no part in our story.

In spite of differences in language and background, the people of the Wood Community have a great deal in common. Their children go to the same schools; their poverty is due to the same economic causes; they attend the same church, Catholics and Protestants alike singing, "I'm a child of the King," out of the same hymnbook in a Non-Progressive Christian meeting, the only available form of public worship; and finally, because of the restrictions of their common poverty and of their common school, they enjoy the same diversions and "socials." These diversions are limited to picnics and revivals in the summer, school socials and church pie- or box-suppers in the winter, and a sprinkling of play-parties whenever there is time to get them in, usually in the fall and spring.

In more recent years, however, the old forms of diversion have become less interesting to the car-minded and movie-minded young people, and where, a few years ago, play-parties were held every week, they are now comparatively rare, and the young people of ten years ago who played the games are so afraid of the stigma of being considered "countrified" that they evade the question or have a convenient lapse of memory when any attempt is made to revive the old songs and games. As automobiles have become more prevalent in the community, more urban forms of amusement have become available, but instead of broadening their outlook, this has only given the people a contempt for rural pleasures. I find that I am unable to agree with the old woman from the Hill Country who surprised me recently with the remark that, "Henry Ford has done more for young people in the country than Jesus Christ ever did."

So it is largely from my own memories of play-parties attended during one unforgettable winter, and from the helpful letters of one or two old friends who still have pride in their traditions, that this collection of play-party songs, still incomplete, and this account of a typical party of the Wood Community, have been written.

II. SWING THOSE PRETTY GIRLS

It was one of those clear, moonlit nights in October when all the senses are exhilarated by the awareness of the change in season. Not that it was cold, for cold weather comes late to the southern cotton-belt of Texas, but the dusty, bitter scent of the broad-leaved burdock weeds and man-high sunflower plants that filled the ditches prickled in the nostrils; the fields in the moonlight showed the skeletons of dried cotton stalks twined about with tie-vines, their bright leaves and purple trumpets gallantly masking the desolation wrought by the last scorching heat of summer; from high in the sky the excited gabbling of wild fowls drifted down as they hurried through the last lap of their long journey to their winter home in the marshes of Matagorda Bay.

On ordinary nights the scene would have been enveloped in silence save for the occasional insect noises or the swish of leaves as a cottontail rabbit dived for safety into the sanctuary of the shadows of a mesquite thicket, but this was no ordinary night. The gravel roads that seldom knew a wayfarer after dark were busy with a varied and pleasure-seeking traffic, for a few days before in each little school of the surrounding communities some overalled small boy or shocky-haired girl had pranced importantly up the aisle to ask teacher if he or she might make the announcement that there would be a play-party "over to Foster's" on the next Friday night. That night had come. There was no time "set," for everyone knew the party would start after the milking was done, the chickens locked up, supper finished, and party clothes put on; no R.S.V.P.'s were requested, for everybody of every age was welcomed and there were no elaborate arrangements to be upset by unexpected guests; no refreshments were expected in this community of tenant farmers where every man's unceasing struggle was to put food in the mouths of his own family; the host's obligation began and ended by furnishing a room for the games.

Along the road, then, in the moonlight of the early evening came the party-guests in all manner of conveyances. Crude farm wagons grated along, pulled by mismatched teams of horses and mules, and filled to overflowing with people of all ages; T-model Fords and rickety Chevrolets rattled by with their loads of families and neighbors; buggies, even a gig or two, and a few young blades on horseback completed the cavalcade.

"Foster's" was one of the many weatherbeaten, unpainted, small farm houses of that region—grey roof, grey walls, grey gallery running the length of the house, a few scraggly rose bushes and perhaps a forlorn perennial or two constituting its only claim to a half-hearted attempt toward beauty. Each arrival was greeted by the baying of a motley collection of dogs, part hound, part terrier, and part plain yellow mongrel, that stretched their way out from under the gallery or from the shadows of the dark umbrella chinaberry trees before the door. The men exchanged laconic greetings and sat or leaned against the house, while the women went inside to a room cleared, for the occasion, of all furniture except a stiff row of chairs and benches arrayed around the walls. The babies were placed in neat rows on a rickety iron bed in the adjoining room, and their mothers returned to where the other women and girls were seated against the wall to take part in the low-voiced talk of births and deaths, church and chickens, that filled the interval before the games began.

* * * * *

"Hello, Bob." ... "Hello, Amelie." ... "Howdy, Miz Carter." ... "We'd about give you out."

The greetings from outside act as a signal to those within. Girls hastily powder noses that are already too heavily whitened, adjust skirts that have turned awry, or twist curls around fingers in a final distrust of the effectiveness of a lamp-heated curling iron. And just in time, too, as the new arrivals enter, closely followed by the entire population of eligible males of the community, dislodged now from their retreat outside by the promise of excitement within. With some scuffling and horseplay, the swains make their way, each to the lady of his choice, and mount guard against possible competition, entertaining their partners with bits of small talk or flirtation, or showing off their own type of wit by calling out personal remarks or mild insults to friends across the room.

Bob, a lanky youth, resplendent in corduroy trousers and a much-laundered white silk shirt topped with a lavender collar, flings back a long, greasy pompadour of hair from his pimply face, and taking his pretty Bohemian partner by the hand, steps to the middle of the floor.

"Well, what'll it be, folks? Name your poison."

This quip is greeted with appreciative giggles from the girls and a clamor of suggestions from the boys:

"Sealy" . . . "Brown Jug" . . . "General Gaines" . . . "Skip-to-my-Lou" . . . "Come on, Bob, give us 'Cinnamon'."

In a nasal drawl with a heavy emphasis on the third and on the last syllables of each line, Bob begins droning out the verse of a favorite:

> "Coffee grows on live oak trees;
> River flows with brandy-o;
> Go choose someone to walk with you
> Sweet as molasses candy-o."

By this time a wide ring has formed, and Bob, taking Amelie by the hand, begins swinging her around the inside of the circle to the quickened tempo of the next movement:

> "One in the middle and got to get about,
> One in the middle and got to get about,
> One in the middle and got to get about,
> Oh turn, Cinnamon, turn."

Is it possible that this "Cinnamon" is a contraction of that "Sinner Man" who occurs in Southern folk songs? Perhaps it is, but the origin of his song is of no importance to him as the singer chooses another couple to join him and his partner within the ring. He continues:

"Two in the middle and both get about . . .
Oh turn, Cinnamon, turn."

Then as other couples are chosen, the song continues:
"Three in the middle and hard to get about . . ."
Then,
"Four in the middle and can't get about . . ."

And finally, as the inner circle becomes larger and the outer circle dwindles proportionately, comes the last verse:

"All hands out and join the ring,
Oh turn, Cinnamon, turn."

At the last line there is a wild scramble to get back in the circle and to get a new and desirable partner.

In the general confusion, Amelie has been snatched from her partner by big blond Emil Hnatek, nearer seven feet in height than six, and overflowing at wrist and ankle from a very new, very mail-order blue serge suit. Bob consoles himself with the buxom daughter of the host, a young lady of too-generous proportions and the life of the party. In an ill-advised moment her parents had named her Faye, but she proves that she can be spry in spite of her size as her black rayon taffeta crackles through the more intricate measures of "Sealy":

"Dr. McCollum's a married man,
A married man, a married man,
Dr. McCollum's a married man.
What makes you do me so?"

Then, the ring having the "feel" of the song, the verses take up the changes of the game and the players follow instructions hilariously as the singer continues:

"Oh wheel and turn, Sealy,
Oh wheel and turn, Sealy,
Oh wheel and turn, Sealy.
What makes you do me so?"

Other figures called are: "Oh do-ce-do, Sealy," "All line up, Sealy," "Oh circle left, Sealy," "Let's balance off,

Sealy," and finally, back to the line again with, "We'll all promenade, Sealy," each verse ending in the same plaintive query, "What makes you do me so?"

As this games reaches its conclusion, the strain of being chief entertainer is beginning to tell on Bob. His silk shirt is clinging damply to his shoulders and his voice is growing husky, but he never gives up his place in the limelight until it is absolutely necessary. Leaving his partner giggling at the blandishments of "one of them Morgans," a young man distinguished chiefly by cowman's boots and a yellow silk neck handkerchief, he dashes "out back," where he drinks hastily from a bucket of well water, using as a matter of course the rusty community dipper that hangs on the wall.

Then, being without a partner upon his return, he starts a new game in which he may be alone in the center of the ring. As the couples slowly march around him in a circle, he sings:

> "Happy is the miller boy that lives by the mill,
> Takes his toll with a free good will;
> One hand on the hopper and the other in the sack,
> Every time the mill turns, he drops two back."

As he reaches the end of the last line there is a scramble as each boy tries to grab the hand of the girl two couples back, and, to complicate matters further, Bob joins the ring by the simple expedient of stepping in and taking Amelie's hand, leaving her tall Bohemian partner alone and very much embarrassed in the center of the ring.

Now everybody joins in the song and the miller boy is put through his paces over and over, sometimes taking a toll of three, sometimes one, but usually two, with the inevitable scramble and the resultant new miller boy at the conclusion of each round. Soon the whole company is breathless and disheveled and the play is stopped while the players squeeze their way in among the older people on the benches along the wall to rest and cool off.

Surely this is the opportunity that Faye has been waiting for. Winking slyly at Lottie Crisp, she disappears into the next room, and Lottie, shaking out her faded gingham dress and adjusting her pink chiffon scarf at a more fetching angle about her neck, takes two chairs to the center of the room and there awaits Faye's return. All the guests know that Faye has gone for her guitar and Lottie's, but they are politely surprised and genuinely delighted when she returns with them. After much preliminary giggling, throat-clearing, and tuning of instruments, the entertainment is under way. Faye leads off in a shrill soprano and Lottie "seconds" in a deep and unnatural basso-profundo to the one-two-three beat of the untiring G-chord of the guitars. The song is "I'll Be All Smiles Tonight." It is of unrequited love, and runs on and on,[1] finally concluding with:

> "And when the feast was ended, oh then I did rejoice,
> And sang the songs he taught me with never a falt'ring voice;
> And even them that know me did think my heart was light;
> Tho' my heart will break tomorrow, I'll be all smiles tonight."

Follows a dramatic song with martial touches, entitled "Custer's Last Stand," which tells of the death of a "fair-haired boy," each stanza ending with the accented assertion that, "He *was* her only son." Several songs succeed, all sad, the themes of which seem to be last words from battlefields, lost letters to loved ones, and lockets containing golden curls. Their repertoire being exhausted, the entertainers beam at their applauding friends and return their guitars to the bedroom.

Now all the young people are ready to begin the games again; all, that is, except little Sophia Puleska, who has spent the evening unnoticed in a corner behind the older people. But not for a moment must you think that Sophia is unhappy. With no thought of joining in herself, she is having a wonderful time watching and listening, for this is her first party; and, to fill her cup

---
[1] The complete text is given toward the end of this article.

quite to overflowing, she is wearing, for the first time, the first pair of shoes she has ever owned. Always she has plodded along on her own bare brown feet, behind the plow, along the cotton rows with hoe or with sack, the long miles to school or to the store, over black sandy fields or hard red gravel roads, without knowing the luxury of shoes. But now that she is fifteen, her father has let her have enough of her cotton-picking money to buy shoes; she has spent delightful minutes reading the mail-order catalog with its profusion of footgear; she has spent days of anxiety waiting for the postman to bring her package; after receiving them and trying them on many times, she has carried her treasures three miles in her arms, carefully wrapped in paper, on her long walk to this party before stopping by the road, in sight of the house, to put them on. She does not know that the over-decorated black and white oxfords were made for a man; nor does she know the reason for the rough crepe soles, nor the meaning of the word "golf." All she knows is a supreme content at owning and wearing the most beautiful possession she has ever had.

But Sophia's evening has not yet reached its peak. Carl Hassendeufel is coming toward her and is asking her to play in the games. Sophia cannot believe it. He is a neighbor and a schoolmate, but never has he noticed her before.

Her round Polish face flaming with blushes, Sophia mutters, "I don' know how." But somehow she finds herself in the excitement of the ring, and she knows from that moment that Heaven is a place where party games are played and that German boys in overalls are the partners.

Bob is still resting, knowing that he must save his voice for more of the old favorites that only he is skilful enough to lead. For the time being, he has graciously abdicated in favor of Jack Lawton, who might be called an apprentice in the art of party singing and who can be trusted to carry on with the simpler plays. He also, as a mark of his profession, is cultivating a long pompadour and is practicing the art of tossing it back with a swing of his head, but his wiry, curly hair is unruly and his efforts are not uniformly successful. With a guarded flip of his forelock, he enters the rapidly forming ring, and with a voice notable more for volume than for beauty, launches into "General Gaines":

>"General Gaines he made a raid,
>He made a raid, he made a raid,
>General Gaines he made a raid,
>And lost many a soldier.

>"Turn back, boys, and save the day,
>And save the day, and save the day,
>Turn back, boy, and save the day,
>And don't forget your partner."

"General Gaines," like the "Miller Boy," becomes wildly hilarious as the boys "turn back" and exchange partners, leaving the unlucky General in the middle of the ring. This game suggests the old familiar "Pig in the Parlor," and the company goes into this so vocally that Jack has to strain his voice to maintain the lead:

>"We got a new pig in the parlor, . . .
>And he is Irish too."

And through the well-known song to:

>"Right hand to the next you meet,
>And we'll all promenade."

As this game ends, it is inevitable that someone calls for "Skip-to-my-Lou"; one seems always to suggest the other:

>"Lost my partner, Skip-to-my-Lou . . .
>Skip-to-my-Lou, my darling.
>"If you can't get a redbird, a bluebird'll do, . . .
>Skip-to-my-Lou, my darling."

Then follow the verses about "Little red wagon painted blue" and "Chicken in the bread-pan," the song concluding with, "Choose your partner, Skip-to-my-Lou"; but by dint of countless repetitions, the game goes on and on.

Just as the weaker members are beginning to fall by the wayside, a commotion at the door attracts general attention, and in bursts a stocky boy in overalls, twanging on a French harp and jigging as he comes. His face is streakily blacked with cork; his lips are reddened in a wide circle; and his blue eyes and the strings of sandy hair escaping from his cap give a contrast to his get-up that is grotesque in the extreme. Quickly the circle opens to give him the center of the floor, and he jigs in, going through muscle-twisting contortions and gyrations as his feet keep up an untiring shuffle-shuffle-thump, shuffle-shuffle-thump.

After the music of his triumphal entry, he jigs on without the French harp accompaniment, saving his breath for his dance, until Albert O'Keefe, the Irish dandy, yells, "I'm bettin' on you, Swede."

Suddenly the jig stops. The sweat of his brow is making the blackened face of the dancer more zebra-like than negroid. Crestfallen, he asks, "How'd you know who I was?"

Albert has a reputation for wit to be maintained. Quick as a flash the answer comes back, "I'd know your hide in a tan-yard."

Howls of laughter follow at the Swede's expense, the familiarity of the joke seeming only to add savor. That Albert is a case, everybody agrees.

The hostess of the evening does not join in the general merriment over the jig. Her face has a set and forbidding look.

Those near enough can hear her say through pursed lips to a neighbor: "Party-games are all right for the young folks, and they ought to have their fun, but I never thought I'd see dancin' in my own house. Dancin', to me, ain't nothing but sin."

Among those who hear is Jack, the substitute singer. Fearing an untimely end to the party, he calls out: "Come on, y'all. Get your partners for "Shudah":

> "Right hands crossed, Shu-dah,
> A long fare-you-well.
> Right hands crossed, Shu-dah,
> A long fare-you-well."

The hostess relaxes; the party is saved; everybody is happy. The game goes on:

> "Left hands back, Shu-dah" . . .

But apparently everybody is not happy. Bob has left his place on the bench and is advancing on Jack with a look, half of annoyance and half of surprise, on his face. Jack knows better than to lead "Shu-dah." Bob learned that one from his mother and taught it to this crowd himself. It is well known that "Shu-dah" is his property. Jack must be put in his place. Too late the upstart realizes his error, and backs into the ring of players with a spuriously welcoming smile to the leader.

Somewhat pacified by this gesture, Bob takes his rightful place and swings into "Brown Jug":

> "I sent my brown jug down to town,
> Sent my brown jug down to town,
> Sent my brown jug down to town,
> So early in the morning.
>
> "It came back all upside down, . . .
> So early in the morning."

His voice is strong again. He has his Public back where it belongs. The figures are followed with dash and a certain grace as he sings:

> "Swing those pretty girls round and round, . . .
> So early in the morning."

Again the call for favorite games is music in his ears. Some of the players want to repeat games played earlier; some are calling for new ones. Bob listens to all with an air of lordly indifference. He is inordinately proud of his seemingly endless repertoire; so he starts a new one:

>"Marching down Tenn-o-see,
>Marching down Tenn-o-see,
>Marching down Tenn-o-see,
>Pretty little girl by the side of me."

He looks around for Amelie and finds her just outside the line, talking with Joe Marraggia. Everybody likes Joe. Of course, everybody knows that he is making bootleg liquor down by the creek, but a fellow has to make a living someway. The only real drawback is that he persists in wearing a little black *mus*-tache, but these Eyetalians are funny. Just the same, everybody likes Joe. So with a friendly smile for his rival, Bob reaches out his hand and pulls Amelie into the line beside him, and "Tenn-o-see" continues:

>"Oh young ladies, won't you go? . . .
>If you go, you'll catch a beau."

Mrs. Humphries is rising from her place and pulling her sweater about her shoulders: "You Jesse, you Lela, you Cecil, come on now. Your Papa'll give you party-games with a broom-handle if you sleep late in the morning."

A chorus of protest arises: "It's early, yet." . . . "It ain't time to go home." . . . "Just one more game." . . . "Come on, Bob, one more."

Bob rises to the occasion. He has a good one that he has saved for a spectacular finish, and he goes into it with vigor:

>"Little log house, nobody living it in,
>Little log house, nobody living in it,
>Little log house, nobody living in it,
>Her name is Susie Brown.

"We'll get married, we'll live in it, . . .
"You'll pick cotton, I'll drag sacks," . . .

The little room is a-flutter with skirts as the boys swing the girls to a grand right and left.

>"Cornstalk fiddle and a shoestring bow, . . .
>Goodbye, Miss Susie Brown."

With a final whirl of partners, the ring breaks up. Players find wraps or locate brothers and sisters. Tired mothers gather their broods together and sort out the babies on the bed. The house begins to empty. A few remember their manners and a spattering of—"Had a good time," and "I sure enjoyed myself," is heard.

As the last of the guests leave, Faye follows to the front gallery and calls after them: "Better not rush off in the heat of the day without your blanket."

Everybody whoops with laughter. That Faye is a clown. Like Albert, she can be depended on to say the smart thing.

* * * * *

Once more the quiet of the Autumn night was broken by the sound of wheels on the gravel. Startled grey rabbits ran across the road and hid trembling in the weeds by the roadside, their eyes dazzled and their minds confused by the lights of the cars. Sleepy birds twittered peevishly at the interruption of their rest and sought more thickly-leaved perches. From the cars and wagons that followed each other so closely came only occasional low-voiced words in place of the laughter and singing that had been heard a few hours before. In the wagon beds children huddled together for warmth in the dew-drenched midnight and dozed. Tired from the unaccustomed gaiety of the party and from the lateness of the hour, the recent seekers after pleasures now sought only home and rest. Soon all had passed. The road again was left to silence and the gleam of moonlight on the cotton stalks.

III. ALL LINE UP

In giving the following songs, with music and directions for playing the games, I have avoided duplicating material in *Swing and Turn: Texas Play-Party Games,* by William A. Owens, 1936.

Brown Jug

(The melody is the same as that used in other parts of Texas, and given by Owens.[2])

1. Sent my brown jug down to town,
   Sent my brown jug down to town,
   Sent my brown jug down to town,
   Sent my brown jug down to town,
   So early in the morning.

2. It came back all upside down, *etc.*
   So early in the morning.

3. Swing those pretty girls round and round, *etc.*

4. Raise big 'taters in the sandy land, *etc.*

5. R'ar back, chicken, and crow for day, *etc.*

6. Flop your wings and fly away, *etc.*

In this game, the players form a circle with girls and boys alternating. On the first stanza, they circle right, changing direction and circling left on the second stanza. For the rest of the song, the boys swing the girls, beginning with the partner and working toward the right, at each line of the song another girl. If the lines and the girls do not come out even, the leader improvises by adding a *do-ce-do* or two when he returns to his original partner, or by repeating some of the verses until all the girls are swung.

This game does not appear to be very widespread, though it is found in several parts of Texas, as well as in Missouri and Arkansas. The Missouri version[3] appears to be the original one, as there is a continuity to the verses and all are about the doings of the brown jug, only the first two verses being like the first two of the Texas version. This is obviously a composite, as the "sandy land" stanza is taken directly from a game called

---
[2] Owens, W. A.: *Swing and Turn: Texas Play-Party Games*, p. 35.
[3] Hamilton, G. M.: "The Play-Party in Northeastern Missouri," *J. A. F. L.,* XXVII, 296.

Sandy Land that is not played in the Wood Community. Dudley and Payne give the "sandy land" lines in their version,[4] also from Texas, but do not include stanzas 3, 5, and 6. In his Texas version, Owens includes a first stanza like that above; his second stanza begins, "It came back with a waltz around"; and the other stanzas all begin with directions for the figures of the game, which is a much more complicated form than that used in Victoria County. The Arkansas version has only two verses, the first like the opening verse of the Texas versions, but the second is an amusing variant which goes:

"Hit come back all flounced around, *(3 times)*
Tral de al de ay."[5]

Charlie

1. Come my love and go with me,
   A trip we'll take together.

2. For Charlie he's nice young man,
   Charlie is a dandy,
   Charlie he's a nice young man,
   And feeds the girls on candy.

3. Five times five is twenty-five,
   Five times six is thirty,
   Five times seven is thirty-five,
   And five times eight is forty.

4. Five times nine is forty-five,
   Five times ten is fifty,
   Five times 'leven is fifty-five,
   And five times twelve is sixty.

5. Higher up the cherry tree,
   Riper grows the berry;
   Sooner young men court the girls,
   Sooner they will marry.

---
[4] Dudley, R. E., and Payne, L. W., Jr., "Some Texas Play-Party Songs," *Pub. of the Texas Folk-Lore Society*, I, 9.
[5] Randolph, Vance: "The Ozark Play-Party," *J. A. F. L.*, XLII, 224.

While this game was played at the same time the others in this collection were used, I was not present at any parties where it was played, and have been able to get only the words, without any idea as to melody or procedure.

Though known in this community as *Charlie,* this game is obviously a fragmentary form of *Weevily Wheat,* one of the oldest of the party-games, and thought to date back to the English songs of Bonny Prince Charlie.[6] The game, as played in other parts of Texas, includes the verses above, Dudley and Payne[7] including all four verses in the same meter, and Owens giving the first three in addition to the regular *Weevily Wheat* verses.

To enumerate the localities in which this song is sung would be a repetition of the bibliography of this paper, for the game was played in practically all the communities studied.

CINNAMON (refrain)

One in the mid-dle and got to get a-bout, O turn, Cin-na-mon, turn.

The first part of the melody is the same as that given by Owens[8] and used in other parts of Texas. As there is some difference in the second movement, the last two lines of the refrain are given below:

1. Coffee grows on live oak trees,
   River flows with brandy-o;
   Go choose someone to walk with you,
   Sweet as molasses candy-o.

2. One in the middle and got to get about, *(3 times)*
   Oh turn, Cinnamon, turn.

---

[6] Wolford, L. J.: *The Play-Party in Indiana,* p. 102; Richardson, Vivian: "The Singing Games Have Eternal Youth," *Dallas News,* April 1, 1928.
[7] Dudley and Payne: *op cit.,* p. 18.
[8] Owens, W. A.: *op. cit.,* p. 37.

PLAY PARTY IN VICTORIA COUNTY 317

3. Two in the middle and both get about, *etc.*
4. Three in the middle and hard to get about, *etc.*
5. Four in the middle and can't get about, *etc.*
6. All hands out and join the ring, *etc.*

At the first stanza, the players circle to the right around the leader, who is inside the ring. At the conclusion of this he chooses a partner, whom he swings, first by the right hand and then by the left to the music of the second stanza. At the conclusion of this, both choose new partners, and the swinging and choosing of partners continue until the inside of the circle becomes too crowded and all go back to the ring at the singing of the last verse.

This song is the only one used in the games of the Wood Community that appears to have any local change in it. It is widely known through the states, but in every other instance the first line runs, "Coffee grown on *white* oak trees"; here the live oak is the most prevalent type, and the white oak is, I believe, unknown; so it follows that the more familiar tree has been substituted in the game. On the other hand, it is possible that this song has come from other Gulf Coast states having the same climate and flora, and that the change occurred before the introduction of the song into this locality. Unfortunately, there were no collections of songs from other Gulf Coast states available for comparison. The refrain, "Turn, Cinnamon, turn," is also unique to this game in this community, though it is used in other parts of Texas in a game called *Turn, Cinnamon, Turn,* which has no further resemblance to the game given above in words, music, or procedure. The usual refrain used with *Coffee Grows on White Oak Trees* is, "Turn those ladies home," or "Swing those ladies round."

This song may be derived from a ballad of the North Carolina mountains, called *Daisy:*

> "Coffee grows on the white oak tree,
> The river runs with brandy;
> My little gal is a blue-eyed gal,
> As sweet as any candy.
>
> Fly around my blue-eyed gal,
> So fly around my daisy;
> Every time I see that gal
> She almost runs me crazy."[9]

But whether the game came from the ballad, or the ballad from the game, its wide diffusion attests to its age. An interesting composite is *Four in the Middle,* a game played in Missouri, of which the stanzas are taken from *Coffee Grows on White Oak Trees, Alabama* and *Josey,* and the refrain is, "Hello, Susan Brown."[10]

Dan Tucker

This, like *Charlie,* was not sung at any games that I attended, though I understand that it was fairly popular at that time. I do not know either the melody or the figures that accompanied it:

> Old Dan Tucker goes to town, stands around,
> Swings those ladies round and round;
> First to the east and then to the west,
> Then to the one that you love best;
> Fly, Tucker, fly; fly, Tucker, fly.

Obviously this is only a fragment, of which even the chorus has been lost, and the refrain, "Fly, Tucker, fly," substituted. The complete form is used in other parts of Texas and is given by Owens, Dudley and Payne, and by Vivian Richardson. A version similar to the complete Texas song, but lacking the chorus, was found in Arkansas.[11] In practically every other collection of songs studied in preparation for this paper, *Dan Tucker,* in various similar forms with many verses and chorus complete, was found to be an old favorite.

---

[9] Edmands, Lila W.: "Songs from the Mountains of North Carolina," J. A. F. L., VI, 131.
[10] Randolph, Vance: *op. cit.,* p. 213.
[11] Wilson, Charles M.: *Backwoods America,* p. 80.

PLAY PARTY IN VICTORIA COUNTY 319

GENERAL GAINES

Gene-ral Gaines he made a raid, he made a raid, he made a raid Gene-ral Gaines he made a raid, And lost many a sol dier

1. General Gaines, he made a raid,
   He made a raid, he made a raid,
   General Gaines, he made a raid,
   And lost many a soldier.

2. Turn back, boys, and save the day,
   And save the day, and save the day,
   Turn back, boys, and save the day,
   And don't forget your partner.

This was also sung occasionally with "General Jackson" substituted for "General Gaines." It was a favorite for use in getting the party started. Partners clasp hands and move in a circle around the leader during the singing of the first part; at "turn back," each boy drops back to catch the hand of the girl behind him, and in the ensuing confusion, the leader usually manages to get the hand of one of the girls, leaving a new "General" in the center of the ring.

References to this game have been found in only two other collections. In Idaho[12] it is sung as *General Price*, and the second stanza goes, "Turn back, boys, and *sail away.*" Owens gives a version like the one used in Idaho but uses "Old John Brown" as well as "General Price." The music given by Owens is somewhat different from the melody given above.

---
[12] Ball, Leona: "The Play-Party in Idaho," *J. A. F. L.*, XLIV, 8.

The origin of this song is difficult to determine because of the conflicting historical references in the different versions. General Andrew Jackson and General Edmond P. Gaines were both active around New Orleans during the War of 1812 and in the local wars against the Indians immediately afterwards. This would tend to date the song earlier than Civil War times, when Owens believes the name, General Price, places it. It is possible, of course, that the local names were substituted in Louisiana to take the place of "General Price" after the Civil War, but Louisiana had Confederate heroes, too, without having to go back fifty years to another war to find familiar names. It seems to me, therefore, that the version used in Victoria County is probably the original form, and that the song came to Texas with the pioneers from Louisiana.

The Girl I Left Behind Me

The melody for this song is the same as that given by Owens.

1. First young man across the ring,
   Take her by the right hand,
   Then your partner by the left,
   And promenade the girl behind you.

2. Oh that girl, that pretty little girl,
   The girl I left behind me,
   Rosy cheeks and curly hair,
   The girl I left behind me.

In this game, the leader swings the girl opposite him in the ring; then he returns to his partner and swings her while all the other boys swing their partners. Then all drop back to promenade the girls behind them.

This game must be of widespread use in Texas. Piper gives a version from Arkansas,[13] beginning:

"O swing that girl, that pretty little girl,
The girl I left behind me;

---

[13] Piper, Edwin F.: "Some Play-Party Games of the Middle West," *J. A. F. L.*, XXVIII, 286.

She's pretty in the face and neat about the waist,
The girl I left behind me."

the same version as Piper's is found also in Missouri,[14] and in a shorter form in Michigan.[15]

GREEN LEAVES

1. Green leaves, green leaves that grow on a vine;
   Go choose you a partner, the prettiest you can find.
2. When you're married, jump for joy, *(3 times)*
   For joy it's bound to be.
3. Now you're married, jump for joy, *(3 times)*
   For joy it's bound to be.
4. Salute your bride and join the ring, *(3 times)*
   For joy it's bound to be.

A ring is formed, which marches slowly around the leader during the singing of the first stanza. The tempo quickens on the second stanza and the leader swings the partner he has chosen within the ring. In the fol-

---

[14] Randolph, Vance: *op. cit.,* p. 231.
[15] Gardner, Emelyn E.: "Some Play-Party Games in Michigan," *J. A. F. L.,* XXXIII, 91.

lowing stanzas, each person in the center chooses a new partner, and the swinging continues, right on the first two lines, left on the next two. A new partner is chosen from the ring on the refrain. At the end of the last stanza, all players return to the ring.

This game seems to be used in Texas only, as there are no references to its being found outside the state. Owens gives a version that is accompanied by a different melody and has only two stanzas, the first of which is like the first above, and the second is:

"Honey in the comb so sweet, so sweet, *(3 times)*
Joy it's bound to be."

Dudley and Payne give a version used in Bowie and Grayson counties which also has only two stanzas, these being identical with the first two of the Victoria County version.

Irish Potatoes

1. Come, my love, and go with me, *(3 times)*
 I will take good care of thee.
2. Oh no, I cannot go, *(3 times)*
 Because I love my mamma so.
3. Irish potatoes, tops and all, *(3 times)*
 Kiss her now or not at all.
4. Cream and peaches twice a week, *(3 times)*
 Kiss her on the other cheek.

This was another of the games I did not see personally, and therefore I can give neither the music nor the procedure. An interesting point is that it is the only kissing game I have come across in this community, though there are many of them recorded from other parts of the state and from other states. This may be due to the fact that the outward and visible morality of the community conformed to a strict standard, or perhaps it was due to the presence at these parties of outlanders such as myself.

This game, under other names, is familiar in a number of other states, and according to Botkin,[16] who gives

---

[16] Botkin, B. A.: "The Play-Party in Oklahoma," *Pub.* of Texas Folk-Lore Soc., VII, 23.

the Oklahoma version, is taken in part from an old English folk-song, "I'm Seventeen Come Sunday," and in part from a hymn, "Consolation Flowing Free." Under this latter title the game has been recorded from northern Texas[17] and from Missouri[18] as well as from Oklahoma. In the North Texas version the game is purged of its kissing stanza. In Indiana[19] it is known as "Oats, Peas, Beans," and takes several stanzas from that old rhyme as well as from "Consolation Flowing Free." The Victoria County version is the only one containing "Irish Potatoes," and alone uses "Irish Potatoes" for a title.

JOSEY

Get in the ring and let's dance Josey, get in the ring and let's dance Josey, get in the ring and let's dance Josey, Oh Miss Susy Brown.

1. Get in the ring, and let's dance Josey, *(3 times)* Oh Miss Susy Brown.
2. Lost my shoe and can't dance Josey, *(3 times)* Oh Miss Susy Brown.
3. Chicken in the breadpan, can't dance Josey, *etc.*
4. Hold my horse while I dance Josey, *etc.*
5. Chew my gum while I dance Josey, *etc.*
6. Get out of the ring if you can't dance Josey, *etc.*

Though the music differs, the procedure in this game and a great many of the verses are the same as those given by Owens, who finds the refrain "Hello, Susan

---

[17] Owens, *op. cit.*, p. 91.
[18] Ames, Mrs. L. D.: "Missouri Play-Party," *J. A. F. L.*, XXIV, 301.
[19] Wolford, L. J.: *op. cit.*, p. 94.

Browny-O" used in the part of the state he writes about. This game seems to belong strictly to Texas, as the only other references found to it are by Dudley and Payne, who give many verses, and by Vivian Richardson, whose refrain is "Hello Susan Brown." As to the music, the score written by Owens is more probably the correct one, as I have noticed a lack of imagination both as to tunes and as to spontaneous additions of words and stanzas among the people dealt with in this paper. When in doubt as to the music, this locality had a tendency to use variants of the *Skip-to-my-Lou* or of the *Mulberry Bush* melodies, changing the tunes just enough to make the words fit.

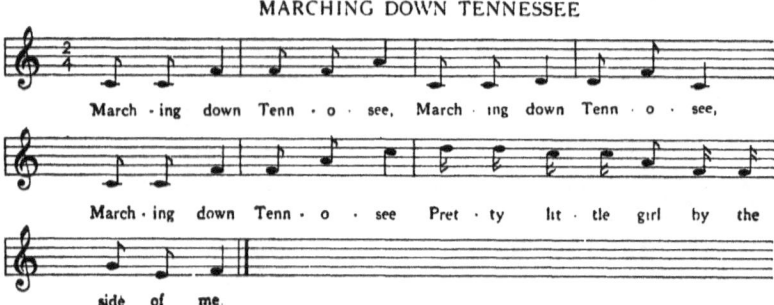

MARCHING DOWN TENNESSEE

1. Marching down Tenn-o-see,
   Marching down Tenn-o-see,
   Marching down Tenn-o-see,
   Pretty little girl by the side of me.

2. Oh young ladies won't you go?
   Oh young ladies won't you go?
   Oh young ladies won't you go?
   If you go you'll catch a beau.

This game was danced to the Virginia reel figures, with the boys and girls lined up in two opposing rows. The boy and girl at the head of the line joined hands and promenaded to the end of the line, walking between the two rows. Then they separated, the boy swinging the ladies one after the other, and the girl swinging the men on the other side. When they returned to the head of the line, they swung each other as all partners came together and joined in the swinging. Then this was repeated by the next couple, and the next, until every couple had gone through the same figures.

I have been unable to find any account of this game in any of the available collections. I heard it only once, at the home of some people who have since moved away from the county. As these people came originally from the depths of the Tennessee mountain country, this game probably came from there also. Although there were several stanzas to the song, the two given above are all that I can recall; and I have been unable to locate anyone else who remembers any more.

It was, however, known in this state, because Dudley and Payne, in a list of songs desired to round out their collection, asked for *Marching down through Tennessee,* which must be the same.

This game has no connection with *Marching down to Old Quebec,* which is given in several collections.

Miller Boy

Happy is the miller boy that lives by the mill,
He takes his toll with a free good will,
One hand on the hopper and the other in the sack,
Every time the mill turns, he drops two back.

The melody used for this is the same as given by Owens for the same game. The procedure is slightly different from his: partners clasp hands and march in a circle with the miller boy inside the ring; then at the line, "He drops two back," each boy tries to catch the hand of the girl two couples back. At this point, the miller boy tries to snatch a partner, leaving another boy in his place. It is sung over and over, the last line being changed to "one" or "three" by way of variation from "two" as given above.

This is an old game and is widely distributed. Wolford, in considering the Indiana version, gives a form identical with the one above and attributes its origin to an early dance-game of England. Though the general context is the same, there are several variants, a number of which are found in Texas. In Cedar Valley, Travis County, the verse runs:

> "Happy is the miller boy who lives by the mill,
> He shakes his toe with a free good will,
> One hand on the hopper and the other in the sack,
> Ladies go forward and gents fall back."

Dudley and Payne give another Texas variation, the first two lines like those used in Victoria County and the last two:

> "One hand on the hopper and the other on the slab,
> Every time the mill turns, grab, boys, grab."

The Owens version is still different:

> "Happy was the miller who lived by the mill,
> Every time the mill turned it turned to his will,
> One hand upon the hopper and the other on the wheel,
> Every time the mill turns, steal, boys, steal."

A version given by Vivian Richardson differs slightly in words and considerably in melody. A Missouri version[20] is another variant:

> "There stands a jolly miller all alone by himself,
> Day by day he is gaining in his wealth,
> One hand on the hopper and the other in the sack,
> Ladies go forward and gents fall back."

Other localities using the *Miller Boy* are Arkansas,[21] which uses the version found in Cedar Valley, given above, and several midwestern states, which use the same version as the Missouri variant, also given above. These states include Illinois,[22] Nebraska and Iowa,[23] and Michigan.[24]

---

[20] Hamilton, G. M.: *op. cit.*, p. 293.
[21] Randolph, Vance: *op. cit.*, p. 206.
[22] Van Doren, Carl: "Some Play-Party Songs from Eastern Illinois," *J. A. F. L.*, XXXII, 489.
[23] Wedgwood, Harriet: "The Play-Party," *J. A. F. L.*, XXV, 269.
[24] Gardner, E. E.: *op. cit.*, p. 101.

Pig in the Parlor

1. My mother and father were Irish, *(3 times)*
   And I am Irish too.

Cho. And I am Irish too, and I am Irish too,
   My mother and father were Irish, and I am Irish too,

2. We got a new pig in the parlor, *(3 times)*
   And he is Irish too.

Cho. And he is Irish too, and he is Irish too,
   We got a new pig in the parlor, and he is Irish too.

3. Oh it's right hand to your partner,
   Left hand to your neighbor,
   Right hand to the next you meet,
   And we'll all promenade.

Cho. We'll all promenade, we'll all promenade,
   Right hand to the next you meet and we'll all promenade.

The melody of this song is the same as that given by Owens and the procedure is the same, the only difference being in the wording of one or two of the stanzas. This game is apparently well known in all parts of the country, being practically the same everywhere except for the additions of various unsavory stanzas reflecting on the rural habits of the Irish, for which the Michigan version[25] may be taken as an example. The Iowa version given by Louise Pound[26] is the only one that shows evidence of mixing with other songs. In this, *Pig in the Parlor* is interwoven with verses from *We'll All Go Down to Rowser's,* the same melody being used with both songs.

---

[25] Gardner, E. E.: *op. cit.,* p. 117.
[26] Pound, Louise: *American Ballads and Songs,* p. 237.

SEALY

1. Dr. McCollum's a married man,
   A married man, a married man,
   Dr. McCollum's a married man,
   What makes you do me so?
2. Oh wheel and turn, Sealy, *(3 times)*
   What makes you do me so?
3. The other way, Sealy, *(3 times)*
   What makes you do me so?
4. We'll all line up, Sealy, *etc.*
5. Oh, circle left, Sealy, *etc.*
6. Oh, balance off, Sealy, *etc.*
7. It's right and left, Sealy, *etc.*
8. We'll all promenade, Sealy, *etc.*

This game is played by partners holding hands and marching around in a circle during the singing of the first stanza, to a melody similar to that of "Here we go round the mulberry bush." The remaining stanzas are sung to a different melody and give directions for the game: At "wheel and turn," the boys swing their partners to the right; at the "the other way," they swing to the left; "we'll all line up" changes the form of the dance to a circle with boys and girls alternating and moving to the right; "circle left" changes the direction of the circle; "balance off" brings the whole circle in toward the middle and then out again; at "right and left," the boys pass to the inside of the circle and move around, catching the right hand of one girl and then the left hand of the next as they pass, until the end of the stanza brings them up to a new partner; "all promenade" begins the game again with the new partner.

There is no mention of this game in any of the available collections, but, in spite of that fact, I do not believe it to be native to this locality. As has been said, there was little or no tendency toward originality in this group of people.

Shoo-Shoo Fly

1. Shoo, shoo, fly, don't bother me, *(3 times)*
   For I belong to somebody.
2. I feel, feel, feel,
   I feel like a morning star;
   I feel, feel, feel,
   I feel like a morning star.

This song was used very rarely and since I did not see the game played at all, I do not know either melody or procedure. All I know is that it was used as a ring game and the two verses given above were sung over and over.

There is no record of this game in any of the available accounts, but I have been told by people of a generation before mine that the song was popular forty or fifty years ago. I have also been told that "Shoo-Fly" was one song, and "The Morning Star" was another, both of them having numerous other verses, but neither being used as a game-song when they first made their appearance.

Shoot the Buffalo

Mention is being made of this song, paradoxical though it seems, because it is *not* used in this community, but it serves to illustrate the attitude of the people and to account for lack of local changes in the songs.

Though *Shoot the Buffalo* is well known in other parts of Texas and throughout the west-central part of the country, it had never been heard in Wood Community until 1935. At that time, a high-school pupil from another county was transferred to Wood School, and at a party tried to introduce the song and game, but the natives refused to have anything to do with it, not because it was difficult, but because it was an importation. I have this information from a teacher who was present, and the attitude seems to me characteristic.

1. Right hands crossed, Shu-dah,
   A long fare-you-well;
   Right hands crossed, Shu-dah,
   A long fare-you-well.
2. Left hands back, Shu-dah, *etc.*
3. Right and left, Shu-dah, *etc.*
4. On to the next, Shu-dah, *etc.*

In this game, the company divided up into fours. The two boys clasped right hands, and their partners caught hands over their arms, forming a cross. At the first stanza, they walked around in a circle, clockwise, changing at the second stanza to cross left hands in the same fashion and walk counterclockwise. At the third stanza, the boys swung their partners and then the other girls of the group one by the right hand and the other by the left. At the fourth stanza, one partner from each group moved to the next group and the same was repeated with a new foursome.

Shu-dah is not found by this name in any of the available collections. However, in Texas and Oklahoma there is a game, called variously *Ju-Tang Ju, Utang, Shoetangle-Shoe,* and *Shoo-Die,* which is obviously the same thing.

Skip-to-My-Lou

1. Lost my partner, Skip-to-my-Lou, *(3 times)*
   Skip-to-my-Lou, my darling.
2. I'll get another one, prettier'n you, *etc.*
3. If you can't get a redbird, a bluebird'll do, *etc.*
4. Little red wagon painted blue, *etc.*
5. Chicken in the breadpan, shoo, shoo, shoo, *etc.*
6. Flies in the buttermilk, shoo, shoo, shoo, *etc.*
7. Gone again, skip-to-my-Lou, *etc.*

The melody used is the same as that given by Owens, but the procedure is slightly different. The couples walk around in a circle without holding hands, one boy being without a partner and wandering around in the circle. He attempts to steal a partner from some other boy, but is successful only if he can grab the girl's hand before her partner does. When he gets a partner, the extra one who is left alone takes his place.

It would take too much space to enumerate here all the references given to *Skip-to-my-Lou* or the verses that have been added as the game was carried from place to place. It is enough to say that it is played from Kentucky to Idaho, and in most of the states between, and that it has grown in number of verses, most of them sheer nonsense, in every community where it has been used. One of the best collections of *Skip-to-my-Lou* verses can be found in Lomax's *American Ballads and Folk Songs,* though to attempt to get a complete file of these would be a colossal, if not impossible, task.

1. Little log house, nobody living in it, *(3 times)*
   Her name is Susie Brown.
2. We'll get married, we'll live in it, *etc.*
3. You'll pick cotton, I'll drag sacks, *etc.*
4. Cornstalk fiddle and a shoestring bow, *etc.*
   Good-bye, Miss Susie Brown.

The procedure in this game depended more or less upon the whim of the leader. It was usually played by beginning with a promenade of the partners in a circle. Boys swung their partners first by the right hand and then, on the second stanza, by the left. Then followed a general right and left swing around the circle, and a return to the partner for a final swing on the last stanza.

Though not to be found in any of the available collections as a complete game, this is obviously a composite of several other games. The first stanza duplicates one in *Virginia*:[27]

"Great big white house, nobody living in it, *(3 times)*
Old Virginia style."

and a variant in *Alabama*.[28] The refrain, "Her name is Susie Brown," or "Oh Miss Susie Brown," is found in the song *Josie,* already considered; it is also used as the refrain of the *Cuckoo Waltz*.[29]

---

[27] Botkin, B. A.: *op. cit.,* p. 21.
[28] Piper, E. F.: *op. cit.,* p. 267.
[29] Wolford, L. J.: *op. cit.,* p. 36.

PLAY PARTY IN VICTORIA COUNTY

The second and third stanzas have not been identified, but the fourth is found in several variants. In Nebraska[30] it is used as a stanza of *Heel and Toe Polka:*

"Buckskin fiddle and shoestring bow,
Makes the very best music you know."

In Iowa,[31] it is found in *Heel and Toe Polka,* in this form:

"Cornstalk fiddle and a shoestring bow,
And I take sugar in my coffee, O."

In Missouri,[32] the line is found in a game called *I'll Come Back and Be Your Beau:*

"Cornstalk fiddle and shoestring bow,
I'll come back and be your beau."

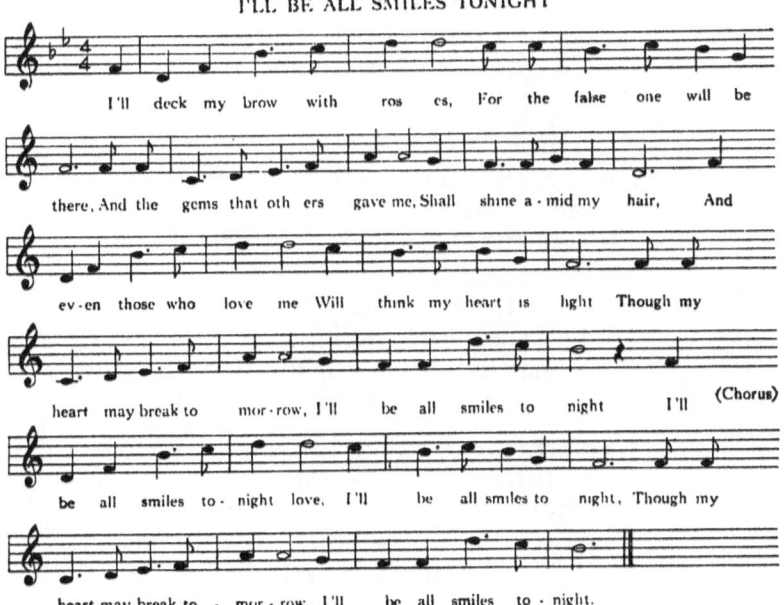

I'LL BE ALL SMILES TONIGHT

I'll deck my brow with ros es, For the false one will be there, And the gems that oth ers gave me, Shall shine a-mid my hair, And ev-en those who love me Will think my heart is light Though my heart may break to mor-row, I'll be all smiles to night I'll (Chorus) be all smiles to-night love, I'll be all smiles to night, Though my heart may break to mor-row, I'll be all smiles to-night.

[30] Piper, E. F.: *op. cit.,* p. 281.
[31] *Ibid.*
[32] Ames, Mrs. L. D.: *op. cit.,* p. 312.

1. I'll deck my brow with roses,
   For the false one will be there;
   And the gems that others gave me
   Shall shine amid my hair,
   And even those who love me
   Will think my heart is light.
   Tho' my heart may break tomorrow,
   I'll be all smiles tonight.

Chorus:
   I'll be all smiles tonight, love,
   I'll be all smiles tonight.
   Tho' my heart may break tomorrow,
   I'll be all smiles tonight.

2. And when the room he enters
   With his bride upon his arm,
   I'll stand and gaze upon him
   As tho' he were a charm.
   As now he smiles upon her,
   So once he smiled on me;
   They know not how I suffer,
   They'll find no change in me.

3. And when the dance commences
   Oh how I will rejoice;
   I'll sing the songs he taught me
   Without one faltering voice.
   When flatterers gather round me,
   I'll hail them with delight;
   Oh none shall know my sorrow,
   I'll be all smiles tonight.

4. And when the dance is over
   And all have gone to rest,
   I'll think of him, dear Mother,
   The one that I love best.
   My love did once believe me;
   Now he's grown cold and strange.
   He sought not to deceive me,
   False friends have wrought this change.

Chorus:

IV. LOOK TO THE EAST AND LOOK TO THE WEST
(BIBLIOGRAPHY)

Books

Lomax, John A., and Lomax, Allan: *American Ballads and Folk-Songs,* New York; The Macmillan Co., 1934.

Owens, William A.: *Swing and Turn: Texas Play-Party Games,* Dallas; Tardy Publishing Co., 1936.

Pound, Louise: *American Ballads and Songs,* New York; Charles Scribner's Sons, 1922.

Sandburg, Carl: *The American Songbag,* New York; Harcourt, Brace & Co., 1927.

Wilson, Charles Morrow: *Backwoods America,* Chapel Hill, N. C.; The University of North Carolina Press, 1934.

Wolford, Leah Jackson: *The Play-Party in Indiana,* Indianapolis; Indiana Historical Commission, 1916.

Periodicals

Journal of American Folk-Lore, Lancaster, P.; American Folk-Lore Society:

Ames, Mrs. L. D.: *Missouri Play-Party,* Vol. XXIV, p. 295.

Ball, Leona N.: *The Play-Party in Idaho,* Vol. XLIV, p. 5.

Edmands, Lila W.: *Songs from the Mountains of North Carolina,* Vol. VI, p. 131.

Gardner, Emelyn E.: *Some Play-Party Games in Michigan,* Vol. XXXIII, p. 91.

Hamilton, Goldy M.: *The Play-Party in Northeastern Missouri,* XXVII, p. 289.

Piper, Edwin F.: *Some Play-Party Games of the Middle West,* Vol. XXVIII, p. 262.

Randolph, Vance: *The Ozark Play-Party,* Vol. XLII, p. 201.

Van Doren, Carl: *Some Play-Party Songs from Eastern Illinois,* Vol. XXXII, p. 486.

Wedgwood, Harriet: *The Play-Party,* Vol. XXV, p. 268.

Publications of the Texas Folk-Lore Society, Austin, Texas; Texas Folk-Lore Society:

Botkin, B. A.: *The Play-Party in Oklahoma,* Vol. VII, p. 7.

Dudley, R. E., and Payne, L. W.: *Some Texas Play-Party Songs,* Vol. I, p. 7.

Transylvania University Studies in English, Vol. II, Lexington, Ky.; Transylvania Printing Co., 1911: Shearin, Hubert, and Combs, Josiah: *A Syllabus of Kentucky Folk-Songs.*

Dallas News, Richardson, Vivian: "The Singing Games Have Eternal Youth," April 1, 1928.

CONTRIBUTORS

JULIA BEAZLEY, a teacher in the Houston schools, may be recalled by "The Uneasy Ghost of Lafitte" in *Legends of Texas* and "The Ballad of Davy Crockett" in *Texas and Southwestern Lore.*

L. D. BERTILLION, Mineola, is one of the original characters of Texas. Years ago he began scouring Mexico and the West for horns of the longhorn cattle. He is probably the foremost collector and dealer of such horns in America. He has a genius for hearing, remembering and telling yarns. His story of "Steinheimer's Millions," which originally appeared in *Legends of Texas,* has been widely read.

As a worker in the rural schools of Texas, while connected with the State Department of Education, G. T. BLUDWORTH, now living in Fort Worth, collected many items of folk-lore. Two tales of his gathering are in the Texas Folk-Lore Society's volume, *Follow de Drinkin' Gou'd.* He is the author of *The Gold Brick,* a story of Bolivian treasure, the Christopher Publishing House, Boston.

CORNELIA CHAMBERS, Dallas, a member of John Lee Brooks' class in Folk-Lore at Southern Methodist University, presented "The Adventures of Little Audrey" before the annual meeting of the Texas Folk-Lore Society in 1935.

Probably the foremost authority in the world on the music and songs of the American Indian is FRANCES DENSMORE, of Red Wing, Minnesota. Since 1907 she has been active with the Bureau of American Ethnology, and has published extensively. Among her works are *Teton Sioux Music*——a noble and beautiful book; *Chippewa Music; Northern Ute Music; Mandan and*

Hidasta Music; Poems from Sioux and Chippewa Songs; Indian Action Songs; The American Indians and Their Music; Handbook of the Collection of Musical Instruments in the United States National Museum; Uses of Plants by the Chippewa Indians; Papago Music; Pawnee Music; Yuman and Yaqui Music.

The only thing better than reading A. W. EDDINS's anecdotes of the Brazos Bottoms is to hear him tell them. In the very first volume issued by the Texas Folk-Lore Society, twenty-one years ago, he had a Negro folk-tale—"How Sandy Got His Meat." In the next volume, 1923, and in *Southwestern Lore* (Vol. IX, 1931), he published collections of "Brazos Bottoms Philosophy." He teaches in the San Antonio public schools.

Certain critical readers with a right to an opinion regard MARTHA EMMONS as the foremost master of Negro dialect that Texas has produced. Among her contributions to the *Publications* of the Texas Folk-Lore Society are "Confidences from Old Nacogdoches," "Dyin' Easy," and "Cats and the Occult." *Tone the Bell Easy,* issued by the Society in 1932, took its title from her lovely Negro spiritual in that volume. She teaches in the State Home, Waco.

MAE FEATHERSTONE, now attending the University of Texas, is a part of the land of which she writes.

DAVID HALL is on the editorial staff of the Fort Worth *Press.* His "Folk Names of Texas Cacti" appeared in "*Spur-of-the-Cock,* the Texas Folk-Lore Society's volume for 1933.

ELMA HEARD, of Lufkin, was associated with Dr. John R. Swanton, of the Smithsonian Institute, in his work among the Creek Indians. She has in manuscript a very large collection of tales from these Indians.

HELEN ASHWORTH (MRS. J. A.) MOORE, now of Austin, absorbed the life and folk amusements of southern Texas while she lived in that region.

Before she married Leon Denny Moses, himself a spinner of folk tales, LOUISE VON BLITTERSDORF MOSES contributed to *Legends of Texas*. She lives in El Paso, where her husband teaches in the School of Mines.

ALICE ATKINSON (MRS. R. S.) NEIGHBORS teaches in the San Antonio public schools. Fortunate children! Her husband's ancestor was the noted Indian agent Major Robert S. Neighbors, and Mrs. Neighbors is writing a History thesis on him, at the University of Texas.

TRUEMAN O'QUINN is full of folk yarns from the Sabine River country that he will write later on. He is a young, but leading, attorney of Austin.

AYLETT ROYAL, Dallas, introduced her heroine, Stella, in person, to the Texas Folk-Lore Society when it met in Dallas, 1935.

CHARLES L. SONNICHSEN, next to being born to the manor—or manner—both are good—took to it like a duck to water when, fresh from the East, he came to the School of Mines at El Paso and found that he had to teach a course in Life and Literature of the Southwest. Then he married the *manor—or manner*. He is still fresh—but not from the East. As an oral deliverer of tales he is simply superb.

MRS. MORGAN SMITH, Austin, is proud of being the mother of Victor Smith, who has built up a remarkable Indian museum at the Sul Ross State Teachers College, Alpine, and whose contributions on Indian lore have been published by the Texas Folk-Lore Society.

About a year ago MYRON W. TRACY sent from Palm Beach, Florida, to the editor of this volume a considerable manuscript on Roy Bean. He thought his manuscript might be appropriate for a centennial book. The editor plead with him not to be guilty of adding another book issued in the name of the Texas Centennial. Mr. Tracy is a reasonable man; he saw how wicked it would be to publish another centennial book. The Roy Bean yarns here presented have been extracted from the manuscript. Mr. Tracy knew Roy Bean and the Pecos country while he was connected with the Southern Pacific Railroad during the eighties.

TRESSA TURNER, now teaching in Dallas, would be marked as a Texan anywhere—from Kildare, Texas, sir. In 1936 she took her Master's degree from the University of Texas, writing a thesis on Alfred Henry Lewis, famous for his Wolfville stories.

AFTON WYNN was born and reared in Parker County, the folk ways of which region she has so thoroughly set down. She is now tutor in Journalism in the University of Texas.

INDEX

Alabama Indians, history, lore, tales, music, etc. of, 270-299. *See* Bludworth, Densmore, Heard.
Alabama Village, 28
Alamo Plaza, San Antonio, 1
Alarcón, explorer, 5
Alazan St., San Antonio, 1
Alfalfa (town), 4
Allseeing Eye (place), 47
Alum (place), 3
Anahuac, 27
Anecdotes, folk, connected with names and places of Texas, 9-70 *passim;* 159, 192. *See* Eddins, Tracy, also Legends, Tales.
Angelina, county, 30; an Indian maid, 29; River, 29, 71
Animals: alligator, 2, 11; antelope, 2; bat, 155, 161; bear, 2, 33, 118; beaver, 2; bee, 37; buffalo, 2, 14, 18-19, 27, 32-33, 42, 60, 61, 206, 217, 281-282; burro, 2, 14; butterfly, 164; cat, 139, 144, 156, 174, 182-184, 211, 240; coyote, 2; crawfish, 7; deer, 2, 33; devil's horse, 158; dog, 36-37, 91, 97, 142, 143, 159, 162, 173, 175, 240, 244; doodlebug, 174; flea, 242; fox, 244; frog, 51, 159, 174, 284; goat, 81, 217, 242; goose, 205; grand-daddy-long-legs, 175; grasshopper, 227; heel-fly, 228-229; hog, 2, 23, 91, 95, 172, 248; horned frog, 139; lizard, 166; lobo, 2, 28, 79-85 *passim;* owl, 11; oyster, 2; panther, 2, 11, 68, 276, 294; polecat, 2, 244; prairie dog, 2; rabbit, 144, 156, 285; rattlesnake, 2; sheep, 87; snakes, 277, 295; spider, 169; squirrel, 221; terrapin, 285; tick, 3; turtle, 172; wasp, 103, 172; weevil, 175; wildcat, 276, 295; wolf, 276, 294. *See* Cattle, Horse.
Animas, Rancho de las, 10
Antelope Draw, 2
Apaches, 24, 26, 29, 121. *See* Indians.
Atascosa, 53
Audrey, Little (folk character), 50; jokes about her, 106-110. *See* Chambers, Cornelia.
Austin, Stephen F., diary, 35; and Brit Bailey, 55
Ayish Bayou, 28

Babyhead Creek, 29-30; Mountain, 29-30, 71
Bailey, Brit, 55
Bailey's Prairie, 55
Baille, Padre Nicolás, 60
Bandera Co., 35-36; Pass. 36
Bañito Creek, 69
Bass, Sam, 203

Baylor, John R., 202
Bean, Roy, "Law West of the Pecos," 111-119. *See* Tracy.
Bear Gulch, 2
Beaver Lake, 2
Beazley, Julia, 337; "The Black Cat of Cole's Plantation," 182-184: a mystery tale of East Texas.
Bedias Creek, 28
Bell Co., 41, 178
Bernardo, 61
Bertillion, L. D., 337; "The Lobo Girl of Devil's River," 79-85: tale of a baby adopted and reared by lobo wolves.
Big Bend, of Texas, 37, 39, 55-56, 61
Big Lump, 47
Big Sandy, 273ff.
Birds: bluebird, 155; buzzard, 2, 155, 159, 171, 244; chicken, 63, 160, 163, 167, 168, 175, 227, 234, 239, 284; crane, 2; cricket, 155; crow, 2, 144, 161; dove, 152; duck, 283-284; eagle, 2, 9, 33; heron, 2; owl, 2, 155, 158, 161, 233; paisano, 2; prairie chicken, 2; redbird, 162; turkey, 2, 282
Blackjack Grove, 44
Blessing, 38, 71
Bloody Hand Print Canyon, 28
Bloys Campmeeting, 61
Bludworth, G. T., 337; "How the Alabamas Came Southward," 298-299: a migration myth.
Boatright, Thos., 34
Boothill Cemetery, 46
Borden, Gail, 63
Bosque Co., 4
Boston, in Texas, 51
Bovina, 49, 71
Bowie Mine, Lost, 13
Brady, 176
Brands, cattle, 4
Brazoria, 50, 71; County, 55
Brazos River, legends of, 12-17, 71; 3, 27, 34, 39, 48, 50, 51, 60, 61, 62, 86, 230
Brewster Co., 36, 54
Bronco (town), 4
Buck Den, 52
Buck Short, 52, 71
Buffalo Gap, 2
Bullhide Creek, 23, 72
Bulltown, 49
Burro Mesa, 2
Butcherknife Creek, 36, 72
Butter Bowl Mt., 3
Butterfield Stage Rt., 24, 39
Buzzard Roost, 2

Caddo Lake, 28; legend of, 68
Calamity Creek, 39, 72
Caldwell Co., 43, 62
California place names, 35n.
Camerón Ranch, 7
Camp Necessity, 39-40, 72
Campo de la Rueda, 8, 72
Canadian River, 31-32, 38, 53, 61
Caney, Big, 3
Cannibal Creek, 35, 72
Carrizo 3; Springs, 11, 81
Casa Blanca Ranch, 6
Casket Mt., 3
Castro, Hy., 55
Castroville, 55
Cathedral Mt., 3
Cattle, 21-23, 45, 49, 172, 175, 225
Cattle thieves, 45
Cedar Hill, 3
Chalk Draw, 3
Chambers, Cornelia, 337; "The Adventures of Little Audrey," 106-110: Character of Little Audrey and prevalence of tales about her, 106; tales related, 106-110.
Chambers, C. W., and wife, missionaries to Alabama Indians, 274ff.
Chambers Co., 46
Chaparro Creek, 35, 72
Checkup, 66
Cherokee County, 28, 42, 66; Indians, 42, 298
Chihuahua Trail, 24, 85
Childress Co., 52
Chiltipin Creek, 3
Chinquapin Creek, 40-41
"Chinquapin Eater," meaning of Nacogdoches, 40
Chisholm Trail, 4, 259
Chisum, John, 50
Chittenden, Larry, 40
Choctaw Creek, 28
Chotilapacquen (Nueces River), 6
Cibola creeks, 52
Clarksville, 46
Coaldale, 4
Coffee Mill Creek, 4
Coffee's Station, 58
Colbert's Ferry, 4, 58
Cole's Plantation, 182-184
Coleman Co., 50
Colorado River, 12, 48, 49, 51, 52, 258ff.
Comal River, 3
Comanche (town), 28; Springs, 28, 72
Comanche Indians, 15, 24, 28, 29-30, 31, 32-33, 36, 39, 64, 203. *See* Indians.
Concan (place), 46
Concho River, 2, 39

Copano, 27
Copperas Grove, 46, 72
Corn Hill, 4
Coronado's Expedition, 18
Corsicana, 22, 42
Coryell Co., 37, 57; Creek, 37, 72
Cotera Well, 55-57, 72
Cottondale, 4
Cow Bayou, 23, 72
Cow Head Road, 22, 72
Cowhouse Creek, 23, 72
Coyote Ridge, 2
Crane Canyon, 2
Crow Flats, 2
Cuero, 23, 72, 148
Cumby, 44
Custer, John, 38
Customs. *See* Wynn, Afton.

Dagger Flats, 3
Dallas, 22
Dances, 43-44, 235-238, 310; Indian, 280-293. *See* Fiddler, Play Party.
Davis, Mollie E. Moore, 16
Dawson Co., 62
Dead Horse Canyon, 26, 72
Dead Man's Canyon, 46; Crossing, 45, 72; Hole, 46; Hollow, 44; Island, 46; Ranch, 45, 72
Dead Nigger Creek, 46
Deer, White, 2
Delaware Creek, 28
Del Rio, 26, 54, 82
Demijohn Bend, 3
Densmore, Frances, 338; "The Alabama Indians and Their Music," 270-293:
    Historical sources, 270-271; history of the tribe, 271-273; the Alabamas in Texas, past and present, 273-276; "The Visit to the Sky," a folk tale, 276-277; musical instruments, 277-278; manner of recording the Alabama songs, 278-280; dances with attendant music— "Green Corn Dance," "Buffalo Dance," "Corn Dance," social dances, "Duck Dance," "Chicken Dance," "Frog Dance," "Rabbit Dance," "Terrapin Dance," "Horse Dance," "Woman Dances," "Nateka Dance"—280-287; summary and analysis of songs, 287-289; the music as recorded, 289-293.
Denton Co., 50, 52
Desdemona (oil field), 47
Devil's River, 45, 53, 73, 80-85 *passim*
DeWitt Co., 23, 26
Diction—dialectal words, provincialisms, Mexicanisms, etc.: all-thorn, 28; *anacahua*, 27; *bandido*, 9; boge, 249; brought on, 248; cabbage, 245; cake bread, 248; *caporal*, 7; *charco*, 10; *chiltipiquin*, 3;

INDEX 343

comal, 3; coon, 245; crumble-in, 215; cush, 215; dipped, 248; dry so, 248; flitters, 216; grapevine telegraph, 43; heelfly, 228-229; *jacal*, 45; joobus, 246; *juajilla*, 27; knock-away, 27; lizard, 199; Mexican hog, 23; mountain dew, 26; mountain oyster, 217; mustang cattle, 23; *pilon*, 7; poor doe, 215; poor doo, 215; *sacahuiste*, 7, 27; saw mill license, 248; *sendero*, 7; shack bully, 248; tarantula juice, 26; *tinaja*, 56; *tortilla*, 3; tote level, 249; tush hog, 248; wash hole, 246; whack, 247; white mule, 26. See O'Quinn.
Dime Box, 53, 73
Dinn, John, 26
Dixon, Billy, 60-61
Doan, C. F., 58
Doan's Crossing, 58; Store, 58
Dobie, J. Frank, 146, 147; "Stories in Texas Place Names," 1-78:
    I. "The Whats in a Name," 1-5. Principles of nomenclature; names record man's history, flora, fauna, geology, elements of the earth, etc. Examples in Texas.
    II. "Spanish Mexican Trails," 5-12. Spanish explorations remembered in names; psychology of Spaniards and of Mexicans as shown in names they give; various examples, including some ranch names and Espantosa Lake.
    III. "The Arms of God," 12-17. Legends of the Brazos River.
    IV. "The Staked Plains," 17-21. Early reputation and character of Staked Plains. Why "staked"? The term Llano Estacado explained.
    V. "Cabeza de Vaca and Horsehead," 21-27. Horses and cattle in Texas history and place names; many examples.
    VI. "Indian Sign," 27-34. The imprint left by Indians on nomenclature not so pronounced as that left by Spaniards and Mexicans. Various Indian names and two legends of Indian character.
    VII. "Downright Circumstantial Evidence," 34-54. The character of Anglo-American name-giving. Numerous anecdotes.
    VIII. "Prolonged Shadows," 54-62. Individualism of certain individuals denoted in names. Anecdotes.
    IX. "Folk Etymology," 62-67. Made-up explanations of names such as Navasota, Texas, Elgin, Wichita, etc.
    X. "Origins of Places," 68-70. Skimmed milk quality of modern myths on origins; examples involving Catholic priests. Sources, 70-78.
Dobie, J. M., 7
Doe Creek, 36, 73; Run, 2
Dog Canyon, 37, 73
Dog Town, 49
Dolores St., San Antonio, 1, 73

Don Patricio Causeway, 60
Double Horn Creek, 52
Driskill Hotel, Austin, 59-60
Driskill, Robert, and sons, 60
Drouth, 13-14
Dry Creek, 81
Dryden, Texas, 54
Dunn, Pat, 60
Duval Co., 6, 10, 45

Eagle Mts., 2
Eagle Pass, 9, 22, 73
Eastland Co., 47
Eddins, A. W., 338; "Anecdotes from the Brazos Bottoms," 86-105; "Wise Saws," 243-244.
Edgar, Capt. Jas., 39
Edgar's Boneyard, 39, 73
Egg-Nog Branch, 41, 73
Egypt, Texas, 51
Elgin, 65-66, 73
El Paso, 3, 54, 112, 120-129 *passim*
Emerson, Texas, 54
Emmons, Martha, 338; "Walk around My Bedside," 130-136: Pictures of two Negro women; their spirituality, spirituals, and belief in spirits.
Encinal, 23
Encinal del Perdido, 8-9, 73
Entraaverlo Creek, 5
Epley Spring, 258ff.
Erath, Geo. B., 27, 37, 88
Erath Co., 25, 37
Espantosa Lake, 11-12, 81

Fairies. See Moses.
Falconer, Thos., 20-21
Farmersville, 4
Featherstone, Mae, 338; "Silver Dreams and Copper Plates," 258-269—a story of buried treasure.
Fiddler, fiddle tunes, etc., 43-44, 235-238. See Dances.
Fisher, S. Rhoads, 55; County, 55
Flatonia, 167
Flores St., San Antonio, 1
Fort Darnell, 57, 73
Fort Elliott, 38
Fort Phantom Hill, 39-40, 73
Fort Spunky, 37, 73
Fort Stockton, 26, 28
Fort Worth, 223
Fossil (place), 3
Fredericksburg, 4
French John Creek, 48-49
Frio River, 46, 49

Gallinas, Arroyo de las, 2
Galveston, 63
Gamble Gully, 46
Garcia, Hipolito, 10

Garcitas Creek, 2
Garrapatas Creek, ῾
Ghosts. See Emmons, Espantosa, Royal, Sonnichsen.
Gibtown, 54, 73
Goacher's Trace, 58
Goliad, 8
Goodnight, Chas., 60
Goodnight-Loving Trail, 24, 60
Goose Creek, 47
Gooseneck Bend, 3
Goshen, community, 193, 194
Granite Mts., 3
Grapeland, 3
Grayson Co., 49
Greasy Neck (place), 47
Gregg Co., 43
Gregg, Josiah, 17, 20
Grimes Co., 62
Groce, Jared E., 61-62
Groce's Retreat, 61-62
Grullas, Rancho de las, 2
Guadalupe River, 3
Gunsight Creek, 47
Gyp Creek, 3

Haley, Lawrence, 61
Haley's Peak, 61
Hall, David, 338; "Witching for Water with the Bible," 176-181: How Bible is used; a water witch in action.
Happy Hollow, 38, 73
Hardeman Co., 32
Harina, Loma de, 7
Harris Co., 47
Harrison, R. C., 146, 147
Haskell Co., 27
Hay Hollow, 4
Hays, Capt. Jack, 53, 112
Haystack Mt., 3
Heard, Elma, 338-339; "Two Tales from the Alabamas," 294-297: "How the Indians First Got Seed," and "The Dice Game."
Hebbronville, 26
Heifer Creek, 73
Hell Roaring Hollow, 48, 74
Hempstead, 38
Hide Town, 48, 74
Hog Creek, 47
Hog Eye, 42, 44, 74
Hog Marsh, 2
Hog Skin (place), 47
Holland, G. A., his book and museum, 203, 223
Hood Co., 28
Horse, 25, 26, 31, 38-39, 44, 56, 114, 162, 167, 169, 171, 242, 285-286; white, 165
Horse Creek, 27

Horsehead Canyon, 25
Horsehead Crossing on Pecos, 24-25, 74
Houston, 22
Huntsville, 59
Hutchinson Co., 61

Indiahoma, 30
Indians, 1, 22, 24, 26-36 passim, 39, 60, 64, 81, 90, 191, 196, 200-203, 213, 258-260, 262-263. See Alabama, Apache, Comanche.
Indian Bend, 30; Bluff, 31-32, 74; Creek, 30, 31; Gap, 30
Indio Ranch, 30
Indios Junction, Los, 30
Irion Co., 28
Isinglass Canyon, 3
Isle d'Bois, 52
Itasca, 53

Jack Co., 43, 57
Jacksboro, 57
James, W. S., cowboy writer, 38
Jernigan's Thicket, 58
Jim Hogg Co., 9
Jim Nail Branch, 58
Jim Ned Creek, 58

Kaolin, 3
Karankawa Bay, 28; Indians, 35
Keechi Creek, 28
Kendall, Geo. W., 61
Kendall Co., 61
Kent, "City of," 4, 74
Kickapoo Road, 28; Springs, 28
Kildare, 146-175 passim
Kiowa Creek, 28; Indians, 32, 203
Koasati Indians, 274. See Alabama Indians.
Kuykendall, Abner, 34

Ladonia, 53
Lafitte, pirate, 46, 63
Lagarto Waterhole, 2
Laguna de Caballo, 26
Lamar Co., 53
Lamesa, 62
Lampasas Co., 44; Springs, 14
Langtry, 111-119 passim
Lariat, 4
Larietta City, 54, 74
LaSalle Co., 6-7
Lavaca River, 8, 51
Lee Co., 53
Legends, connected with Brazos River, Staked Plains, and other Texas place names, 9-70; around El Paso (Mexican), 120-129; "Lobo Girl of Devil's River," 79-85; "Irish Fairies in Texas," 185-189. See Tales.

INDEX 345

Lick Skillet, 49-50, 74
Lipan Flats, 28
Little Audrey. *See* Audrey.
Little Emma, 106
Little Gertrude, 106
Live Oak Co., 44, 46
Livermore Mt., 56
Livingston, 273
Llano Estacado. *See* **Staked Plains.**
Llano Co., 29-30, 36-37; River, 14
Lobo (place), 2; (wolf), 79-85 *passim*
Log City, 54, 74
Loma Grande, 8, 74
Long, S. H., 17
Longfellow, Texas, 54
Longhorns. *See* Cattle.
Lost Prairie, 29
Loving, Oliver, 60
Loving's Bend, 60
Luce, slave, 29, 74
Luce's Bayou, 29, 74
Luck. *See* Turner, also **Royal.**
Luling, 62, 74
Lytton Springs, 43

Maltby, Jeff, 39
Mansanet, Fray D., 6
Maravilla Canyon, 39
Marble Falls, 3
Marcy, R. B., 18
Margil, Fray Antonio de Jesús, 68-69, 74
Marion Co., 52
Matagorda Bay, 59, 302
Maverick Creek, 23
McLennan Co., 23, 37
McMullen Co., 45, 49
Medicine Mounds, 32-34, 75
Medina River, 5, 65
Menard, 15, 180
Menger Hotel, San Antonio, 59
Mesmeriser's Creek, 42, 75
Metheglin Creek, 41-42, 75
Mexican Springs, 56
Mexicans, 1-70 *passim*, 81-85 *passim*, 113, 117-119; spooks of, 120-129, 158, 258-269 *passim*
Midland, 51
Milam Co., 27
Milam Square, San Antonio, 1
Mills Co., **258ff.**
Mineral Wells, 3
Mission River, 4
Mooar, J. Wright, 61
Mooar's Draw, 61
Moore Co., 54

Moore, Helen Ashworth, 338; "The Play Party in Victoria County," 300-336:
   I. Character of the Wood community, in Victoria Co., where the games are played, 300-302.
   II. Description of a particular play party—characters, talk, dress, games, etc., 302-313.
   III. Words, music, and comparative analysis of various games, 313-334. *See* Songs.
   IV. Bibliography, 335-336.
Moses, Louise von Blittersdorf, 338; "Irish Fairies in Texas," 185-189: Irish fairies move to Texas.
Moss, Tate, 36
Mound Prairie, 28
Mud (place), 47
Mud Dig, 47
Muerto Creek, 46
Mulberry Canyon, 25
Mule creeks, 26, 27
Mule, white, 165, 167
Muleshoe, 47
Murderer's Creek, 46
Mustang Bayou, 25; Gray, 112; Island, 25; Pens, 4, 25
Mustangs, 10, 21, 25. *See* Horse.

Nacogdoches, 40-41, 68, 69, 75
Nana Creek, 69
Natchitoches, 40
Navasota River, 62-63, 75
Navidad, 51
Negro folk-lore, 147, 170, 174. *See* Emmons, Royal.
Neighbors, Alice Atkinson, 339; "'Old Obadiah' and 'My Juanita,'" 250-257: songs remembered out of childhood. *See* Songs.
New Year's Creek, 34, 75
Nipple Peak, 3
Nogalus Prairie, 62
Nopal, 3
Norse (place), 4
Norton, Uncle Jim, 37
Nueces River, 5-6, 10, 11, 58

Oakville, 3
Oglesby (town), 178
Oilery, 4
Olmos Ranch, 6
O'naga, 50, 75
One Eye Creek, 42
Onion Creek, 3
O'Quinn, Trueman E., 339; "Colloquialisms along the Sabine," 245-249: A list of words and phrases. *See* Diction.
Ox Skull Hill, 22
Oyster Bay, 2

Padre Island, 60
Padre Mine Canyon, 4
Page's Tree, 46, 75

Paisano Pass, 2
Palestine, Texas, 28
Palo Duro Canyon, 3, 34, 60
Palo Pinto Co., 48, 60
Panther Canyon, 2
Paris, Texas, 51
Parker, county of, 191-238 *passim;* Cynthia Ann, 29, 199-200, 203; Isaac D., 199-200; Quanah, 29
Peach Point, 3
Pease River, 32, 34
Pecos River, 23-25, 26, 60, 111-119 *passim*
Peg Leg Crossing, 47
Pepper Creek Camp, 2-3
Perryman Thicket, 57, 75
Peyote (place), 3
Pierce, John, and place named for him, 38
Pierce, Shanghai, and place named for him, 59
Pike, Albert, on Brazos, 12
Pilot Grove, 50; Knobs, 50
Pinhook, 51
Pipe Creek, 36, 75
Plant life: all-thorn, 28; *anacahua,* 27; apple, 149; balmonia, 234; bean, 172; bear grass, 167, 168; blackberries, wild, 214; black gum, 153; blackjack, 222, 234; bois d'arc, 138; broom corn, 226; buckeye, 138; cane, 3, 275; careless weed, 213; cedar, 3, 162; chinquapin, 40; *coma,* 7; corn, 172, 215, 216, 223, 224, 232, 247, 248, 277, 280-283; cotton, 220, 244; cottonwood, 3; cucumber, 172; cypress, 278; dewberry, wild, 1-2; dock, 213; elderberry, 168, 232; elm, 153, 208, 232; gourd, 211, 223, 278; hackberry, 153, 232; haw, 214; holly, 148; huisache, 27; Irish potato, 167, 172; John-the-Conqueror, 137; *juajilla,* 27; *junco,* 28; lamb's quarter, 213; *lechuguilla,* 3; lobelia, 234; lovevine, 152; Margil vine, 68; mesquite, 3, 6, 27; mulberry, 1, 222; mullein, 169; mustang grape, 70, 214; night shade, 234; oak, 3, 8, 44, 208; onion, wild, 3; *palo duro,* 3; pea, 172; peach, 243, 247; peach, wild, 3, 276; pecan, 9; pepper, 2, 174, 175; persimmon, 243; peyote, 3; pine, 175; plum, wild, 214; poison oak, 167; poke-berry, 204, 213; popcorn, 50, 213; postoak, 191, 246; prickly ash, 168; prickly pear, 30, 234; purslane (pursley), 213, 222; roses, 227; *sacahuiste,* 7, 27; senna, 234; sheep sorrel, 213; slippery elm, 277, 295; snake root, 167; Spanish dagger, 234; Spanish moss, 8; Spanish oak, 44; squash, 277, 296; sumac, 222, 276; sweet potato, 277; sycamore, 3; tobacco, 226; tule, 3; turnip, 172; walnut, 168; watermelon, 228; willow, 162; yucca, 3

Play party, 230, 300-336. *See* Moore.
Poker Flats, 46-47
Polecat Creek, 2
Polk Co., 273ff.
Polvo, 3
Pool, The, in Parker Co., 191ff.
Popcorn Patch (Brazoria), 50, 75
Popher, Indian chief, 30, 75; Creek, 30, 75
Possum Kingdom, 48-49
Post Oak Point, 3
Powder Horn Bayou, 3
Poverty Flat, 52
Prairie Chicken Creek, 2
Prairie Dog Town Fork, 2
Preston's Bend, 58
Privilege Creek, 36, 75
Proverbs, 239-244
Pulltite (place), 37, 75

Quanah, 29. *See* Parker.
Quarry (place), 4
Quitaque, 27

Rake Pocket, 50, 75
Randado Ranch, 9-10, 76
Rangers, Texas, 11, 24, 113
Rattlesnake Cave, 2
Raven Cafe, 59
Rawhide, 221
Razor, Texas, 53, 76
Real Co., 52
Red Bluff Creek, 35
Red River, 2, 46, 58
Remedies, pioneer, 233-234
Remlig, 54
Rio Grande, 26, 56, 111-119 *passim,* 120-129 *passim*
Robinson, "Popcorn," 50
Rope Pen Creek, 26
Ross, Sul, 13
Roundup Creek, 4
Royal, Aylett, 239; "I'se Sho' Nuff Lucky," 137-145: Stella, Negro mammy, on luck, hoodoo, love, hants, dreams, and the "Seven Sisters."
Rusk Co., 50

Sabinal, 22
Sabine River, 245
Sal de Rey, 3
Sallie Keaton Slough, 58
Salsipuedes Creek, 5
Salt War, 128
San Antonio, 1-2, 15, 20, 22, 65, 68, 69, 112; River, 70
San Bernard, 51
San Elizario, 121, 128
San Francisco Creek, 56
San Jacinto Bayou, 29
San Juan Mission, 15

INDEX 347

San Marcos River, 68
San Norbeto (Nueces), 6
San Patricio, 5
San Saba Co., 28; Mine, 258; Mission, 13, 15; River, 13, 15, 16, 176
Sánchez, diarist name-giver, 8
Sandia, 4
Santa Fe Expedition, 21
Santa Niña Ranch, 26
Santa Rosa St., San Antonio, 1
Sawlog Creek, 4
Scalp Creek, 28
Scary Lane, 44-45, 76
Seego, Wiley, 7
Seminole, Texas, 28
Seven Heart Gap, 4
Shawnee Creek, 28
Sheep Ranch Hollow, 4
Shelby Co., 52
Simmons, Frank E., 178-179
Siringo, Chas. A., 59
Sixshooter Creek, 38; Draw, 47; Junction, 38
Skinout Creek, 47
Slag (place), 4
Smith, Mrs. Morgan, 339; "Wise Saws from Texas," 239-243.
Smoothing Iron Mt., 3
Smuggler's Gap, 47
Snyder, 48, 76
Soap Creek, 4
Socorro, 121-128
Sodville, 47
Soledad St., San Antonio, 1
Songs: "Brown Jug," 311, 314-315; "Charlie," 315-316; "Cinnamon," 304, 316-318; "Coffee Grows on Live Oak Trees," 304, 316-318; "Dan Tucker," 318; "G e n e r a l Gaines," 309, 319-320; "Girl I Left Behind Me, The," 320-321; "Green Leaves," 321-322; "I'll Be All Smiles Tonight," 307, 333-334; "Irish Potatoes," 322-323; "Josey," 323-324; "Little Log House," 312; "Low-Backed Car, The," 253-255; "Miller Boy," 306, 325-326; "My Juanita, I Must Leave You," 255-257; "Old Obadiah," 250-251; "Once There Was a Man He Came From the West," 250-252; "Pig in the Parlor," 309, 327; "Sealy," 305, 328-329; "Shoo-Shoo Fly," 329-330; "Shu-dah," 310-311, 330-331; "Skip-to-My-Lou," 309, 331; "Susie Brown," 332-333; "Tennessee," 312, 324-325; "Walk around My Bedside," 131-132; "When I Lay My Burden Down," 136. See Alabama Indians.
Sonnichsen, Charles L., 339; "Mexican Spooks from El Paso," 120-129: Five delightfully told tales.
Sorgum Flats, 4
Sour Lake, 68, 76
Spaniards, 1-70 *passim*, 123-125

Sparerib Creek, 47
Spur, 4
Squabble Mt., 47
Squaw Creek, 28-29, 76
Staked Plains, 13, 17-21, 76-77
Stampede Creek, 57; Mesa, 39
Starvation Creek, 38, 77
Stephens Co., 38
Steal Easy Mt., 47
Straddlebug Mt., 4
Sunday Creek, 34, 77
Sun-Kee, Alabama chief. See Thompson.
Superstitions, 68-70. See Beazley, Emmons, Hall, Moses, Royal, Sonnichsen, Turner.
Swedes in Texas, 4

Tahoka, 27
Tales, folk, of Alabama Indians, 276-277, 294-299; general, under Beazley, Chambers, Dobie, Moses, Sonnichsen, Tracy. See Anecdotes, Legends.
Tallow Face Mt., 47
Tanyard Branch, 4
Tascosa, 46, 53
Taylor, T. U., 237
Tecolote Ranch, 2
Tehuacana Hills, 28
Tejas Indians, 64
Tell, 52, 77
Tepee Butte, 3; Draw, 28
Terán, explorer, 5
Tesnus, 54
Texas, name, 63-65, 77
Texian *vs.* Texan, 65
Thompson, Chas., Alabama chief, 275-289 *passim*, 294
Thorndale, 185
Tilden, 49
Tin Rag, 54
Toadloop Draw, 51-52, 77
Tockonhono (Brazos) River, 16-17
Toewash Creek, 47
Tonk Valley, 28
Tonkawa Bottom, 28
Tracy, Myron W., 339; "Roy Bean: Law West of the Pecos," 111-119: Some facts about Old Roy and first-hand versions of some of the Bean yarns that have become traditional.
Trading House Creek, 4
Treasure, buried, 13-15, 258-269
Trick 'em, 50-51, 77
Trickham, 50-51, 77
Trinity Co., 62; River, 5, 191ff.
Troublesome Creek, 47
Tule Canyon, 3
Tulip Bend, 2
Tumlinson, Joe, 25-26

Turkey Creek, 2
Turner, Tressa, 340; "The Human Comedy in Folk Superstitions," 146-175:
  How and where superstitions were collected, 146-147.
  I. Marriage, Love, and Courtship, 148-155.
  II. Good Luck Signs, 155.
  III. Bad Luck Signs, 155-160.
  IV. On Death, 160-162.
  V. Letters, News, and Company, 162-164.
  VI. Wishes, 164-165.
  VII. Money, 165-166.
  VIII. Remedies and Cures, 166-170.
  IX. Weather Signs, 170-172.
  X. Miscellaneous Superstitions, 172-175.
Turnover, 37, 77

Uvalde Co., 46

Vaca, Cabeza de, 21-22
Victoria, Apache chief, 29; County, 300-336 *passim;* Peak, 29
Vingt Un Island, 46

Waco, 13-15, 22
Waco Indians, 13-15
Wagon Timber Creek, 4
Wall Eye Creek, 47
Wallace, Bigfoot, 47, 57
Ward Co., 3
Washita River, 67
Wasp Creek, 37, 77
Watch Mt., 36-37, 77
Waukarusa, Kansas, 67, 77
Waxahachie, 27
Way, Back, 47
Weather lore, 88-89, 170-172
Weatherford, 197ff.
Webb Co., 23
Welch, Mike, 185ff.
Wends, German, in Texas, 53
Wharton Co., 51
Whiskey Creek, 42
White Mule Creek, 26
Wichita Falls, 66, 77
Wichita Indians, 66-67, 77; River, 66-67, 77

Williams, O. W., 24
Wise Co., 43
Witch, for water, 233. *See* Hall.
Wood community, 300-336 *passim*
Wynn, Afton, 340; "Pioneer Folk Ways," 190-238:
  Suggested readings on folk-ways of Texas, 190; historical background of Parker County, where the frontier lingered long, and The Pool, a representative community, 191-193.
  Religion, singings, campmeetings, observance of the Sabbath, Sons of Temperance, 193-199.
  Effect of Indian horse-stealing and scalping on pioneer ways of life; John R. Baylor and his anti-Indian newspaper; the Double Log Cabin at Weatherford as a preserver of articles connected with Indian days, 199-203.
  House-building, 203-205; furnishings, 205-206; weaving, 206-208; beds, shelves, gourds, dishes, candles, fireplace, etc., 208-213.
  Cooking, foods, 213-219; home industries and home-made articles, 219-223; washing and bathing, 223-224; fencing in the farm, 224-226; plants for use and beauty, 226-227; chickens, cotton, watermelons, diversification in work, 227-230.
  Social life: games, sociables, literary and debating societies, badger fights, cards, "playing house" (children), gossip, superstitions, home remedies, gatherings at school house, fiddling, dances and dance calls, 230-238.
Wynn, Mrs. W. P., 214, 218, 222, 227
Wyres, Roy H., 178ff.

X I T Ranch, 49

Yearling Head, 47
Yegua Creek, 25, 52-53
Yo-lo-digo Creek, 9, 78
Young Co., 42
Yucca Siding, 3

Zarzamora St., San Antonio, 1-2, 78
Zavala Co., 9
Zephyr, 3
Zilly Boy, 52

www.ingramcontent.com/pod-product-compliance
Lightning Source LLC
Chambersburg PA
CBHW030302080526
44584CB00012B/403